# Personality *and* Intellectual Competence

# Personality *and* Intellectual Competence

**Tomas Chamorro-Premuzic**
*Goldsmiths, University of London*

**Adrian Furnham**
*University College London*

**LEA**

LAWRENCE ERLBAUM ASSOCIATES, PUBLISHERS
2005    Mahwah, New Jersey                    London

Lawrence Erlbaum Associates, Inc., Publishers
10 Industrial Avenue
Mahwah, New Jersey 07430
www.erlbaum.com

Cover photo: "Dasolog" by Tomas Chamorro-Premuzic
Cover design by Kathryn Houghtling Lacey

**Library of Congress Cataloging-in-Publication Data**

Chamorro-Premuzic, Tomas.
    Personality and intellectual competence / Tomas
    Chamorro-Premuzic, Adrian Furnham.
        p. cm.
Includes bibliographical references and index.
ISBN 0-8058-5136-4 (cloth : alk. paper)
1. Personality and intelligence. I. Furnham, Adrian. II. Title.
BF698.9.I6C55   2005
155.2—dc22                                    2004053322
                                                   CIP

Printed in the United States of America
10  9  8  7  6  5  4  3  2  1

*To Mylene, and more summers*
*in Juan-les-pins*
—TCP


*To Benedict, Godspeed my fair one*
—AF

# Contents

# Preface

After a century of psychometric testing (Binet, 1903), the prediction of future achievement still remains a relatively unaddressed issue. In applied settings, workers in organizations and academic institutions are uncertain about the choice of robust instruments to maximize the prediction of success and failure. At a theoretical level, differential psychologists, historically divided by different methods of research, have made isolated progress in personality and intelligence research, yet only a few have attempted to conceptualize a comprehensive, integrative model to explain cognitive and noncognitive individual differences underlying human performance (Ackerman & Heggestad, 1997; Chamorro-Premuzic & Furnham, 2004).

This volume provides an extensive review of the literature on personality and intelligence research (in the past 100 years), looking not only at the independent theoretical and empirical developments of both constructs, but also their interactions—namely, the psychometric interface between personality traits and cognitive ability measures. Nevertheless, it is argued that this interface (which has been increasingly examined by differential psychologists during the last 5 years) represents only one level of integration between cognitive and noncognitive traits. Two other important perspectives are the focus on academic performance (the criterion, par excellence, for the validation of ability measures) and self-assessed or subjective assessed ability. Hence the title of this book, which deals with the relationship between personality and *intellectual competence*—a term we chose to encompass the three different aspects of psychometric intelligence (cognitive ability tests), academic performance, and self-assessed ability—although it should be noted that other constructs (e.g., leadership, creativity, art judgment) may also be considered indicators of intellectual competence.

This book, then, looks at the relationship between salient personality traits (mostly within the Gigantic Three and Big Five framework) and ability test scores, examination grades (in school and university), as well as other indicators of academic performance, and at the individuals' estimations of their own intellectual abilities and those of others. In that sense, the authors go well beyond recent efforts of "bridging the gap" between the two historically unrelated fields of personality and intelligence. Rather, the authors attempt to establish the foundations for the development of a comprehensive taxonomic conceptual framework to account for observable performance-related individual differences across a variety of occupational and academic settings. It is thus hoped that this book will improve, not only our ability to predict an individual's performance (at work, school, or university), but also our understanding of the traits that play an important role in the Development of adult skills and knowledge.

## ACKNOWLEDGMENTS

We are grateful to Phillip Ackerman, Elizabeth Austin, Nathan Brody, and Gerald Matthews for their valuable advice and helpful correspondence on many of the preliminary thoughts that inspired us to write this book. We also thank Emily Wilkinson and Lawrence Erlbaum for their patience and encouragement during the evolution of this book. Finally, we would like to register our thanks to Joanna Moutafi, Georgia Dissou, and, in particular, Nadia Bettega for their helpful assistance.

—*Tomas Chamorro-Premuzic*
—*Adrian Furnham*

# 1

# Overview: Predicting Future Achievement

For more than a century, psychologists have attempted to identify and understand systematic, observable differences between individuals that seem stable over time. Among these *individual differences*, personality and intelligence have received widespread attention, not only in an academic, but also in a lay, forum. Values, beliefs, and attitudes are all important, but may seem systematically related to the more fundamental and stable factors of abilities (intelligence) and traits (personality).

Loosely defined, *personality* refers to stable patterns of behaviors or traits that predispose an individual to act in a specific (more or less consistent) manner. We often describe and explain our own behavior and that of others in terms of personality traits: "she is responsible," "he is very creative," "she is very shy," or "he is very talkative." In contrast, *intelligence* refers to an individual's capacity to learn new things and solve novel (Gf) as well as old (Gc) problems. It is also often referred to as accumulated knowledge and is used widely in everyday life to describe ourselves and others: "he is very bright," "she is very knowledgeable," or "he learns quickly." In that sense, intelligence could be regarded as a fundamental characteristic of an individual and considered part of personality (as has indeed been the case; see Barratt, 1995; Cattell, 1971; Eysenck & Eysenck, 1985). Nevertheless, methodological and applied issues, concerning the way in which personality and intelligence have been assessed and measured, as well as the purpose for which they are usually examined, have determined a major division in the field of individual differences. As a consequence, the study of personality and intelligence has followed two different research paths, and there has been little significant communication between researchers from one field and the other, at least until recently (Ackerman & Heggestad, 1997; Chamorro-Premuzic & Furnham, 2004a, 2004b; Zeidner & Matthews, 2000).

This book is essentially aimed at integrating the concepts of personality and intelligence in what could be defined as an attempt to provide a conceptual framework for understanding individual differences underlying intellectual competence. In that sense, it plans to go beyond initial efforts of "bridging the gap" between both constructs by setting the empirical and theoretical foundations for a comprehensive model for understanding individual differences research and predicting future achievement. This model is based not only on the interface between personality and intelligence (as traditionally conceived in terms of psychometric scores of standardized inventories or tests; see chap. 4), but also academic performance (see chap. 5), and subjectively assessed intelligence (see chap. 6).

Although mainly theoretical, this book is not only aimed at experts in the area of individual differences, but to a wider public, which includes social science students with an interest in human performance, and anyone interested in the prediction of intellectual competence as well as the understanding of the psychological theories underlying individual differences in intellectual competence.

Starting from an introductory examination of the topics of personality (chap. 2) and intelligence (chap. 3) as two major independent areas of research in psychology (or what is usually referred to as differential psychology or individual differences), it continues with an in-depth discussion of the core of this book—that is, the personality–intelligence interface (conceptualizing intellectual competence in terms of the traditional psychometric approach; chap. 4), as well as academic and work performance (chap. 5). Subjective indicators of intellectual competence, notably self-assessed—as opposed to psychometrically measured—intelligence, are the topic of another major section (chap. 6). Finally (chap. 7), constructs such as leadership, creativity, and art judgment, not traditionally associated with individual differences in intellectual competence, are examined in terms of their theoretical and applied implications for the development of a wider conceptual framework to understand various individual differences in human intellectual competence—specifically, whether they represent a fertile area of research for differential psychologists concerned with the integration of cognitive and noncognitive determinants of future achievement. Concluding remarks are presented in a final chapter (chap. 8).

**2**

# Personality Traits

As with most widely used words, the definition of *personality* may seem both complex (particularly compared with the easiness of its use) and unnecessary. Further, because of the ubiquitous use of the term, it may almost be impossible to encompass all connotations. It is, however, clear that a scientific approach to the study of personality should provide a clear and comprehensive definition of the term beyond the discrepancies of prescientific knowledge and the lay uses (and misuses) of the term. Luckily (as it is also the case with most frequently used terms), definitions of personality have already been attempted, in many cases by experts in the field. Because this book only focuses on the relationship between personality traits and intellectual competence, we suggest that readers with an interest in personality consult any of the excellent books on the topic (e.g., Hogan, Johnson, & Briggs, 1997; Matthews & Deary, 1998; Pervin, 1996). Here we only provide an overview of the major issues in personality research, its history, and its assessment.

The study of personality traits is concerned with the structural differences and similarities among individuals. Starting from a general classification of these stable and observable patterns of behavior (*taxonomy*), it attempts to assess the extent to which individuals differ on these dimensions to predict differences in other observable behaviors, outcomes, or constructs, such as happiness, health, reaction time, or academic and job performance. Thus, personality refers to an individual's description in general and provides a universal taxonomy or framework to compare individuals and account for everybody's individuality at the same time.

Traits are used to describe *and* explain behavior—they are *internal* (associated with characteristics of the individual, rather than the situation or context) and *causal* (influence behavior). From the first known attempts to identify major individual differences and elaborate a taxonomy of personality (usually acknowledged to the ancient Greek classifi-cation of *humours* and temperaments) to the current *state-of-the-art* dif-ferential and behavioral genetic approaches, personality theorists have attempted to identify, assess, explain, and predict systematic differences and similarities between individuals, looking for the fundamental and general causes of human behavior. Specifically, they have aimed to (a) identify the main dimensions in which people differ or can be compared, (b) test that these dimensions remain relatively stable over time, and (c) explain the etiological basis of these universal and stable differences among individuals (Cooper, 1998). The forthcoming sections provide an introduction and overview to personality research. After this introduction to the topic of personality, we examine the salient taxonomies or systems of personality traits, which have dominated the field for decades. The final model to be examined in this chapter, the Big Five personality traits, is the focus of most of this book, specifically in relation to psychometric intelligence (chap. 4) and academic performance (chap. 5).

## 2.1   HISTORY OF PERSONALITY TRAITS

As is the case in most modern disciplines, the beginnings of personality the-ory date back to the times of the ancient Greeks. This conceptualization of personality traits, credited to Hippocrates (460–370 BC), was an attempt to classify the major descriptors underlying individual differences in terms of four different types, which were a function of biological differences in fluids or "humours"—namely, the *sanguine, choleric, phlegmatic,* and *melan-cholic* temperaments. According to the Greek physician Galen (130–200 AD), who reinterpreted Hippocrates' theory, differences in personality were a direct reflection of constitutional differences in the body.

The *sanguine* personality described enthusiastic, positive, and cheer-ful individuals, satisfied with life and generally enjoying good mental as well as physical health. This type of personality was associated with high levels of blood supply (or the strength of the blood), hence the term *san-guine* from the Latin *sanguis* (blood). A second type of personality, the *choleric* one, was used to characterize aggressive, tense, volatile, and hot-tempered individuals and was believed to be caused by levels of the bile chemical released by the gall bladder during the processes of diges-tion. A third personality type, the *phlegmatic*, referred to individuals with a tendency to be dull, lazy, and apathetic, and who live a slowly paced life. This personality type was associated with the mucus from the lungs or phlegm, typical during flu or lung infection. Phlegmatic individuals are the opposite of sanguine and choleric ones, the former being cold (both phys-ically and psychologically), and the two latter types being warm. The fourth type of personality (also believed to be warm), the *melancholic* one, appears more familiar to our everyday language surely because it is the origin of a widely used word in our times. Melancholic individuals were believed to be chronically sad or depressed, reflective, and have a pessimistic approach to life. The biological origin of melancholy was believed to be the malfunctioning of an organ called *black bile*, but this idea was probably abandoned after the middle ages. Figure 2.1 depicts a representation of the ancient Greek typology and Galen's interpretation of the four types of temperaments as described here.

Despite the preliminary and prescientific basis of the ancient Greek theory of personality, their classification persisted for many centuries and inspired several leading intellectual figures of the modern era, notably Imannuel Kant (1724–1804). Influenced by the readings of Galen and the ancient Greeks, Kant (1796/1996) published his *Anthropology From the Pragmatic Viewpoint*, echoing the classification of the four types of personality as a fundamental description of individuality. However, Kant's major contribution was his philosophical or metaphysical work, and it was not until modern psychology that personality became a central topic in science.

The most notable psychologist and personality theorist to be influenced by the Greek classification of humours was Hans Eysenck (1916–1997). In the early developments of his personality theory, which was strictly empirical and psychometrically founded, Eysenck identified two major universal personality traits that could be used to account for a general description of individual differences. These traits are Neuroticism

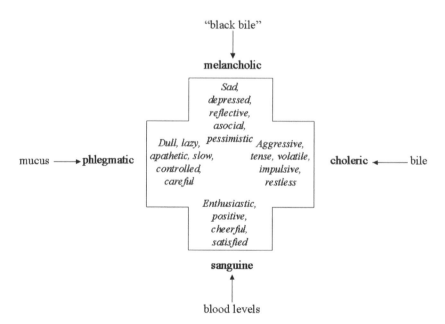

FIG. 2.1.    Ancient Greek classification of humours and personality types (after Hippocrates and Galen).

and Extraversion; they still persist in most well-established personality taxonomies (although sometimes under different names). Figure 2.2 depicts the taxonomic overlap between Eysenck's two early dimensions of personality (*temperament*) and the ancient classification of Hippocrates, later expanded by Galen and Kant.

As can be seen, the four Greek typologies can be mapped onto Eysenck's two personality factors, such that low Neuroticism is represented by a combination of sanguine and phlegmatic types, whereas high Neuroticism is represented by a combination of melancholic and choleric types. In contrast, low Extraversion overlaps with phlegmatic and melancholic types, whereas high Extraversion would seem a mix of choleric and sanguine types.

Before Eysenck's theory is discussed in more detail, it is important to emphasize that the ancient Greek typologies have also had an impact on many notorious predecessors of Eysenck, such as the early experimental psychologist Wilhem Wundt (1832–1920), the animal behaviorist Ivan Pavlov (1849–1936), and the psychoanalyst Karl Jung (1871–1961). It was Jung (1921) who first supported the main typological differences between introverts and extraverts, although in terms of psychodynamic processes. Introverts, he thought, were characterized by a tendency to direct their instinctual energies or *libido* toward their own mental self, whereas extraverts would be identified by their tendencies to transfer these energies to real-world objects (notably individuals) other than the self.

Despite the little impact of psychoanalytic theory in modern scientific psychology, the preliminary distinction between extraverts and introverts would persist in most psychometrically validated theories of personality,

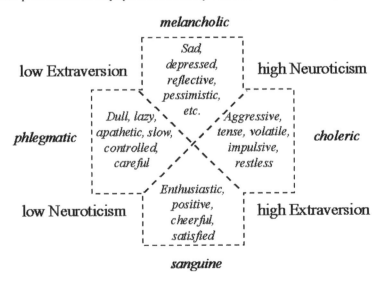

FIG. 2.2. The ancient Greek and Eysenck's early personality traits.

even when the identification of other traits has seemed an issue of debate and controversy between exponents of different taxonomies. Two of these major taxonomies are the Gigantic Three and Big Five personality traits, which are discussed in Sections 2.3 and 2.5, respectively.

## 2.2   PERSONALITY TRAITS AND STATES

Unlike the idea that individuals can be described in terms of traits that refer to their consistent preferences or patterns of behaviors, some researchers have preferred to conceptualize personality in terms of a series of unrelated (and ungeneralizable) *states*. These refer to sporadic or ephemeral acts of behaviors (lasting perhaps no more than a few hours) or even occasional moods such as joy or anger. It has even been argued that biological instincts such as hunger, sex drive, and aggression may also be indicative of an individual's personality in terms of his or her motivational states (Cattell, 1957). This idea has often been used to refute trait theories of personality, arguing that individuals may respond to the same situation in different ways, and that behaviors may be more determined by a situation rather than stable personal dispositions to act in a consistent manner (see Brody, 1988, for a review of this debate).

Paradoxically, however, the only evidence in support of personality as a mere function of unrelated states of behavior derives from the lack of evidence on the stability of traits. Thus, if longitudinal data failed to provide significant and substantial correlations between traits assessed across the life span, state advocates would somehow be victorious. However, this requires the use (a priori) not only of personality traits, but also of self-report instruments to assess them. Figure 2.3 illustrates the conceptual representation of a sample trait (Extraversion) as derived or deducted from a set of observable and correlated states. Different behaviors (smile, touch, move, talk) that occur in some intensity across different situations and circumstances can be grouped together under the same concept (Extraversion), to which these states are then attributed. Thus, traits are conceptualized from a series of related states.

One major advantage of trait approaches and theories to personality is their rigorous empirical methodology and usefulness to assess individual differences. This is why they have been exposed to criticisms and why failure to empirically support a system or taxonomy has often led one to question the theory. However, scientific theories should produce testable hypotheses, and a theory based on sound empirical observation is superior to those based on speculation. It must be emphasized that one should not judge the very nature of trait approaches to personality in terms of the poor validity or reliability of specific systems or instruments, especially if these have proved to be poor (see Block, 1977). Studies with reliable instruments provide sufficient evidence for the invariance of major personality traits across the adult life span (see Costa & McCrae, 1980; Leon,

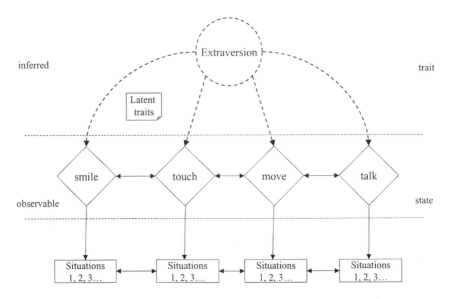

FIG. 2.3.   Traits and states psychometrically and conceptually represented.

Gillum, Gillum, & Gouze, 1979; McCrae & Costa, 1982). These studies have examined not only self-report, but also other ratings of personality traits, and they have concluded that there is little change in personality traits across different situations and an individual's life.

Further evidence for the stability of traits has been provided by behavioral genetic studies, which suggest that there is a substantial genetic influence on personality traits, which persist even in adulthood, and that environmental factors seem to play a minor role in determining personality changes (Cooper, 1998; Costa & McCrae, 1992; Loehlin, 1992; Zuckerman, 1991). As Costa and McCrae (1988) argued:

> Many individuals will have undergone radical changes in their life structure. They may have married, divorced, remarried. They have probably moved their residence several times. Job changes, layoffs, promotions, and retirement are all likely to have occurred for many people. Close friends and confidants will have died or moved away or become alienated. Children will have been born, grown up, married, begun a family of their own. The individual will have aged biologically, with changes in appearances, health, vigor, memory, and sensory abilities. Internationally, wars, depressions, and social movements will have come and gone. Most subjects will have read dozens of books, seen hundreds of movies, watched thousands of hours of television. *And yet, most people will not have changed appreciably in any of the personality dispositions measured by these tests.* (p. 61)

Thus, after many decades of theoretical debate (1941–1990) on the nature of personality structure (a debate that was predominantly centered around the stability or consistency of behavioral patterns attributed to individual differences in personality and derived in the division between trait and state advocates), the psychometrics of personality seem to have led most researchers to conceptualize individual differences in personality in terms of the Gigantic Three (Eysenck & Eysenck, 1985) or the Big Five (Costa & McCrae, 1992) personality dimensions. Both these taxonomies posit that major personality traits are determinants of an individual's behavior, although there is disagreement on the number of traits or fundamental dimensions in which people differ. Hence, there is a reference to either three or five major factors, although it should be noted that the lack of consensus underlying attempts to develop a taxonomy for personality assessment has been such that virtually any number of personality dimensions has been proposed (see John, 1990).

## 2.3  EYSENCK'S GIGANTIC THREE AND THE BIOLOGICAL BASIS OF PERSONALITY TRAITS

The Gigantic Three framework derived from Eysenck's ground-breaking and long-standing empirical investigations on personality and individual differences (Eysenck, 1947, 1952, 1977, 1982). According to this personality theory, there are three major dimensions of personality or aspects in which individuals differ: Neuroticism, Extraversion, and Psychoticism. Eysenck also provided a psychometric tool to assess these dimensions; the Eysenck Personality Questionnaire–Revised (EPQ–R; Eysenck & Eysenck, 1991) is the latest version of this instrument. The EPQ–R is a self-report inventory comprising items about typical behavior (preferences and dispositions) that are answered on a 2-point Likert scale (*yes/no*). Theoretically, the three dimensions assessed by the EPQ–R are orthogonal (i.e., uncorrelated), although positive correlations among the three personality domains have been reported, particularly in male samples (see Eysenck & Eysenck, 1991). Nevertheless, correlations are relatively low, and it is thus assumed that a full description of an individual would not be fulfilled unless the three personality traits were assessed. Due to the self-report nature of this instrument, Eysenck also included a measure of *dissimulation*, often referred to as the fourth scale of the EPQ–R. Nonetheless, for the purposes of this book, we focus on the three Gigantic personality traits only.

The major advances in Eysenck's personality theory with regard to the ancient and classic (but also psychoanalytical) approaches to personality were a consequence of his strictly empirical, systematic, and quantitative research methodology. Starting from theoretical readings and systematic clinical observations, Eysenck applied robust statistical techniques of data reduction to account for his dimensions of personality, providing one of the first and certainly the most long-standing scientific theory of personality traits. Self-report questionnaires ask subjects to describe themselves (or others) on a number of behaviors and preferences, and large sets of responses can be correlated to extract common underlying factors, which represent the latent personality traits (see Fig. 2.4). In that sense, items replace observation and statistical data reduction substitutes common sense or inferential associations. Further, because it is virtually impossible to observe large numbers of people all the time, and starting from the assumption that we know ourselves relatively well (certainly better than we know others), self-reports should provide a more accurate description of an individual's typical behavior than partial, unsystematic, and often biased observation.

Another advanced (and, to some extent, unique) element in Eysenck's theory is that it attempts to explain individual personality differences in biological terms. According to Eysenck and Eysenck's (1985) theory, there are biological and inheritable individual differences in personality, specifically in levels of arousability. Different levels of Neuroticism, Extraversion, and Psychoticism (the three major dimensions of what Eysenck referred to as *temperament*) are directly caused by genetic factors and account for similarities and differences among individuals. Thus, the biological basis of temperament would explain the life-long impact of personality traits in the observable and nonobservable aspects of our individuality.

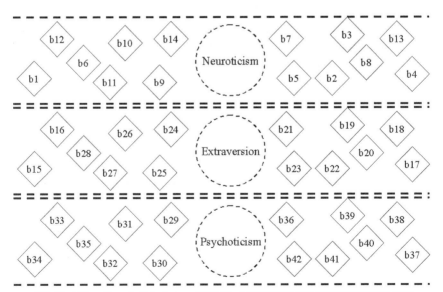

*Note.* b1…b42 = self-reported behaviors or preferences. Correlated behaviors are located within the same psychometric space (Neuroticism, Extraversion or Psychoticism, the three independent/orthogonal traits).

FIG. 2.4.    Eysenck's Gigantic Three psychometrically assessed.

Eysenck argued that Extraversion was the psychological consequence of physiological differences in the ascending reticular activating system (located in the brain-stem reticular formation). The cerebral cortex, which is excited by this system, determines levels of motivation, emotion, and conditioning according to either inhibitions or excitations, and these consistent patterns of arousability determine the extent to which an individual is extraverted or introverted. Introverts have a greater tendency to be cortically aroused than their extraverted counterparts and vice versa. This is because, under equal conditions of external stimulation (i.e., in exactly the same situation), introverts will generate greater arousal than extraverts. Thus, introverts need more time (and effort) to adapt to external stimuli, and thus benefit from quiet environments. Conversely, extraverts, who have the need to compensate for their lower levels of arousal, tend to seek external stimulation and are more comfortable (and able to deal) with distracting environments or rich stimulation. As a consequence, extraverts' and introverts' differential levels of arousability and inhibition would lead them to avoid or seek stimulus intensity, which in turn would enhance or reduce their innate levels of habituation to stimuli, resulting in a physiopsychological feedback.

In contrast, individual differences in Neuroticism could be explained in terms of brain activity in the visceral area (composed of the amygdala, hippocampus, septum, cingulum, and hypothalamus) and reticular formation, which generate activation perceived as arousal. Levels of arousability are associated with emotionality, and the arousing activities in the brains of neurotic individuals can be translated in the experience of (or a predisposition, at least, to experience) intense emotions. Thus, Neuroticism can be understood in terms of the relationship between excitability and emotional responsiveness (reflected in the autonomic activation of the neurotic system). In the same way that differences in Extraversion/Introversion are more evident in stimulus-intense environments, individual differences in autonomic activation leading to Neuroticism are more clearly observed under stressful or anxiety-evoking conditions. Because neurotic individuals are characterized by a hyperarousable visceral system (the area of the brain involved in emotional regulation), they are more sensitive to reproduce emotional reactions than stable individuals (low in Neuroticism). Thus, the same event may elicit intense emotional reaction in neurotic, but not in stable, individuals, and observable indicators such as sweat or galvanic skin response (apart from the very experience of intense negative emotions) are believed to be the consequence of the visceral-brain activation and its consequent activation of the nervous system.

Evidence for the biological basis of Neuroticism has not been provided as extensively and consistently as for Extraversion, certainly not by Eysenck. Further, Eysenck did not elaborate a theoretical framework to understand the biological basis of his third trait, Psychoticism. Thus, claims that personality traits have inheritable and biological roots (an idea that, as we observed, has been present since ancient civilizations) remained somehow untested.

Some other problems and inconsistencies with Eysenck's psychobiological theory were its complexity, the physiological interdependence of the processes underlying two supposedly unrelated or orthogonal traits (such as Neuroticism and Extraversion), and the lack of sufficient technological instruments—at the time—to test his hypotheses. Because of the fast-paced technological advances in neuropsychology, several of the concepts underlying Eysenck's theory now seem as out of date as those used by Galen and Hippocrates in the times of Eysenck's theoretical developments. However, some interesting research in this line is still being conducted, and there are some—notably Robinson (1991)—concerned with the reinterpretation and reexamination of Eysenck's biological theory of temperament with state-of-the-art technology and from an up-to-date neuropsychological perspective (see Section 4.1).

Rather than following up the much-heated debate on the biological nature of personality traits (a question already covered in the relevant personality textbooks and handbooks; e.g., Brody, 1988; Matthews & Deary, 1998), in the present book we concern ourselves with the relationship between personality and intellectual competence at the psychometric or descriptive, as opposed to the psychobiological, level, for which it is crucial to identify the dimensions of personality in psychometric (rather than biological) terms. It is in psychometric terms that Eysenck's contribution to personality theory has been more influential and may only be challenged by a handful of rival taxonomies.

As mentioned earlier, Eysenck's taxonomy of *temperament* (the noncognitive aspects of personality, where personality also includes the cognitive aspects of intelligence) is based on three major, uncorrelated dimensions—namely, Neuroticism, Extraversion, and Psychoticism. These dimensions can be assessed through self-report inventories such as the EPQ–R, EPP (Eysenck Personality Profile), and so on (see Table 2.1) and are believed to be universal (Eysenck & Eysenck, 1985). Further, as much as these dimensions are thought to be inherited, they may be expected to remain stable over time. There is impressive longitudinal evidence for the stability of these traits across the life span and their identification as major personality dimensions across cultures, too (see Matthews & Deary, 1998). Neuroticism refers to an individual's level of emotionality and his or her tendency to be moody, touchy, and anxious. Extraversion assesses the degree to which individuals show a preference and tendency to be talkative, outgoing, and optimistic (as well as energetic). Psychoticism (only introduced to the taxonomy in 1976) refers to emotionally cruel, risk-taking, impulsive, and sensation-seeking individuals. Characteristics of high and low scorers are presented in Table 2.2.

**TABLE 2.1**

**Sample Items for the Gigantic Three Personality Traits (EPQ-R)**

| Trait | Sample items |
|---|---|
| Neuroticism | "Does your mood often go up and down?"<br>"Are you often troubled about feelings of guilt?"<br>"Are you a worrier?" |
| Extraversion | "Do you tend to keep in the background on social occasions?"<br>"Can you usually let yourself go and enjoy yourself at a lively party?"<br>"Do you enjoy meeting new people?" |
| Psychoticism | "Would you take drugs which may have strange or dangerous effects?"<br>"Do you enjoy hurting people you love?"<br>"Have you ever taken advantage of someone?" |

*Note.* Table is based on Eysenck and Eysenck (1985).

**TABLE 2.2**

**Eysenck's Gigantic Three (Characteristics of High and Low Scorers)**

| | Neuroticism | Extraversion | Psychoticism |
|---|---|---|---|
| High | Anxious, moody, depressed, pessimistic, tense, shy, low self-esteem | Energetic, sociable, lively, active, assertive, confident, dominant | Tough-minded, unempathetic, creative, sensation-seeking, aggressive, cold |
| Low | Stable, positive, calm, optimistic, confident, relaxed | Asocial, passive, slow, reflective, introspective, socially unconfident | Altruistic, rational, patient, conformist, organized, down-to-earth, empathic |

*Note.* Table is based on Eyenck and Eysenck (1991).

The first psychometric instrument to assess Neuroticism and Extraversion was the Maudsley Medical Questionnaire (MMQ), but the late versions of the Eysenck Personality Inventory (EPI) and the most recent Eysenck Personality Questionnaire–R (EPQ–R) introduced advances and improvements in the assessment of all three dimensions, including Psychoticism (see Eysenck & Eysenck, 1985). It was precisely this third dimension in the Eysenckian system that would be the focus of largely unresolved psychometric dispute and open the field to another major taxonomy—namely, the Five Factor or Big Five personality traits.

Five Factor advocates (who increased substantially after the 1980s) have claimed that the Psychoticism dimension needs to be *broken down* into Openness, Agreeableness, and Conscientiousness, suggesting that individuals may be high on some, but low on other, of these traits (Borkenau, 1988; Digman & Inouye, 1986; Goldberg, 1982; McCrae & Costa, 1987). Thus, there are three novel personality traits identified and included in the Big Five taxonomy, not present—but arguably represented—in the Eysenckian model. Specifically, Eysenck's idea of Psychoticism would be conceptualized in terms of low Agreeableness, high Openness, and low Conscientiousness, but Eysenck considered Openness an indicator of intelligence (i.e., the cognitive aspect of personality, according to his theory), rather than temperament. A great deal of the disputes with regard to Openness—specifically, whether it should be considered as part of personality (or temperament) or intelligence—are discussed in detail in forthcoming sections (see particularly Section 4.7) and are especially relevant to understanding the personality–intelligence interface. In contrast, Eysenck and Eysenck (1985) considered Agreeableness a combination of the Gigantic Three—namely, low Psychoticism, low Neuroticism, and high Extraversion, rather than a major personality dimension.

Table 2.3, a psychometric comparison between the Gigantic Three and Five Factor taxonomies, shows that Neuroticism and Extraversion are overlapping dimensions in both systems, suggesting that the Big Five and Gigantic Three are assessing two similar traits. However, Agreeableness and Conscientiousness are only moderately correlated with Psychoticism ($r = -.45$ and $r = -.31$, respectively), and Openness is uncorrelated with Psychoticism ($r = .05$). Thus, both systems seem to differ in their assessment of traits other than Neuroticism and Extraversion. Before looking at the Five Factor model in detail, let us examine another major taxonomy to conceptualize individual differences—namely, Cattell's 16PF.

**TABLE 2.3**
**Correlations Between the Gigantic Three**
**and Big Five Personality Traits**

|  | Neuroticism | Extraversion | Psychoticism |
|---|---|---|---|
| Neuroticism | **.75** | −.05 | .25 |
| Extraversion | −.18 | **.69** | −.04 |
| Openness | .01 | .15 | **.05** |
| Agreeableness | −.18 | .04 | **−.45** |
| Conscientiousness | −.21 | −.03 | **−.31** |

*Note.*   Table is based on Costa and McCrae (1985).

## 2.4  CATTELL'S 16PF
## AND THE LEXICAL HYPOTHESIS

Although many differential psychologists have approached the psychometrics of personality in terms of the Gigantic Three or the Big Five taxonomies, other systems and instruments have also been used. One of these systems has been that of Raymond Cattell (1905–1998), a leading figure of factor analysis and a very skillful statistician. According to Cattell, there are not 3 or 5, but 16 major dimensions of personality (including intellectual ability; see Cattell et al., 1970). The universality of these personality traits was based on a large empirical examination and consequent data reduction of the factors underlying a vast combination of words to describe individuals. This approach is based on an exhaustive and systematic analysis of the English language, and it assumes that every aspect of an individual's personality can be described with existing words. Starting from 4,500 words, Cattell obtained 180, then 42 to 46, and eventually 15 personality traits to which he added intellectual ability. Factors from Cattell's taxonomy, the 16PF, are presented in Table 2.4

Despite the wide aspects of behaviors covered by Cattell's 16 factors, moderate and high intercorrelations between several of these dimen-

### TABLE 2.4
### Factors in Cattell's 16PF

| | |
|---|---|
| 1 | Factor A Warmth (Reserved vs. Warm) |
| 2 | Factor B Reasoning (Concrete vs. Abstract) |
| 3 | Factor C Emotional Stability (Reactive vs. Emotionally Stable) |
| 4 | Factor E Dominance (Deferential vs. Dominant) |
| 5 | Factor F Liveliness (Serious vs. Lively) |
| 6 | Factor G Rule-Consciousness (Expedient vs. Rule-Conscious) |
| 7 | Factor H Social Boldness (Shy vs. Socially Bold) |
| 8 | Factor I Sensitivity (Utilitarian vs. Sensitive) |
| 9 | Factor L Vigilance (Trusting vs. Vigilant) |
| 10 | Factor M Abstractedness (Grounded vs. Abstracted) |
| 11 | Factor N Privateness (Forthright vs. Private) |
| 12 | Factor O Apprehension (Self-Assured vs. Apprehensive) |
| 13 | Factor Q1 Openness to Change (Traditional vs. Open to Change) |
| 14 | Factor Q2 Self-Reliance (Group-Oriented vs. Self-Reliant) |
| 15 | Factor Q3 Perfectionism (Tolerates Disorder vs. Perfectionistic) |
| 16 | Factor Q4 Tension (Relaxed vs. Tense) |

sions make it possible to reduce the taxonomy to fewer, second-order, factors—notably, QI, QII, and QVIII. This can be achieved through oblique rotation, a technique championed by Cattell. QI (*exvia-versus-invia*) and QII (*adjustment-versus-anxiety*) are comparable to Extraversion and Neuroticism, respectively, whereas QVIII (*super-ego*) seems to overlap with Eysenck's Psychoticism trait (referring to levels of ego-strengths, discipline, and self-concepts). However, several researchers, including Cattell, failed to replicate both the primary and secondary solutions of the 16PF (see Byravan & Ramanaiah, 1995; Eysenck & Eysenck, 1985; Matthews, 1989). Besides, the idea that intelligence should also be conceptualized in terms of personality and assessed through self-reports has proved controversial and runs counter to a well-established line in differential research that is concerned with the measurement of cognitive ability in terms of power tests or objective performance measures (Cronbach, 1984; Deary, 2001; Hofstee, 2001). This is discussed further in Sections 4.7 and 4.8.

If personality psychology were to advance from a preliminary classification of universal traits to the real-world outcomes and other psychological constructs that can be predicted by consistent personality definitions (exploring the validity of personality in the prediction of other events), it would be essential to establish consensus on the number of traits that are used to describe the basic individual differences underlying human behavior. The system that appears to have won the vote of most differential psychologist is the Big Five factor model no doubt because of the extensive longitudinal and cross-cultural evidence in support of the universality of the five higher order dimensions of personality proposed by Costa and McCrae (1985, 1992), as well as the psychometric failure of Eysenck's Psychoticism dimension.

## 2.5   THE FIVE FACTOR MODEL (BIG FIVE)

Like Cattell's 16PF, the Big Five personality framework originated from the lexical hypothesis—the assumption that the major dimensions of behavior could be mapped onto (or derived from) the words that exist in our language to describe a person. Almost 70 years ago, Allport and Odbert (1936) reported 18,000 *descriptors* of an individual in the English language. This group of words was later reduced to approximately 8,000 and then 4,500 (see Norman, 1967) based on the elimination of evaluative, ambiguous, and unfamiliar words, as well as terms that referred to physical (rather than psychological) aspects. As explained, the lexical hypothesis refers to the idea that these words (derived from lay rather than scientific knowledge) would provide a comprehensive frame of reference to establish a taxonomy for the underlying personality dimensions of human beings. This method, combined with sophisticated and complex data-reduction techniques, would have a direct impact on the psychometrics of personality traits and how research would approach the study of individual differences (Cattell, 1946, 1957; Cattell, Eber, & Tatsuoka, 1970).

After Cattell's initial version of a lexical-based personality model, Norman (1967), based on Tupes and Christal (1961),[1] identified 1,431 major descriptors that could be collapsed into a more fundamental list of 75. Rather than an exploratory factor analysis, this solution was the result of a subjective confirmatory analysis of five major underlying dimensions, which were later psychometrically confirmed through self-report inventories (Goldberg, 1990). Despite the lack of theoretical rationale for the etiology of traits identified by the Five Factor model, there has been enough consensus and empirical evidence in support of the identification of the Big Five as the universal dimensions of personality (Costa, 1997; Costa & McCrae, 1992; Deary & Matthews, 1993; McCrae & Costa, 1997b). Thus, most personality researchers (e.g., Busato, Prins, Elshout, & Hamaker, 2000; De Raad, 1996; Digman, 1990; Furnham, 1996a, 1996b, 1997) have agreed on the psychometrical advantages of the Big Five taxonomy proposed by Costa and McCrae (1992), often concluding that the Five Factor model is universal (Costa, 1997; Costa & McCrae, 1992; Deary & Matthews, 1993; McCrae & Costa, 1997b). As in Cattell's and Eysenck's models, the Big Five conceptualizes individual differences that refer to stable patterns of behavior and are independent from each other.

The Big Five model proposed by Costa and McCrae derived from the re-analysis (via a statistical technique called *cluster analysis*) of Cattell's 16PF (Costa & McCrae, 1976). According to the Five Factor taxonomy, there are five higher order personality traits (or factors)—namely, Neuroticism, Extraversion (these two dimensions are replications of the two equivalent traits in Eysenck's and Cattell's systems and were identified in the first re-analysis of Cattell's 16PF), Openness to Experience (added in Costa & McCrae, 1978), Agreeableness, and Conscientiousness. Table 2.5 presents the complete NEO–PI–R (Neuroticism-Extraversion-Openness Personality Inventory–Revised; Costa & McCrae, 1992) super and primary traits with their respective checklist. Sample items for each subfacet are presented in Table 2.6.

The first main personality trait is *Neuroticism*. It can be described as the tendency to experience negative emotions, notably anxiety, depression, and anger (Busato, Prins, Elshout, & Hamaker, 2000). It is a widely conceptualized personality factor and can be assessed through both the EPQ (Eysenck & Eysenck, 1985) as well as the NEO–PI–R (Costa & McCrae, 1992). Furthermore, Neuroticism finds its equivalent or similar expression in the Anxiety trait of Cattell's model (Cattell, Eber, & Tatsuoka, 1970). Neurotic individuals can be characterized for their tendency to experience anxiety, as opposed to the typically calm, relaxed, and stable (low Neuroticism) personalities. The primary facets of

---

[1]Published as Tupes and Christal (1992).

# TABLE 2.5
## NEO–PI–R Super and Primary Traits (Facets) With Checklist Items

*Neuroticism Facets*

| | |
|---|---|
| N1: anxiety | anxious, fearful, worrying, tense, nervous, –confident, –optimistic |
| N2: angry hostility | anxious, irritable, impatient, excitable, moody, –gentle, tense |
| N3: depression | worrying, –contented, –confident, –self-confident, pessimistic, moody, anxious |
| N4: self-consciousness | shy, –self-confident, timid, –confident, defensive, inhibited, anxious |
| N5: impulsiveness | moody, irritable, sarcastic, self-centered, loud, hasty, excitable |
| N6: vulnerability | –clear-thinking, –self-confident, –confident, anxious, –efficient, –alert, careless |

*Extraversion Facets*

| | |
|---|---|
| E1: warmth | friendly, warm, sociable, cheerful, –aloof, affectionate, outgoing |
| E2: gregariousness | sociable, outgoing, pleasure-seeking, –aloof, talkative, spontaneous, –withdrawn |
| E3: assertiveness | aggressive, –shy, assertive, self-confident, forceful, enthusiastic, confident |
| E4: activity | energetic, hurried, quick, determined, enthusiastic, aggressive, active |
| E5: excitement-seeking | pleasure-seeking, daring, adventurous, charming, handsome, spunky, clever |
| E6: positive emotions | enthusiastic, humorous, praising, spontaneous, pleasure-seeking, optimistic, jolly |

*Openness Facets*

| | |
|---|---|
| O1: fantasy | dreamy, imaginative, humorous, mischievous, idealistic, artistic, complicated |
| O2: aesthetics | imaginative, artistic, original, enthusiastic, inventive, idealistic, versatile |
| O3: feelings | excitable, spontaneous, insightful, imaginative, affectionate, talkative, outgoing |
| O4: actions | interests wide, imaginative, adventurous, optimistic, –mild, talkative, versatile |
| O5: ideas | idealistic, interests wide, inventive, curious, original, imaginative, insightful |
| O6: values | –conservative, unconventional, –cautious, flirtatious |

## TABLE 2.5    (continued)

| Agreeableness Facets | |
| --- | --- |
| A1: trust | forgiving, trusting, −suspicious, −wary, −pessimistic, peaceable, −hard-hearted |
| A2: straight-forwardness | −complicated, −demanding, −clever, −flirtatious, −charming, −shrewd, −autocratic |
| A3: altruism | warm, soft-hearted, gentle, generous, kind, tolerant, −selfish |
| A4: compliance | −stubborn, −demanding, −headstrong, −impatient, −intolerant, −outspoken, −hard-hearted |
| A5: modesty | −show-off, −clever, −assertive, −argumentative, −self-confident, −aggressive, −idealistic |
| A6: tender-mindedness | friendly, warm, sympathetic, soft-hearted, gentle, −unstable, kind |

| Conscientiousness Facets | |
| --- | --- |
| C1: competence | efficient, self-confident, thorough, resourceful, confident, −confused, intelligent |
| C2: order | organized, thorough, efficient, precise, methodological, −absent-minded, −careless |
| C3: dutifulness | −defensive, −distractable, −careless, −lazy, thorough, −absent-minded, −fault-finding |
| C4: achievement striving | thorough, ambitious, industrious, enterprising, determined, confident, persistent |
| C5: self-discipline | organized, −lazy, efficient, −absent-minded, energetic, thorough, industrious |
| C6: deliberation | −hasty, −impulsive, −careless, −impatient, −immature, thorough, −moody |

*Note.* Adapted from Costa and McCrae (1992).

Neuroticism are anxiety, angry hostility, depression, self-consciousness, impulsiveness, and vulnerability.

The second major personality dimension is *Extraversion*. This factor refers to high activity (arousal), the experience of positive emotions, impulsiveness, assertiveness, and a tendency toward social behavior (Busato, Prins, Elshout, & Hamaker, 2000). Conversely, low Extraversion (Introversion) is characterized by rather quiet, restrained, and withdrawn behavioral patterns. Like Neuroticism, Extraversion is present in both Eysenck and Eysenck's (1985) and Costa and McCrae's (1992) personality models. The subfacets of Extraversion are warmth, gregariousness, assertiveness, activity, excitement-seeking, and positive emotions.

## TABLE 2.6
## NEO–PI–R Primary Traits (Facets) With Sample Items

### Neuroticism Facets

| | |
|---|---|
| N1: anxiety | "I am not a worrier." – |
| N2: angry hostility | "I often get angry at the way people treat me." |
| N3: depression | "I rarely feel lonely or blue." – |
| N4: self-consciousness | "In dealing with other people, I always dread making a social blunder." |
| N5: impulsiveness | "I rarely overindulge in anything." – |
| N6: vulnerability | "I often feel helpless and want someone else to solve my problems." |

### Extraversion Facets

| | |
|---|---|
| E1: warmth | "I really like most people I meet." |
| E2: gregariousness | "I shy away from the crowds of people." – |
| E3: assertiveness | "I am dominant, forceful, and assertive." |
| E4: activity | "I have a leisurely style in work and play." |
| E5: excitement-seeking | "I often crave excitement." |
| E6: positive emotions | "I have never literally jumped for joy." – |

### Openness Facets

| | |
|---|---|
| O1: fantasy | "I have a very active imagination." |
| O2: aesthetics | "Aesthetic and artistic concerns aren't very important to me." – |
| O3: feelings | "Without strong emotions, life would be uninteresting to me." |
| O4: actions | "I'm pretty set in my ways." – |
| O5: ideas | "I often enjoy playing with theories or abstract ideas." |
| O6: values | "I believe letting students hear controversial speakers can only confuse and mislead them." – |

### Agreeableness Facets

| | |
|---|---|
| A1: trust | "I tend to be cynical and skeptical of others' intentions." – |
| A2: straight-forwardness | "I am not crafty or sly." |
| A3: altruism | "Some people think I am selfish and egotistical." – |
| A4: compliance | "I would rather cooperate with others than compete with them." |
| A5: modesty | "I don't mind bragging about my talents and accomplishments." – |
| A6: tender-mindedness | "I think political leaders need to be more aware of the human side of their policies." |

**TABLE 2.6**    (*continued*)

| Conscientiousness Facets | |
|---|---|
| C1: competence | "I am known for my prudence and common sense." |
| C2: order | "I would rather keep my options open than plan everything in advance." |
| C3: dutifulness | "I try to perform all the tasks assigned to me conscientiously." |
| C4: achievement striving | "I am easy-going and lackadaisical." – |
| C5: self-discipline | "I am pretty good about pacing myself so as to get things done on time." |
| C6: deliberation | "Over the years I have done some pretty stupid things." – |

*Note.*   Adapted from Costa and McCrae (1992).

A third[2] dimension—namely, *Openness to Experience*—derived from the ideas of Coan (1974) and represents the tendency to involve oneself in intellectual activities and experience new sensations and ideas (Busato, Prins, Elshout, & Hamaker, 2000). This factor is also referred to as Creativity, Intellect, or Culture (Goldberg, 1994; Johnson, 1994; Saucier, 1994a, 1994b, Trapnell, 1994) and Tender-Mindedness or Affection (Brand, Egan, & Deary, 1993). It comprises six scales—namely, fantasy, aesthetics, feelings, actions, ideas, and values. In a general sense, Openness to Experience is associated with intellectual curiosity, aesthetic sensitivity, vivid imagination, behavioral flexibility, and unconventional attitudes (McCrae, 1993). People high on Openness to Experience tend to be dreamy, imaginative, inventive, and nonconservative in their thoughts and opinions (Costa & McCrae, 1992). Poets and artists may be regarded as typical examples of high Openness scorers (McCrae & Costa, 1997a).

A fourth factor, *Agreeableness* (also known as Sociability), refers to friendly, considerate, and modest behavior. This factor is associated with a tendency toward friendliness and nurturance (Busato, Prins, Elshout, & Hamaker, 2000). It comprises the subfacets of trust, straightforwardness, altruism, compliance, modesty, and tender-mindedness. Agreeable people can thus be described as caring, friendly, warm, and tolerant

---

[2]Although throughout most of this book Openness is listed in the third place, this order is only in accordance with the denomination of Costa and McCrae's (1992) questionnaire (i.e., the NEO [Neuroticism-Extraversion-Openness] personality inventory). It is, however, noteworthy that most of the literature tends to refer to Openness as Factor Five.

(Costa & McCrae, 1992). This personality trait is negatively related to Psychoticism and (together with Conscientiousness) is a main exponent of social behavior in general.

Finally *Conscientiousness* is associated with responsibility and persistence (Busato, Prins, Elshout, & Hamaker, 2000). This factor includes the second order dimensions of competence, order, dutifulness, achievement striving, self-discipline, and deliberation. Conscientious individuals are best identified for their efficiency, organization, determination, and productivity. No wonder, then, that this personality dimension has been reported to be significantly associated with various types of performance (see chap. 5).

As mentioned earlier, the Five Factor model has sometimes been criticized for its lack of theoretical explanations on the development and nature of the processes underlying some of its personality factors—in particular, Openness, Agreeableness, and Conscientiousness (see Matthews & Deary, 1998, for a detailed discussion). However (perhaps as a consequence of its good validity and reliability), most of the recent literature dealing with the personality–intelligence interface has focused on the relationship between psychometric intelligence and the Big Five personality factors (Ackerman & Heggestad, 1997; Brand, 1994; Zeidner & Matthews, 2000). Further, most researchers seem to agree on the existence of five main personality dimensions as well as the advantages of assessing these dimensions through the NEO–PI–R (e.g., Busato, Prins, Elshout, & Hamaker, 2000; De Raad, 1996; Digman, 1990; Furnham, 1996a, 1996b, 1997). Perhaps the most obvious advantage of this is the agreement, which allows researchers to compare and replicate studies on personality and other variables because there is a shared or common framework and instrument to assess personality. Thus, even if the theoretical conceptualization of personality may lack explanatory power, systematic data collection with the same instrument may help answer some of the questions underlying personality traits. In that sense, the choice of a unique instrument to assess individual differences in personality may be compared to that of a single, universal currency or software, which provides a common ground for trading and decoding (of goods, information, or knowledge). Besides, the advantage of the NEO–PI–R Five Factor model is that it accounts not only for a lay taxonomy of personality (based on the lexical hypothesis), but also other established systems that can somehow be translated into the Five Factor system. Thus, other findings with other scales may also be interpreted in terms of the Big Five personality traits, like other currencies that can be converted into dollars or euros according to a given exchange rate.

Therefore, most of this book focuses on the psychometric evidence for the relationship between intellectual competence and the Big Five personality traits, although other relevant traits are also examined.

## 2.6  SUMMARY AND CONCLUSIONS

In this chapter, we examined the concept of personality, reviewing the salient historical aspects and dominant taxonomies of personality traits. As observed, the idea that there are consistent patterns of behavior that may be ascribed to latent variables or traits is as old as ancient Greek medicine. Further, the notion that these individual differences have biological causes is equally ancient and has dominated prepsychological conceptualizations of personality.

Although several modern psychological theories have questioned this idea, differential psychology as a robust empirical discipline is based entirely on the principle of traits, which are useful to understand and predict human behavior in a variety of aspects. Nevertheless, debate on the number of independent or major dimensions of personality has dominated the field since Eysenck and Cattell, two major figures in the field with unmatched contributions to personality theory and research.

Eysenck's biological theory of personality comprised three main dimensions—Neuroticism, Extraversion, and Psychoticism—and is still used in differential research, although the biological aspects of the theory seem out of date and the conceptualization of Psychoticism has been debated (Brody, 1988; Matthews & Deary, 1998). Cattell's approach, based on the lexical hypothesis (the assumption that all aspects of personality are mapped onto words and language), was abandoned on psychometric grounds, but gave birth to the current state of the art taxonomy, the Five Factor or Big Five model.

Despite the lack of theoretical explanatory power of the Big Five framework (in particular compared with Eysenck's theory), its robust psychometric properties, reflected in a substantial body of evidence in support of the validity and reliability of the NEO–PI–R (Costa & McCrae, 1985, 1992), have persuaded most personality researchers to investigate personality with the NEO–PI–R, which assesses the five major personality traits of Neuroticism, Extraversion, Openness to Experience, Agreeableness, and Conscientiousness (and underlying subfacets). Given the obvious advantages of employing a universal language for the study of personality traits, and the growing consensus on the choice of a reliable and validated tool, the present book examines the relationship between personality and intellectual competence in terms of the Big Five personality traits.

# 3

# Intellectual Ability

Although the idea that some individuals are more talented, bright, gifted, or clever than others probably always existed in human society, the concept of intellectual ability has its roots in scientific psychology. More specifically, the psychological notion of intelligence derived from the use of psychometric instruments to predict future scholastic achievement, which may perhaps explain why there are almost as many definitions of *intelligence* as types of ability tests. It is not surprising, then, that one of the best-known definitions has referred to intelligence as that which intelligence tests measure (Boring, 1923). Despite the circular and operational emptiness of this definition (which often overlooks the fact that Boring also conceptualized and defined intelligence in terms of a general mental power factor that develops mainly in the first 5 years of life), it will help as a good starting point to understand how the psychological concept of intelligence developed approximately 100 years ago and the great extent to which measurement and theory are intertwined.

Intelligence is only an inferred notion—that is, a latent variable, a theoretical construct. However, it refers to observable behavior, and the extent to which intelligence is or is not a meaningful concept ultimately depends on empirical data or observable behavior. Typically, this behavior is measured in terms of individual differences in standardized performance and test results correlated with real-life outcomes, such as academic exam grades or job performance (although we see that this constitutes only one—namely, the psychometric approach to intelligence). Figure 3.1 depicts the latent concept of intelligence in terms of both test and real-world performance, and any definition of intelligence will have to conceptualize the underlying or latent processes to which these individual differences can be attributed. Although there are several, rather than one, definitions of intelligence (even within differential psy-

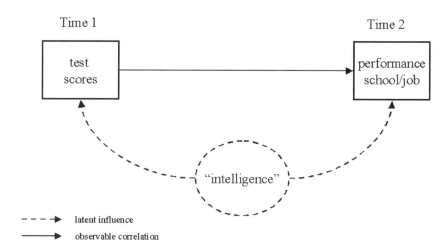

FIG. 3.1.   Graphical depiction of the latent concept of intelligence in relation to both test scores and real-world performance.

chology), it may be appropriate to think of intelligence as a general ability or capacity to know, comprehend, or learn. Intelligence then does not refer to specific abilities, but to an "indivisible quality of mind that influences the execution of all consciously directed activities" (Robinson, 1999, p. 720).

Definitions of *intelligence* are examined more closely throughout this book, but it should suffice for an overview and preliminary understanding of the concept to define it as a "general ability to reason, plan, solve problems, think abstractly, learn quickly, and learn from experience" (Gottfredson, 2000, p. 81).

## 3.1   HISTORY OF INTELLIGENCE TESTING

As said, the idea that some individuals are brighter than others certainly precedes the development of psychometrics. This is reflected in the number of words referring to able and unable individuals in virtually every language. The Oxford Thesaurus, for instance, provides the following synonyms of intelligence: "clever, bright, sharp-witted, quick-witted, talented, gifted, smart, capable, able, competent, apt, knowledgeable, educated, sagacious, brainy, shrewd, astute, adroit, canny, cunning, ingenious, wily, inventive, skillful." Nevertheless, the beginnings of scientific psychological research on intelligence are psychometric in nature and easy to trace in both time and space (we concern ourselves with lay theories of intelligence throughout chap. 6).

The first scientific attempt to conceptualize individual differences in cognitive ability was that of Francis Galton (1822–1911), who argued that "genius" was hereditary and normally distributed in the population (two ideas still shared by most experts in the field). Further, Galton (1883) designed a laboratory to measure differences in basic cognitive functions; he believed that these differences could be used as proxy measures of a man's intellectual capacity, and he applied several statistical methods (most based on Quetelet, 1796–1874) to compare individuals in what he believed were scientific indicators of genius.

A similar method was employed by James McKeen Cattell (1890) to identify 10 basic psychological functions (e.g., tactile discrimination, hearing, and RT) and devise the first known "mental test." However, most of the variables measured by this test were more elemental than mental, and they referred to basic cognitive processes that are now known to be related to intelligence, but certainly fail to define the concept in broad terms.

In an attempt to elaborate a measure of intelligence as a whole—that is, accounting not only for basic cognitive processes, but also for the more abstract and higher order ability to perform mental operations—Alfred Binet (1857–1911) would set the foundations of modern intelligence testing. As Cronbach (1984) pointed out, "a history of mental testing is in large a history of Binet's scale and its descendants" (p. 192). Thus, Binet's (1903) pioneering research in France, 100 years ago, is usually regarded as the starting point of psychometrics and intellectual ability research.

In 1904, the government of France commissioned Binet the creation of a method to identify children with learning difficulties in regular classes. The result was the creation of a standardized test to measure reasoning ability and the use of judgment. This test contained items or questions (six per year level) that could be answered by average children of different ages. For instance, 3-year-olds would be asked to point their eyes or nose; 7-year-olds, to describe a picture. Children were tested and interviewed individually and responded to items in order of increasing difficulty. The last level of difficulty they could answer correctly determined their level of reasoning and learning ability. The child's score was calculated in terms of the average age of children who answer the same number of questions—that is, by comparison to other children. Specifically, this was scored in terms of years and months, so that answering correctly all questions of Level 7 plus three in Level 8 would indicate that the child's ability or mental age is that of someone age 7.5 or 7½ years.

Although Binet's test is usually referred to as the first psychometric intelligence test (and a milestone in the history of intelligence theory and research), it was the American adaptation of this test, introduced in Stanford by Terman (1916), that would have a greater impact on the psychometrics of intelligence (and still exist in revised versions until today). The major modifications of this version were the inclusion of an adult scale and the way scores were calculated. A child's score would now be expressed as intellectual quotient (IQ—a term introduced by Stern, 1912)—that is, the mental age divided by the chronological or real age multiplied by 100.

Thus, someone age 10 who responded correctly up to Level 10 would have an IQ of 100 (average), someone age 10 who responded correctly up to Level 8 would have an IQ of 80 (below average), and someone age 10 who responded correctly up to Level 12 would have an IQ of 120 (above average). In the 1960s, these normative differences were standardized through a measure called *standard deviation* (a comparative indicator of a person's score with regard to the general population), which would eventually replace Terman's formula and is still being used to compare individuals in intelligence (not just according to age, but also specific population groups such as gender, ethnicity, and nationality). Today the concept of IQ is almost a synonym of intelligence and is used widely by both lay people and academics. It is graphically represented by a normal distribution or *bell curve* of scores, with a mean of 100 and an *SD* of 15 (set for all IQ tests), which is virtually ubiquitous to psychometric intelligence testing (see Fig. 3.2).

Despite their usefulness in the prediction of school grades, Binet's instruments were mainly an applied tool and did not refer to any theory— not even to operationally defined constructs. Thus, even after Terman's (1916) American adaptation of Binet's scale, a test that would prove a reliable measure for the prediction of school performance for many decades, there had been little efforts to define intelligence or elaborate a theory for understanding individual differences in intellectual ability.

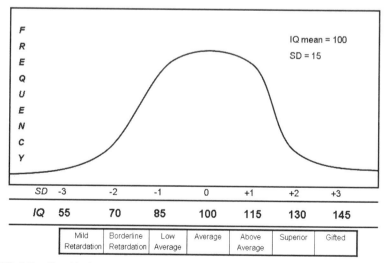

FIG. 3.2.   Graphical representation of the *bell curve* or normal distribution of IQ scores.

## 3.2   PSYCHOMETRIC INTELLIGENCE
## AND THE NOTION OF *g*

In Britain, Spearman's (1863–1945) early application of factor analysis and data-reduction procedures allowed him to show that different ability tests were significantly intercorrelated, and that the common variance could be statistically represented in terms of a single, general, factor (see Fig. 3.3). Like Galton and Cattell, Spearman (1904) started from basic individual differences in information processing, looking at elementary cognitive processes such as olfactory and visual sensory discrimination. Like Binet, however, he contrasted these scores with academic performance indicators, enabling a criterion to examine the validity of his measure (i.e., whether it could accurately distinguish between high and low performance or level of education).

Deary (1994) showed that Spearman's interpretation of elementary processes as the basis of individual differences in ability was supported by studies correlating these processes with academic performance. It is now believed that basic cognitive processes, such as inspection time, may account for approximately 20% of the variance in an IQ test (see Davidson & Downing, 2000). Perhaps the main advantage of focusing on elementary processes to define individual differences in intellectual ability is the possibility of designing robust experiments in laboratory conditions. This led to the increase of cognitive experiments on intelligence in the 1970s and early 1980s, causing a paradigmatic revival of early concep-

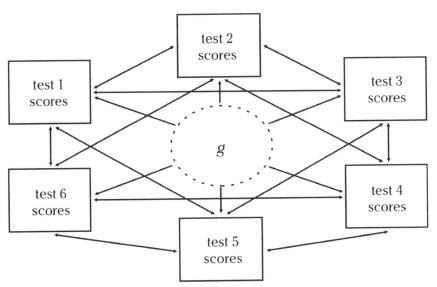

FIG. 3.3.   Illustration of the concept of *g* (general intelligence) as underlying common variance to different cognitive tests.

tualizations, such as Spearman's and Cattell's. Thus, rather than measuring intelligence through a series of abstract and unobservable mental operations that are assumed to take place while participants complete an ability test, researchers attempted to define intelligence in terms of reaction time (Jensen, 1982) or inspection time (Deary, 1986).

Spearman (1927) argued that, although there may be different aspects of cognitive performance (or abilities), intelligence could be represented as a general underlying capability. Unfortunately, much of the following research on psychometrics focused on the statistical properties of standardized performance test, producing a lack of theoretical knowledge on the nature of the processes underlying individual differences in intelligence. Furthermore, the existence of Spearman's general intelligence factor was questioned directly by Thurnstone (1938), who devised a (very useful) statistical technique called *multiple factor analysis*. This method, which is still largely represented in the American educational approach to the measurement of abilities in Grades 1 to 12, was in contradiction to Spearman's procedure of data analysis based on decomposition of the variance and multiple factor loadings and identification, attributing great portions of a matrix covariance to an independent group of factors. However, both methods could be combined to overcome the initially excluding solutions and establish a hierarchical model of abilities, which acknowledged both general and specific factors.

## 3.3  CATTELL'S THEORY OF FLUID AND CRYSTALLIZED INTELLIGENCE

Spearman's (1904, 1927) findings had a crucial impact on one of the most influential theories of intelligence until this date—namely, Cattell's (1987) theory of crystallized (Gc) and fluid intelligence (Gf). Based on the idea that there are different types of ability tests, Cattell distinguished between Gf or the ability to perform well on nonverbal tasks, which do not require previous knowledge, but measure a rather *pure*, culture-free element of cognitive performance (to some this aspect of intelligence is comparable to Spearman's notion of a general intelligence factor; see e.g., Jensen, 1982) and Gc or the ability to do well on verbal tasks, which are substantially influenced by previous knowledge and acculturated learning (rather than being a raw measure of basic mental capabilities).

Broadly speaking, Gf represents information processing and reasoning ability (i.e., inductive, conjunctive, disjunctive reasoning capability used to understand relations and abstract prepositions; Stankov, 2000). Conversely, Gc is used to acquire, retain, organize, and conceptualize information, rather than information processing. Gf is dependent on the efficient functioning of the central nervous system, whereas Gc is dependent on experience and education within a culture. A useful metaphor to understand the relationship between Gf and Gc, as well as their meaning, is that of a computer. Gf would represent the processor, memory, and other characteristics of the hardware. In contrast, Gc would be equivalent to the software as well as the data and information contained in the files and other software. Hence, Gf, like the processor of a PC, refers to processes rather than content. Conversely, Gc, like the data files and software stored and loaded onto a PC, would refer to content (or information) rather than processes. Measuring both Gf and Gc is beneficial in the sense of indicating both a person's learning potential as well as his or her accumulated learning (Stankov et al., 1995). In addition, Cattell (1987) added Gsar, a third dimension of intelligence, to conceptualize performance on short-term memory and retrieval tasks—namely, tests that require manipulation and information retrieval in short-term memory. Figure 3.4 depicts Cattell's three-component theory of intelligence.

Although there has been a tendency for almost 50 years (approximately between 1940 and 1990) to employ tests of Gf or nonverbal abilities, rather than Gc or verbal abilities, the last 10 years have been dominated by a rein vindication of measures of Gc (see Ackerman, 1999; Ackerman & Heggestad, 1997). Several researchers have argued that previous attempts to focus on the measurement of Gf were politically, rather than scientifically, founded (Anastasi, 2004; Robinson, 1999), and that there is long-standing evidence for the predictive power of Gc over and above Gf (see also McNemar, 1942). Furthermore, it has been shown that intelligent individuals tend to do better on verbal than nonverbal measures, whereas the opposite is true for lower IQ scorers (see Matarazzo, 1972).

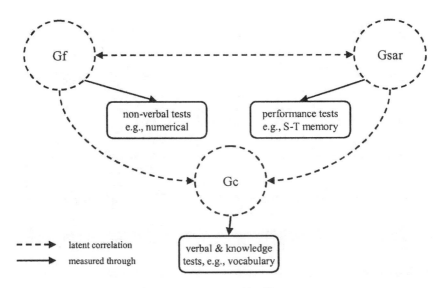

FIG. 3.4.   Cattell's (1987) three components of intelligence.

Thus, Gc measures would be a better tool to distinguish between high and low intelligence, and would therefore represent a better instrument for the measurement of individual differences underlying intellectual ability (this is true even in Binet's data). Moreover, it has been argued (Robinson, 1999; Terman & Merrill, 1937) that one cannot understand adult human intelligence without reference to any conceptual knowledge (i.e., individual differences in comprehension, use, and knowledge of concepts would constitute the essence of intelligence). Hence, verbal ability tests (e.g., tests of verbal comprehension, general knowledge, and vocabulary) would represent an optimal single measure of general intellectual ability.

## 3.4 GENETIC VERSUS ENVIRONMENTAL CAUSES OF INTELLIGENCE

Much more than personality, the idea that intelligence may be inherited has powerful and social implications and has thus been exempted of objective scientific examination at times. Rather, the genetic basis of intelligence has been the center of heated, often irrational, debate to the extent that it is probably impossible to know with certainty how many results have been faked, misreported, or censored because of these implications.

Both Binet and Spearman, pioneers in the psychological study of intelligence, believed that there was a strong hereditary basis for individual differences in intellectual ability; however, they also acknowledged the influence of sociocultural (i.e., environmental) factors on the development of specific skills. Thus, although individuals with the same education may differ in ability due to biological causes, two individuals with the same IQ may experience different intellectual developments if exposed to unequal—in particular, opposite—training or environments. Such is the case of social class, long identified as a significant correlate of intelligence, although (as with most correlational studies) the causal direction underlying this relationship has been a topic of ideological, rather than scientific, scrutiny. Thus, there has been a long-standing debate on whether social class determines intelligence or vice versa—a debate of political and almost moral (but rarely scientific) nature that has affected the reputation of IQ tests and even differential psychology. Figure 3.5 depicts several possible causal paths for understanding the relationship among social class, education, and intelligence.

There has been evidence both in favor and against the hypothesis that intelligence can be inherited, and this ambiguity has probably increased the debate. Besides this controversy, several adoption and twins studies provided interesting results in support of both genetic and environmental theories of intelligence, suggesting that individual differences in ability can be determined by genes as well as the environment. Early evidence for the genetic basis of intelligence was reported by Newman,

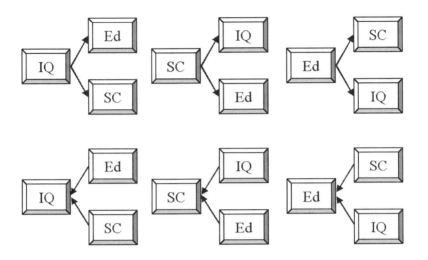

*Note:* IQ = intelligence, Ed = education, SC = social class (only unidirectional causations are presented)

FIG. 3.5. Some possible combinations for the causal relationships underlying the significant correlations among intelligence, education, and social class.

Freeman, and Holzinger (1937), who found that monozygotic twins were more similar in intelligence than dizygotic twins even if they were raised apart. Studies on adopted children confirmed these findings, reporting larger correlations between natural parents and children than between adoptive parents and children (even when children had virtually zero contact with their natural parents). The data suggest that only 17% of the variance in IQ could be accounted for by environmental (nongenetic) factors.

However, Kamin (1974) noted that several studies by Burt (a great supporter of the idea that intelligence had a strong genetic basis) reported fake data on monozygotic twins, inflating the correlations of intelligence. This encouraged a new wave of researcher (undoubtedly helped by the technological advances of behavioral genetics) on adopted children and twins. Twin studies have shown that, although intelligence is largely inheritable, there are some environmental influences that cause siblings raised in the same family to have different intelligences (Plomin, Fulker, Corley, & DeFries, 1997). However, adoptions studies have yielded conflicting results as correlations were found to be variable, ranging from as little as $r = .22$ up to as high as $r = .77$ (see Grigorenko, 2000).

## 3.5  PIAGET AND THE DEVELOPMENTAL THEORY OF COGNITIVE ABILITY

Although most sections in this chapter focus on the psychometric development of the concept of intelligence, the contribution of Jean Piaget (1896–1980), a famous developmental psychologist, cannot be neglected. Piaget (1952; Piaget & Inhelder, 1969) identified various developmental stages in the evolution of adult intellect with its underlying abilities mapped throughout childhood. Thus, he was concerned with the question of how individuals arrive to the adult processes of intellectual functioning. His theory of intellectual development is based on four universal stages—namely, *sensorimotor, preoperational, operational* and *formal operational*—that describe a baby's intellectual transition from a nonverbal, preconceptual elementary stage in the early 4 years of life to the complex stages of language skills and conceptual reasoning of young adolescence.

Like Spearman, Piaget also believed in a single, general intelligence factor. However, Piaget focused on the evolutionary or developmental aspects of this factor, which he considered the result of a series of ubiquitous qualitative stages. Further, unlike most early psychologists concerned with intelligence, Piaget was more interested in the elaboration of a theoretical framework for understanding the development of adult intelligence from early childhood than the actual study of individual differences. Thus his theory was more about similarities (in the development of skills) than differences, learned or inherited, between individuals.

The essence of Piaget's (1952) theory is that there is a universal interaction between biological and environmental variables that accounts for the progressive development of adult human intelligence. At each evolutionary stage (sensorimotor, preoperational, concrete operational, and formal operational), there are certain cognitive functions that individuals are able to do, and the acquisition of some is a precondition of others. Therefore, this theory explains the passage from basic sensorial and motor skills (at the age of 2 years) to very abstract (formal/logical) mental operations. This passage is explained mainly in terms of adaptation (assimilation and accommodation) and organization (linking mental structures that can be applied to the real world).

Despite the theoretical importance and robust nature of Piaget's findings, his theory remained virtually unrelated to differential approaches to intelligence, with few attempts of applying it to individual differences taxonomies. This may be due not only to Piaget's different approach to intelligence, but also to the fact that his theory applies entirely to children and adolescents (with final stages of intellectual development at approximately age 15). Thus, albeit a fundamental contribution to developmental psychology, the applied implications of Piaget's theory to individual differences in intellectual ability remain of secondary importance. However, it is important to bear in mind that, because Piaget's theory does not overlap with differential approaches to intelligence (rather it provides a qualitative explanation of the development of the processes underlying universal cognitive functions that are present in adult mental operations), it can be used to understand structural aspects of human intelligence. Once these structural aspects are present, we can concern ourselves with testing individual differences in intelligence and attempt to answer the question of how and why some people are more intelligent than others.

## 3.6 DEBATE: *g* VERSUS MULTIPLE ABILITIES

Although the predictive validity of well-established IQ measures is well documented, several critics have argued that the traditional conception of intelligence is not comprehensive and refers mainly to academic abilities or being "book smart" (Gardner, 1983; Goleman, 1995; Sternberg, 1985, 1988, 1997). Furthermore, it has been argued that individual differences in intellectual ability should be conceptualized in terms of multiple intelligences, rather than a single, general intelligence because individuals may be good at some, but bad at other, ability tests.

This idea has gained support in the last two decades, but was most emphatically defended by Guilford (1967, 1977, 1981, 1985), who proposed the most comprehensive catalogue of human abilities, describing up to 150 different types. This model was based on the preliminary distinction among the three dimensions of *operations*, *products*, and *contents*. According to Guilford, there were five types of operations (cognition, memory, divergent production, convergent production, and evaluation), five types of contents (auditory, visual, symbolic, semantic, behavioral), and six types of products (units, classes, relations, systems, transformations, implications; see Fig. 3.6). This extensive classification would result in a combination of 150 abilities (Guilford, 1977). However, Guilford's (1981) revision of the model eventually acknowledged the existence of a hierarchy including 85 second-order and 16 third-order factors, although evidence for this model is yet to be provided (Brody, 1992, 2000).

Although there have been a variety of theories in the last 20 years to propose that intelligence should be understood in terms of many abilities— rather than a single ability (see Section 3.6)—the scientific study of intelligence has provided substantial evidence for both the positive manifold of correlated ability test scores derived from Spearman's original *g* hypotheses, as well as the predictive power of general intellectual ability with regard to academic outcomes.

In a large psychometric study that tested 2,450 individuals (across the United States), on the third revised version of the *Wechsler Adult Intelligence Test* (*WAIS–III*), one of the most established and prestigious measures of intelligence, all correlations among the 13 subtests of this measure (vocabulary, similarities, information, comprehension, picture completion, block design, picture arrangement, matrix reasoning, arith-

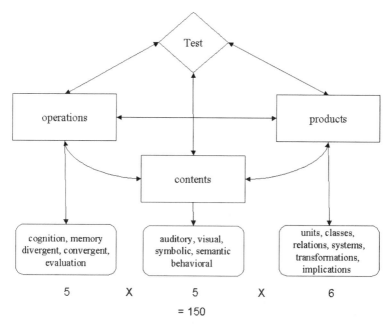

FIG. 3.6.    A graphical depiction of Guilford's (1977) model of intelligence.

metic, digit span, letter-number sequencing, digit-symbol coding, and symbol search) were significant and positive (ranging from $r = .30$ to $r = .80$ approximately; see Wechsler, 1997). The pattern of correlations also supported Cattell's idea that some types of tests (verbal on one hand and nonverbal on the other) are more interrelated than others, but the underlying general intelligence factor hypothesized to be the source of variations between individuals' cognitive performance was clearly identified in this large and representative data set. This hypothesis refers to the general tendency of individuals to perform consistently well, modestly, or poor on different types of intellectual ability tests. Thus, mental abilities, as tested by different ability tests, tend to be closely associated so that they cluster together in one common factor (see again Fig. 3.3). This factor, which accounts for approximately 50% of the variance in IQ test performance, is the best existent measure of individual differences in human intelligence.

Perhaps the most convincing source of evidence for the existence of a general intelligence factor derived from Carroll's (1993) book on human intelligence—a great meta-analytic review of the salient 20th century studies on intellectual abilities. After reanalyzing more than 400 sets of data, results reveal that a single, general intelligence factor emerges to account for a considerable amount of variance in ability test performance. This factor was identified at the highest hierarchical level of the pyramid and may be thought of as the determinant of different types of cognitive performance—namely, fluid intelligence, crystallized intelligence, general memory and learning, processing speed, broad cognitive speediness, broad retrieval ability, broad auditory perception, and broad visual perception (see Fig. 3.7).

These eight types of abilities or ability clusters constitute the second level of the hierarchy, which is noteworthy because the theory of general intelligence does not, by any means, deny the existence of these different and differentiable types of abilities. What it does suggest, however, is that although these types of abilities at the second level of the hierarchy refer to different aspects of human performance, all these aspects tend to be significantly correlated so that, in any large and representative sample, those individuals who do well in some tests will also show a tendency to do well on the other tests and vice versa.

Thus, the debate about whether there are one or many intelligences is often based on the fallacy that these two hypotheses are exclusive of each other, when in fact both things are true. There are many identifiable and distinctive types of abilities (not only the Level 2 abilities summarized earlier, but also narrower, Level 3 abilities, which can be mapped onto Level 2), but there is also a general intelligence factor that accounts for most of the variance in different ability test performance. Accordingly, a great deal of the nature of the debate on the number of factors to conceptualize human intelligence is relative because the structure of human intellectual ability can be conceptualized in terms of different levels or stratums, which support the idea that there are many specific abilities, as well as one underlying intelligence factor. In that sense, it can be said that there is

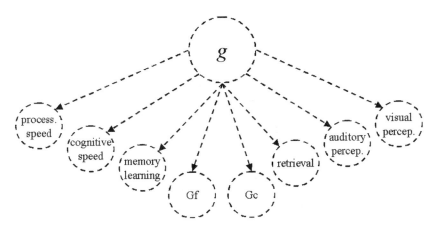

FIG. 3.7.  Conceptual representation of Carroll's (1993) hierarchical structure of intelligence.

a lack of justification for the arguments against the existence of a general intelligence factor: The data clearly show it does exist (Carroll, 1993; Deary, 2001; Wechsler, 1997). Another issue is whether it is useful—that is, whether it can be effectively used to predict real-life outcomes, particularly beyond academic performance or school success, but this is discussed elsewhere (see chaps. 5 and 7).

### 3.7   OTHER APPROACHES: EMOTIONAL, SOCIAL, AND PRACTICAL INTELLIGENCE

Considering the vast amount of psychometric evidence in support of the idea of a general intelligence factor that accounts for a substantial amount of variance in different types and aspects of intellectual performance, it is perhaps no surprise that the principal dissidents of the $g$ factor have preferred to ignore existent data sets and focus on the design of novel abilities. Hence, rather than directing any effort to explaining the positive manifold of correlated ability tests, they have insisted on identifying new types of intelligences, which they believed to be uncorrelated with $g$. Although most of these efforts have had a poor impact on the development of individual differences research, in particular intelligence, it should be noted that this rather original area of research has had a substantial influence on the personality–intelligence interface and may be regarded as a preliminary approach to the integration of noncognitive and cognitive individual differences.

Although this theoretical line is not novel (Gardner, 1983), it has generated much enthusiasm in recent years, particularly since the conceptualization of *emotional intelligence* (Goleman, 1995; Hein, 1997; Salovey & Mayer, 1990; Steiner, 1997). Nevertheless other types, notably *social intelligence* (Thorndike, 1920), may be more representative of the original or preliminary efforts to include traditionally nonability components within the realm of human capabilities. Thorndike defined *social intelligence* as an individual's ability to understand and manage others, as well as a general tendency to act wisely in human relations. Despite the theoretically innovative and attractive nature of social intelligence (an ability that referred to individuals rather than mathematical or logical problems), several measurement problems led to the progressive vanishing of this construct from individual differences research (Cronbach, 1984). However, Gardner (1983, 1999) reinvented the concept in terms of *interpersonal intelligence*, which he defined as one's ability to deal with others and act wisely in interpersonal relations. These types of nontraditional abilities (conceptualized as independent abilities from verbal and mathematical abilities) are often grouped under the label of *hot* intelligences, as opposed to the rather mathematical, cognitive, and *cold* characteristics of traditional intellectual ability. Although it is not the aim of this book to discuss theories of multiple abilities, hot intelligences are an interesting and original example of an attempt to broaden the concept of intellectual ability, and most of these abilities were essentially conceptualized to emphasize that there is much more to human performance than intellectual ability (as conceived of in terms of IQ test scores), but is there?

Even when researchers and lay people may both agree that the measurement of human ability in terms of IQ test results may only provide limited information about a person's capability to perform in the future—that is, about her or his potential for future achievement—and even if other necessary components for real-world success have been identified (such as in social and emotional intelligence theories), the psychometrics of hot abilities have yet to provide reliable and valid methods to quantify and assess these noncognitive individual differences *in ability*. The fact is that many of Gardner's multiple intelligences (notably verbal, musical, and mathematical abilities) have been reported to be significantly intercorrelated, in which case the term *multiple intelligences* would only be correctly applied to the second stratum or hierarchy within the structure of intelligence. As regarding the other types of intelligences he conceptualized (e.g., kinesthetic, spiritual, personal), their particular independence from general intelligence is predominantly due to the fact that they cannot be measured psychometrically. Thus there are no power tests[1] for many of these multiple intelligences (e.g., musical), and their classification within the realm of intellectual abilities is highly questionable not only empirically, but also theoretically (because they would seem to be part of personality rather than intelligence).

To date there is more enthusiasm about the usefulness of emotional and social intelligence than evidence for their existence as independent ability factors (which account for unique variance in real-life outcomes). There are usually two types of problems—one is the unreliability of power measures of emotional or social intelligence, and the other is the low validity of preference inventories in predicting real-life criteria. Furthermore, self-report inventories of emotional and social intelligence tend to overlap substantially with established personality traits, which questions the usefulness and need to design and assess novel constructs.

Thus, sound claims that hot abilities represent a novel type of abilities within the realm of human intelligence must at least address two psychometric issues. First, they must show moderate correlation with measures of traditional intellectual ability (thus, they should be expected to correlate in the order of $r = .30$ with measures of $g$), showing that, albeit referring to novel abilities or skills, they are still representing something of the intelligence domain. Second, they should not be highly correlated with established personality traits. Hot abilities, as any other novel type of abilities put forward, must then be shown to be closer to intellectual abil-

---

[1]The expression *power tests* refers to standardized, timed performance measures with objectively and unique correct responses for each item (Cronbach, 1989).

ity than to personality traits without, however, being too close to psychometric intelligence (*g*) and without being explained in terms of individual differences in personality traits. Further, to be classified within the realm of intelligence, hot abilities should be *measured* rather than *assessed*—that is, through power tests including correct and incorrect responses, rather than assessed through inventories of preferences containing Likert scales or items referring to typical behaviors, rather than correct and incorrect answers.

Petrides and Furnham (2000) proposed that the study of emotional intelligence should follow *either* the path of assessment/personality *or* measurement/intelligence, but not both simultaneously. This methodological distinction would, a priori, determine two different options of study. So-called *mixed conceptualizations* of emotional intelligence should therefore be replaced by either trait (nonability) or information-processing (ability) models. Accordingly, Petrides and Furnham (2001) developed a self-report inventory to assess trait emotional intelligence, which has been shown to be significantly correlated with Neuroticism (negative) and Extraversion (positive), albeit accounting for unique variance in individual differences—that is, 60% of the variance in trait emotional intelligence has been shown to be independent of both Neuroticism and Extraversion.

Progress on the measurement of emotional intelligence (through power or maximal performance test) has been more problematic. As mentioned earlier, the difficulties associated with the design of items with objectively correct and incorrect responses have made power test of emotional intelligence infrequent and unreliable (Davies, Stankov, & Roberts, 1998). Thus, inventories of trait EI would comprise self-report items and refer to self-perceived emotional intelligence, whereas information-processing measures should include items with correct and incorrect responses, such as those in Mayer, Salovey, and Caruso (2000) or the face-recognition test used to measure emotion perception.

Finally another salient exponent of hot intelligences—namely *practical intelligence*—can be found in Sternberg's (1985; see also Sternberg & O'Hara, 2000) triarchic theory of intelligence, which also includes *analytical/academic* and *creative intelligences*. Practical intelligence refers to one's ability to make solutions effective, solve real-world problems, and apply ideas to real-world contexts and problems. Thus, it refers to tacit, practical, and everyday knowledge, and Sternberg believes this type of intelligence to be independent of academic or traditional cognitive ability. Sternberg and Wagner (1993) provided a detailed comparative distinction between academic/analytical and practical tasks, which would refer to the need of conceptualizing an independent, more applied type of ability, different than that defined in terms of traditional cognitive ability. As they argued, academic problems tend to be well defined, possess a single correct answer, and are of little intrinsic interest, whereas practical problems tend to be ill defined, have multiple correct responses, and require personal motivation to be solved. Although these different aspects of ability were well mapped (factor analyzed) onto lay conception's of intelligence (Sternberg et al., 1981), there is little empirical evidence for the existence of testable individual differences in practical intelligence, particularly in terms of psychometric instruments. Furthermore, claims that individual differences in practical problem solving can be better explained in terms of practical, than academic or general, intelligence have yet to be supported empirically (see Gottfredson, 2002, for a close examination of this topic).

## 3.8  SUMMARY AND CONCLUSIONS

Before we summarize the salient points discussed in this chapter, it is worth looking at a major benchmark in intelligence research, often quoted in textbook and handbooks on intellectual ability. This refers to the 1996 publication, in the *Wall Street Journal*, of a dossier compiled by experts in the field of intelligence to install some order in the literature and attempt to establish a state-of-the-art consensual view on the *known* and *unknowns* of intelligence. This occurred as a consequence of heated popular and scientific debate on a widely researched topic (and after almost a century of research on intelligence at that time).

Despite apparent contradictions and semipopular criticisms, this dossier showed that there is great consensus on the nature of intellectual ability. Although definitions can vary and there is a lack of clear-cut, simple, predominant definitions of intelligence (a fact that may be attributed to both the latent and complex nature of this construct), there is substantial agreement among experts on a variety of issues surrounding the concept of intelligence. Thus, 52 eminent researchers in the field agreed that:

> Intelligence is a very general mental capability that, among other things, involves the ability to reason, plan, solve problems, think abstractly, comprehend complex ideas, learn quickly and learn from experience. It is not merely book learning, a narrow academic skill, or test-taking smarts. Rather, it reflects a broader and deeper capability for comprehending our surroundings—"catching on," "making sense" of things, or "figuring out" what to do.

In light of the issues discussed in this chapter, we can only agree with this definition. After a close examination of the literature and both theoretical and empirical published material on intelligence, we have seen that intellectual ability, as measured psychometrically, does indeed refer to a general, overall capability that reflects individual differences in reasoning, problem solving, and learning. We have also observed that, although this ability has been mainly examined with regard to academic performance—where both theories and instruments were developed as a pragmatic scientific effort to predict future success and failure in scholastic settings, an anticipation based on differences in children's learning capacity—psychometric intelligence is a powerful predictor of human performance.

Further, the reliability and validity of psychometric intelligence compares to no other psychological measure of individual differences, and efforts to develop novel constructs of ability (notably hot intelligences, such as social, practical, or emotional intelligence) have yet to provide robust evidence for both the predictive power and the usefulness (incremental validity) of these psychological constructs in the wider realm of individual differences.

Thus, although there have been claims that intelligence should be conceptualized as a set of independent/orthogonal abilities (rather than a single intellectual capacity), it is clear from the positive multiple intercorrelations between different measures of cognitive performance that there is a general factor in which people can be measured and compared.

At the same time, there are two major aspects of intelligence—namely, the ability to learn new things and solve novel problems (irrespective of previous experience, knowledge, or education) (Gf), and the accumulated content (information) that can be used to solve problems related to what one has already learned (Gc) (Cattell, 1987). Because these are two wide, easily distinguishable components of intelligence, which nonetheless acknowledge the existence of a general underlying factor, we emphasize this distinction in relation to personality traits in particular throughout chapter 4 (which deals with the personality–intelligence interface).

# The Personality-Intelligence Interface

The most traditional approach to the integration of cognitive and noncognitive traits has been the psychometric interface between established ability measures and personality inventories. Rather than identifying and putting forward novel constructs that may expand the conceptualization of intellectual ability beyond individual differences in abstract reasoning or spatial, verbal, and mathematical ability, researchers have often attempted to identify links between personality and intelligence by *correlating* both types of constructs. Although the last decade has produced more research on the interface between intelligence and personality than any other, evidence for the specific relationship between the Big Five and psychometric intelligence is far from conclusive, proving that this is still a fertile area for research.

For instance, Hofstee (2001) reported that between 1991 and 1997 the terms *personality* and *intelligence* combined in the title of no more than 25 papers (only 6 of which attempted to relate the constructs). In the last 6 years, there have been another dozen papers published that included the terms *personality* and *intelligence* in the title, but no more than six looked at the actual interface between the constructs. Moreover, only a few quantitative studies (notably Ackerman & Heggestad, 1997; Austin et al., 2002) have analyzed large and representative data sets employing modern, well-validated, and reliable psychometric instruments, providing sound correlational evidence for the relationship between personality and intelligence (see also Austin, Hofer, Deary, & Eber, 2000). On the contrary, most studies have employed diverse psychometric instruments and analyzed data from samples that were often not large enough for the statistical analyzes performed (e.g., correlations, factor analysis), leading to some apparent contradictions. One of the aims of this chapter is to review and evaluate the current literature. To this end, the results of the most robust studies on the relationship between personality and psychometric intelligence are discussed.

Before examining the salient empirical evidence on the relationship between personality traits and psychometric intelligence, it is important to look at some of the (few) existent theoretical frameworks to conceptualize the link between personality and ability variables—namely, cerebral arousability and top–down approaches.

## 4.1 AROUSABILITY THEORY AND THE BIOLOGICAL BASIS OF PERSONALITY AND INTELLIGENCE

The theory of arousability has been formulated and extensively developed and tested by Eysenck (1957, 1967; Eysenck & Eysenck, 1985), one of the most eminent differential psychologists of the 20th century (see Section 2.3). More recent research on this framework has been followed up by Robinson (1999). The theory of arousability is indirectly related to sex differences in both personality and intellectual ability. Tests of general intelligence or IQ are carefully designed to avoid or counterbalance sex difference in performance (Matarazzo, 1972; Robinson, 1999), whereas females and males have frequently been reported to differ in their working memory, spatial, and verbal ability scores, with women having an advantage in the latter, but a disadvantage in the former measures (see also Maccoby & Jacklin, 1974, 1980). However, a larger meta-analytic article by Snow and Weinstock (1990) provided conflicting evidence for females' superiority on verbal ability tests.

There is also a substantial body of evidence suggesting that there are modest, but relatively consistent, sex differences in personality traits, particularly Neuroticism (where females tend to score significantly higher than males) and Psychoticism (where the opposite pattern is often reported; see Claridge, 1983; Eysenck & Eysenck, 1976; Lynn, 1959). Eysenck explained these differences in terms of differential levels of sympathetic activation of the autonomic nervous system; this has been particularly well documented for the Neuroticism trait (Eysenck, 1957, 1967; Eysenck & Eysenck, 1985). Thus, individual differences in Neuroticism are primarily understood in terms of the biological etiology of personality traits.

Robinson (1996) also provided evidence for the relationship between cerebral arousability and the Psychoticism trait, reporting that higher Psychoticism scorers tend to have less persistent cerebral potentials and lower cerebral arousability than their lower counterparts. Because this pattern of arousability differences in the two personality traits of Neuroticism and Psychoticism seems to map that of sex differences in these traits (with lower arousability levels associated with males, rather than females, stability, rather than Neuroticism, and high, rather than low, Psychoticism), arousability has been hypothesized to be a prime cause of sex differences in personality and intelligence.

Robinson (1989, 1991, 1993) conducted systematic EEG research on the relationship between intellectual ability and cerebral arousability. Further, this hypothesis was also extended to the second Gigantic trait— namely, Extraversion, in Eysenck's taxonomy. With regard to intelligence, Robinson (1989) argued that the correlation between different ability tests (Spearman's $g$) is a direct consequence of differences in arousability. More specifically, it has been suggested that high IQ scores are related to intermediate or moderate levels of cerebral arousability, whereas both high and low levels of arousability would be linked to lower IQ scores. This is consistent with the Yerkes–Dobson law that performance is best at an intermediate level of arousal, thus it can be graphically represented by an inverted-U curve. According to this law, the effects of moderate or intermediate levels of arousal on performance would be positive because of their motivational function for the individual, providing an optimal level of concentration. At low arousal, however, individuals would be easily distracted and attention would shift away from task-oriented goals, whereas at high levels of arousal individuals would be likely to experience anxiety. Furthermore, the mechanisms associated with arousal can influence not only the processes underlying performance, but also the level and content of conscious experience in general, including acquisition, retention, and utilization of information.

A recent study (Robinson, 1999) showed that sex differences in cerebral arousability were significantly related to both differences in Neuroticism *and* intelligence test performance. The term *intelligence test performance* is crucial because it implies that females' higher arousability would lead them to experience greater anxiety, which in turn impairs cognitive performance. Thus, arousability theory implicitly distinguishes between actual intelligence and intelligence test performance (i.e., it posits that trait arousability may lead to states of arousal that are detrimental for performance on cognitive tests, but it does not imply that females or neurotics are inherently less able than their male or stable counterparts). We return to this discussion later.

It should be noted that arousability theory conceptualizes a close link between nonability and ability variables, such that neither can be completely understood without some reference to the other (Robinson, 1999). In line with the Yerkes–Dobson law, this link is a direct consequence of biologically derived individual differences in cerebral activity, such that a moderate level of arousal would be beneficial for optimal information processing with regard to both elementary and higher order tasks (Robinson, 1999). Hence, arousability theory offers a theoretical explanation for the biological differences in intelligence proposed by Cattell's concept of

Gf. Figure 4.1 depicts an illustration of the theoretical framework underlying the biological basis of Cattell's intelligence theory—that is, how the theory of Gc and Gf can be understood in terms of arousability.

As can be seen in Fig. 4.2, individual differences in cerebral arousability would lead to individual differences in test performance ($g$) on both verbal and nonverbal ability tests, Gc and Gf, respectively. Although it is not clear whether these differences are due predominantly to the effects of arousability on test performance (such that intermediate levels of arousal would facilitate performance on ability tests) or the results of long-term effects of arousability on learning, it is a fact that different intelligence tests are significantly intercorrelated, and the shared variance of these test results can be explained primarily in terms of the $g$ factor. As Cattell (1987) observed, nonverbal and verbal ability scores tend to cluster relatively independently, giving origin to the Gf and Gc hypotheses (but still supporting the idea of a general intelligence factor; see Section 3.3).

Additional evidence for the existence of a lower order, biological basis of intelligence and personality can be found in multivariate (behavioral genetic) studies on twins—for instance, those looking at the relationship between genetic factors and IQ test or academic exam performance. These studies suggest that the substantial correlation between cognitive ability measures and academic performance can be explained in terms of genetic influences because of the large hereditary origin of both intelligence and academic performance (Brooks, Fulker, & DeFries, 1990;

The biological basis of Cattell's intelligence theory

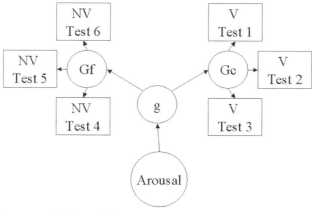

*Note:* NV = non-verbal, V = verbal

FIG. 4.1.    The biological basis of Cattell's intelligence theory.

Cherny & Cardon, 1994; McGue, Bouchard, Iacono, & Lykken, 1993; Plomin & DeFries, 1979; Thompson, Detterman, & Plomin, 1991). Recent research has also looked at intelligence differences in terms of brain structure or functioning through positron emission tomography. This technique has shown that the same brain areas are activated during performance on different types of ability tests, supporting the idea that intelligence is a general property of mental functioning.

## 4.2   TOP–DOWN APPROACHES

A second theoretical framework to conceptualize the personality and intelligence interface is represented by the so-called *top–down* approaches, clearly influenced by Cattell. Cattell (1971, 1987) conceived of personality and intelligence as separate individual differences factors and predictors of human behavior.[1] Thus, both variables could have a joint influence on academic, work-related, or social behavior. Although this conceptualization posits that personality and intelligence should be kept separate (because they are clustered and unrelated), it also implies that certain types of behavior (notably performance) may not be classified under the domain of personality or intelligence, but of necessity as a mix of both. Accordingly, IQ test results, which are obtained through performance, cannot be considered a "pure" measure of intelligence (because performance may also be influenced by personality traits; see Strelau, Zawadzki, & Piotrowske, 2001). This approach posits that nonability factors may affect the results of IQ tests (Rindermann & Neubauer, 2001). A typical example is anxiety, which is likely to impair test performance particularly under extremely arousing situations (Zeidner, 1995; see Section 4.1).

However, because a diversity of variables—from test conditions and distractability to physical illness—may have a significant influence on test results, problems arise when it comes to interpreting the results of IQ tests (we cannot assume that the score is a true reflection of the tested person's ability). As a consequence, top–down approaches may question the very nature and essence of intelligence. This problem was already considered by Wechsler (1950), who proposed that IQ tests should be redesigned to include (rather than exclude) nonability factors. In doing so they would not only facilitate interpretation, but also increase validity with regard to other types of performance. Nevertheless, Wechsler's advice appears to have had little or no effect on most test constructors, administrators, and testers no doubt because of the difficulties of measuring personality traits objectively. Because the assessment of noncognitive traits is associated with self-report invento-

---

[1]Although as seen in Section 2.4, Cattell's 16PF also included a measure of intelligence.

ries, a modification of IQ tests to include personality traits would require an abrupt methodological change, which most intelligence researchers would not happily accept. Yet IQ skeptics have used the argument that "ability test performance does not equal *real* intelligence" to produce a variety of novel theories about intelligence and define several hot abilities (see Section 3.5), without developing sound psychometric instruments to measure these abilities. Further, it is perhaps the very success of (good) traditional intelligence tests that undermines Wechsler's concern about the need to assess relevant noncognitive traits that may affect performance on IQ tests and made this a trivial suggestion. Pragmatically, IQ tests are effective predictors of performance. Hence, even if theoretically we knew that test performance may be affected by variables other than intelligence, psychometric intelligence remains a sound indicator of an individual's ability.

Following top–down approaches to the interface between personality and intelligence, it seems that the theoretical construct of intelligence is founded on the paradoxical fact that we can only measure intellectual ability through performance, but that human performance will always be affected by a variety of nonability traits and states.

We recently proposed a two-level conceptual framework to overcome this theoretical paradox (Chamorro-Premuzic & Furnham, 2004a, 2004b). This model (see Fig. 4.2), which refers to the relationship of Cattell's Gf and Gc with the Big Five personality traits, is based on the differentiation between ability as latent (immeasurable) capacity and ability as (measur-

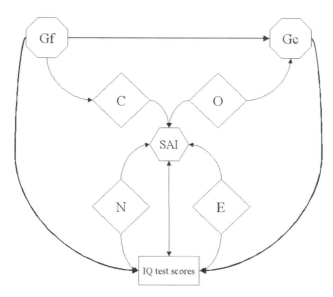

FIG. 4.2.    A two-level conceptual model for the personality–intelligence interface.

able) performance output.[2] Although this distinction may, at first, seem problematic because it is based on the assumption that the latent construct of intelligence is a purely theoretical, immeasurable variable, it is neither controversial nor an obstacle for empirical research in the area. On the contrary, it is a mere reflection of the implicit assumption underlying a substantial body of reliable research evidence. Moreover, it considers IQ tests and other psychometric ability measures an accurate indicator of individual differences in (latent) ability, and the same applies to academic performance (this is discussed throughout chap. 5).

The distinction between latent intelligence and IQ test performance has nonetheless been silently excluded from both theoretical and psychometric research papers on personality and intelligence to only be part of the skeptical criticisms of anti-IQ writings. As is noted throughout the rest of this chapter (and most of this book), conceptualizing both latent and psychometric intelligence is largely beneficial to understand the apparent equivocal body of correlational evidence for the relationship between noncognitive and cognitive traits. Hence, there are at least two connotations for intelligence—one refers to ability as a latent capacity (actual intelligence; i.e., Gf and Gc), the other to ability as output (cognitive or IQ test performance). Theoretical approaches to the personality–intelligence interface differ according to their representation of actual ability or ability as output/performance (although the two are related). This implicit distinction can also be found in the lay conceptions of intelligence of everyday life, specifically in the connotations of terms such as *underperforming* or expressions such as "she could have done much better" or "he is a wasted talent," used to describe the discrepancy between what a person can do and what he or she actually does.

The following sections discuss the empirical associations between personality and intelligence in terms of either test results or actual intellectual ability. Thus, they examine two types of evidence—one that refers to the possible impact of personality traits (such as Extraversion and Neuroticism) on IQ or ability test performance, and one that refers to the long-term effects of personality traits on actual intellectual competence (this is also the topic of most of chap. 5).

## 4.3 PERSONALITY AND IQ TEST PERFORMANCE

In this section (and Sections 4.4 and 4.5), we discuss the psychometric studies referring to links between personality traits and cognitive performance on ability tests. As mentioned earlier, most of these studies are concerned with the effects of Neuroticism and Extraversion on IQ test

---

[2]The concept of subjectively assessed intelligence (SAI), also represented in Fig. 4.2, is dealt with throughout chapter 6.

performance, although the correlational nature of most studies is a considerable limitation to this theory.

Although the meaning of what IQ tests measure is now exempted from most scientific controversy (see chap. 3), at least among differential psychologists, there has been a long-standing debate on the measurement of intelligence regarding how various states, such as mood and illness, can affect the reliability and validity of IQ scores (Furnham, 1994). According to the comprehensive taxonomies of personality (e.g., Big Five, Gigantic Three, and 16PF), several of these states can be accounted for and consequently predicted by personality traits. Furthermore, a number of key variables that have been assumed to have an effect on IQ test performance can also be understood in terms of the cerebral arousability hypothesis previously discussed.

Thus, individual differences in arousability may determine particular *test-taking styles* or strategies, which in turn may affect performance on cognitive tests (Eysenck, 1967a, 1967b; Furnham, Forde, & Cotter, 1998a, 1998b). The most salient and replicated cases refer to the relationship of speed and accuracy to the Extraversion trait and associations between Neuroticism and test anxiety.

In a large meta-analysis that examined 135 studies, Ackerman and Heggestad (1997) reported a significant, albeit modest, correlation between psychometric intelligence and Neuroticism ($r = -.15$). The authors also found that $g$ was negatively and moderately correlated with self-report measures of test anxiety ($r = -.33$). This is consistent with the findings of what is considered the most important paper on the relationship between test anxiety and intelligence—namely, Hembree's (1988) review of 273 studies. Here correlations between test anxiety and ability test performance ranged from $r = -.06$ up to $r = -.29$ (with a mean correlation of $r = -.18$). These correlations were replicated by the results of another large study ($N = 36,000$) by Siepp (1991; see also Austin et al., 2002).

With regard to Extraversion, Ackerman and Heggestad (1997) concluded that this personality trait is weakly but positively and significantly related to $g$ ($r = .08$). This correlation may be larger in younger samples, reaching $r = .21$ for males and $r = .19$ for females. Nevertheless, Austin et al. (2002) found relatively few (and negative) correlations between psychometric intelligence and Extraversion. As is seen later (Section 4.5), these inconsistencies can be partly explained in terms of different types of ability tests and their specific relation to Extraversion/Introversion.

## 4.4  NEUROTICISM AND TEST ANXIETY

There are several studies presenting evidence for the significant correlation between Neuroticism and ability tests. They show essentially that trait anxiety is likely to impair performance under arousing conditions. Callard and Goodfellow (1962) were among the first to find a low but statistically significant association between IQ and Neuroticism. In a study that examined the relationship between IQ and the Junior Maudsley Personality Inventory, in a sample of 11- to 14-year-old school children ($N = 3,559$), results show that there were group differences in Neuroticism, such that higher IQ scorers tended to be low in Neuroticism and vice versa. Interestingly, within the high IQ group, Neuroticism was positively related with intelligence, whereas in the low IQ group, the relationship between Neuroticism and IQ was negative. Kalmanchey and Kozeki (1983) examined a large sample ($N = 642$) of similarly aged children and reported low but significant correlations between Neuroticism (as assessed by the EPQ) and psychometric intelligence. More recently, Furnham, Forde, and Cotter (1998a; $N = 233$) obtained modest but significant correlations between Neuroticism (as assessed by the EPQ) and the Wonderlic Personnel (Wonderlic, 1992) and Baddeley Reasoning (Baddeley, 1968) tests, two well-established measures of IQ and Gf, respectively.

Without salient exceptions, and even when the correlation does not reach significance levels (e.g., Matarazzo, 1972), the relationship between Neuroticism and psychometric intelligence is negative, implying that intelligence would decrease with negative affectivity (e.g., anxiety, worry, tension, depression, anger, etc.; Zeidner & Matthews, 2000). As mentioned earlier, this does not necessarily mean that neurotic individuals are inherently less intelligent than stable ones. Rather, it is likely that negative affects such as anxiety and worry, which are typical of neurotic individuals, would interfere with the cognitive processes (e.g., memory, attention) required to solve ability tests. Indeed Hembree (1988) found moderate to high correlations between trait and test anxiety, on the one hand and IQ test performance and test anxiety, on the other hand (see Table 4.1).

Thus, the negative relationship between Neuroticism and psychometric intelligence has mainly been attributed to the anxiety components

### TABLE 4.1
**Correlates of Test Anxiety**

| Correlate | Test Anxiety |
|---|---|
| IQ Test performance | $r = .23$ |
| General anxiety | $r = .56$ |
| Trait anxiety | $r = .53$ |
| State anxiety | $r = .45$ |
| Worry | $r = .57$ |
| Emotionality | $r = .54$ |

*Note.*   Table is adapted from Hembree (1988).

of the Neuroticism scale (Sarason, 1980; Zeidner, 1995, 1998), which have been found to impair intellectual functioning not only on intelligence tests, but also in school and university exams (Entwistle & Entwistle, 1970; Eysenck & Eysenck, 1985; Sharma & Rao, 1983; see also Section 5.3).

Boekaerts (1995) explained neurotics' impairment of intellectual functioning in terms of attentional interference. However, this interference may only be affected by *states* of anxiety. It is thus necessary to distinguish between trait (chronically anxious) and state (currently anxious) anxiety because only the latter individuals may experience a decrement of intellectual performance (Zeidner, 1995). Although performance may be a function of state rather than trait anxiety (Eysenck & Eysenck, 1985), Hembree (1988) showed that there is a close relationship between the two constructs. Hence, neurotic individuals would be particularly likely to experience states of anxiety, notably exam or test anxiety (see Table 4.1). It should also be noted that predicting performance from trait rather than state anxiety may be more beneficial than state anxiety because it would facilitate intervention and prevention at an earlier stage (see Section 2.2).

The relationship between test anxiety and IQ test performance may be interpreted in terms of the *underlying worry*, as opposed to emotionality, components of the Neuroticism trait (Zeidner, 1998). A useful distinction is that of Eysenck's (1981b), who conceptualized worry as the cognitive aspect of anxiety, whereas emotionality represents the physiological aspect (e.g., tension, nervousness). It is likely that worry and negative expectations (e.g., fear of failure) make it difficult for neurotic individuals to focus on their task (De Raad & Schowenburg, 1996). Particularly the working memory system would be affected by worry (task-irrelevant processing) components (Eysenck, 1979; see also Darke, 1988). It is noteworthy that the impairment of performance by worry may be significantly enhanced when pressure is involved (Matthews, 1986; Morris & Liebert, 1969).

As Strelau, Zawadzki, and Piotrowske (2001) explained, individuals who complete an ability test are usually presented with difficult tasks, exposed to the judgment of others, and affected by the consequences of their performance. Sarason (1975) likewise suggested that anxiety may affect performance on ability tests only in competitive settings, whereas under neutral conditions the differences between anxious and nonanxious individuals would be marginal. This was confirmed in a study by Markham and Darke (1991), who found that high anxiety inhibited verbal reasoning but only under highly demanding circumstances. In a similar way, Dobson (2000) showed that only under stressful situations (e.g., time pressure or when the results have important consequences for the individual) is Neuroticism associated with lower performance on numerical reasoning tests, and that these situations underestimate neurotics' true intellectual ability.

As Zeidner (1995) pointed out, the fact that Neuroticism may impair test performance should not question the validity of ability tests, but rather provide additional information about the individual who completes the tests (see also Furnham, Forde & Cotter, 1998a). This argument is based on the assumption that anxiety affects real-world performance in the same way that it affects (impairs) test performance. Although Neuroticism may be more related to IQ test performance than to actual intelligence (Child, 1964; Eysenck, 1971), measures of trait anxiety could still be useful to predict performance under stressful conditions. If noncognitive components may influence test results, including personality traits in the assessment of intellectual competence, they may provide additional information on the individual, as well as improve the prediction of his or her performance in real-life settings (Wechsler, 1950).

An alternative interpretation to the significant correlation between Neuroticism and intelligence has been proposed by Muller (1992). The author argued that the correlation between Neuroticism and psychometric intelligence may be indicative of the influence of actual intellectual competence on anxiety, rather than the effects of anxiety on ability test performance. Hence, Muller inverted the causal direction usually attributed to this correlation. The central argument for this hypothesis is based on the concept of *self-efficacy* (Bandura, 1986). Muller's (1992) theory posits that, at an early stage, Neuroticism is negatively associated with self-efficacy (individuals high on trait anxiety would be more likely to have lower self-efficacy), but not with intellectual competence. However, low self-efficacy may lead to worry and impair test performance through test/state anxiety. At a second stage, these individuals would be less likely to invest in preparation and engage in intellectually stimulating activities. This lack of engagement would lead to low intellectual competence. Finally, a third stage is conceived in which low competence affects both test performance and trait anxiety, in that it would lead to both low self-efficacy and poor test results. Hence, poor performance may be regarded as a self-fulfilling prophecy: The initial fear of failure is eventually justified by objective low competence. This feedback or vicious cycle can be illustrated by Fig. 4.3.

Some researchers (e.g., Lynn & Gordon, 1961) have also suggested that the relationship between Neuroticism and psychometric intelligence may be curvilinear rather than linear. Such suggestions are mainly based on Eysenck's (1957) and Eysenck and Eysenck's (1985) theory on the biological basis of personality and intelligence, which attributes individual differences on these constructs to differences in cerebral arousability. Recent support for this theory can be found in the numerous papers by Robinson (e.g., 1989, 1998; see Sections 2.3 and 4.3). As discussed, Eysenck (1957) argued that higher Neuroticism is associated with greater activation on the sympathetic division of the autonomic nervous system. Because the sympathetic activation may increase cerebral activation

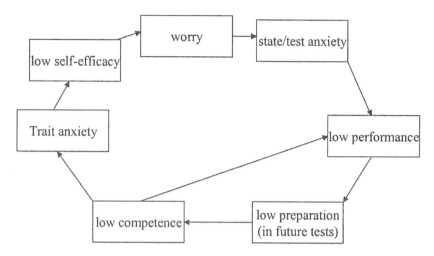

FIG. 4.3.   A hypothetical model for the processes underlying the relation between anxiety and test performance (based on Muller, 1992).

(and vice versa), it is implied that there is a positive relationship between Neuroticism and cerebral arousal. Furthermore, because psychometric intelligence is associated with intermediate arousability (Robinson, 1989), extreme (i.e., very high and very low) levels of Neuroticism would be negatively associated with psychometric intelligence.

Another interesting approach to the relationship between Neuroticism and psychometric intelligence has been proposed by Austin, Deary, and Gibson (1997), who pointed out that $g$ seems to be stronger at higher levels of Neuroticism. This would imply that the magnitude of the correlation between different ability tests (e.g., measures of Gc and Gf) should be expected to increase with levels of Neuroticism (see also Austin et al., 2000).

It may be argued that the increase in the correlation between different ability tests may be a consequence of Neuroticism—specifically, high test anxiety. That is, the consistent effect of anxiety on different ability measures may increase the correlation between these measures, in that it reduces cognitive sources of variability between tests. Conversely, at low levels of Neuroticism, the effects of test/state anxiety would be practically irrelevant, allowing for a greater cognitive variability between measures. Thus, anxiety is regarded as a source of distortion in the measurement of abilities and may influence not only test results, but also correlations among these tests. An array of experimental difficulties may complicate the feasibility of experimentally testing and replicating these results; notably, the fact that state (rather than trait) anxiety is assumed to inflate the correlation of different ability measures. Thus, it would require not only reliable measures of state anxiety, but also replicable levels of state anxiety across studies and individuals (E. J. Austin, personal communication, December 7, 2002).

## 4.5    EXTRAVERSION AND TEST-TAKING STYLE (SPEED vs. ACCURACY)

Unlike Neuroticism, the correlation between psychometric intelligence and Extraversion has been found to vary from positive to negative. That is, the results are equivocal. Revelle, Amaral, and Turriff (1976) were among the first to observe these contradictory results caused by the use of different types of ability tests. They suggested that the link between psychometric intelligence and Extraversion was, to an important extent, dependent on the test conditions. This interaction was later explained by Eysenck and Eysenck's (1985) arousal theory, which states that the resting level of cortical arousal for introverts is higher (i.e., have lower reactive inhibition) than that of extraverts. Hence, introverts tend to avoid arousing stimuli, whereas extraverts tend to seek them (Eysenck, 1991; see Section 2.3). Therefore, one may predict that the relationship between psychometric intelligence and Extraversion will differ in arousing and nonarousing situations, favoring extraverts or introverts, respectively.

Extraverts also show greater vigilance decrement than introverts and, consequently, trade off speed for accuracy when taking an ability test. Thus, extraverts may have slightly different results than introverts depending on the style of the test (in particular, whether it is timed and how long it takes). Extraverts would seem to have an advantage when tests are short (2–5 minutes) and timed, whereas introverts would benefit from long (e.g., 40 minutes) and untimed tests. Accordingly, introverts can be expected to outperform extraverts on verbal tests and problem-solving tasks that require insight and reflection (Matthews, 1992), whereas extraverts would outperform introverts on speed (i.e., timed) tests. This hypothesis was tested by Rawlings and Carnie (1989), who showed that the relationship between Extraversion and IQ is partly a function of time pressure. The authors found that the timed version of the *WAIS* favored extraverts, whereas the untimed version favored introverts. Eysenck (1994a) also showed that Extraverts have a general tendency to spend less time doing a test (and even tend to give up toward the end of a test), concluding that Extraversion is related to speed of working. Table 4.2 (adapted from Matthews, 1999) resumes some of the strong and weak test features associated with high and low Extraversion.

However, studies by Rawlings and Skok (1993) and Furnham, Forde, and Cotter (1998a; $N = 233$) failed to replicate these results. Further, Furnham et al. (1998a) showed that, although it could be that the relationship between Extraversion and psychometric intelligence is influenced by the type of test used or the type of intelligence being measured, introverts can also outperform extraverts on speed tasks. It is arguable that the type of test used by Furnham et al. (1998a; i.e., the Baddeley Reasoning Test [Baddeley, 1968]) may also have tapped aspects of verbal ability because this measure is based on grammatical transformations, not just speed. This may have helped introverts' performance (Matthews, 1992). In any case, the relationship between Extraversion and psychometric intelligence is far from well established and therefore remains an interesting topic of research for differential psychologists.

It has been suggested that the correlation between Extraversion and psychometric intelligence may be determined by the type of ability measures employed (see Table 4.2). Zeidner (1995) argued that introverts have an advantage in tasks related to superior associative learning ability (verbal tasks), whereas extraverts have an advantage in tasks related to ready acquisition of automatic motor sequences (performance tasks). As discussed, this argument had been previously exposed by Eysenck (1971) and Robinson (1985), who attributed these differences to interpersonal variation in cerebral arousability (excitation/inhibition of the autonomic system). Thus, extraverts, who are naturally less aroused, find it harder to concentrate for a long time and end up trading speed for accuracy. The opposite should apply to introverts.

In this sense, the positive correlation between Extraversion and psychometric intelligence would be consistent with the representation of intelligent individuals as characterized by higher speed of information processing (Neubauer, 1997; Roth, 1964; P. A. Vernon, 1987). Most researchers would agree, however, that there is certainly more to intellectual ability than processing speed (Ackerman, 1996, 1999; Stankov, 1999). In fact even those who adopt RT-based approaches to intelligence have found only modest correlations between short RT measures and psycho-

**TABLE 4.2**
**Test–Related Features to High and Low Extraversion**

| Extraversion Level | High | Low |
|---|---|---|
| Divided attention | + | − |
| Long-term memory | − | + |
| Reflective problem solving | − | + |
| Resistance to distraction | + | − |
| Retrieval from memory | + | − |
| Short-term memory | + | − |
| Vigilance | − | + |

*Note.* Table is adapted from Matthews (1999).

metric intelligence ($r = -.12$ to $r = -.28$ in Jensen's [1987] meta-analysis). Thus, further research is needed to clarify the inconsistencies in the relationship between psychometric intelligence and Extraversion (M. J. Roberts, 2002; Stough et al., 1996).

## 4.6 INVESTMENT THEORIES

A third conceptual framework to interpret associations between personality and intelligence has also derived from Cattell's findings, but has been thoroughly elaborated by R. Snow (1995) and Ackerman (1996, 1999; Ackerman & Heggestad, 1997). This approach, technically defined as *investment* theories, posits that personality traits may have long-term effects on the development of intellectual abilities—in particular, crystallized intelligence.

As mentioned earlier, Chamorro-Premuzic and Furnham (2004) considered this approach within a two-level theoretical framework for understanding interactions between personality and intelligence, also based on a major aspect of Cattell's (1971, 1987) theory—namely, investment. This approach deals with the influence of personality on actual ability, rather than IQ test results (see Fig. 4.2). In this respect, it is important to emphasize again Cattell's distinction between fluid (Gf) and crystallized (Gc) intelligence. Another useful definition is that of Gf as "the neurological structures and processes underlying mental activity" and Gc as "the sum of acquired knowledge and experience" (Rolfhus & Ackerman, 1996, p. 175; other definitions were given in Section 3.3). Furthermore, Cattell also believed Gc to be the result of applying Gf over time. Accordingly, individual differences in Gc could be determined by the amount and quality of investment of Gf. This theory was further developed by Ackerman (1996, 1999), who distinguished between intelligence as processes (Gf) and intelligence as content/knowledge (which is similar, but not equivalent, to Gc). Like Cattell, Ackerman viewed intelligence as partly the result of engaging (investing) in intellectual activities. However, more emphasis is placed on the role of personality, interests, and motivation in determining the acquisition of knowledge (see Ackerman's theory of PPIK—i.e., Intelligence as Process, Personality, Interests, and Knowledge). Thus, theories of investment are concerned with the cognitive processes and nonability traits that underlie the development of human intellect in a broad sense.

## 4.7 OPENNESS TO EXPERIENCE (NEED FOR COGNITION)

As much as Neuroticism and Extraversion were the focus of long-standing evidence for the relationship between personality and IQ test performance, the association between personality and actual intelligence (i.e., intellectual investment) can be primarily understood in terms of Openness to Experience. Despite its "late arrival" to the realm of personality, Openness to Experience is the factor most frequently associated with intelligence (Ackerman & Heggestad, 1997; Austin, Hofer, Deary, & Eber, 2000; Brand, 1994; Goff & Ackerman, 1992; Zeidner & Matthews, 2000).

Ackerman and Heggestad (1997) reported an overall correlation of $r = .33$ between Openness to Experience and $g$. This correlation was replicated in a recent study by Austin et al. (2002), who examined several large data sets. Kyllonen (1997), examining a large sample of Air Force recruits, found the correlation between Openness to Experience and IQ to be even higher ($r = .45$). As discussed later, interpretation of this correlation may be ambiguous because Openness to Experience may be regarded as a self-report measure of ability (subjectively assessed intelligence; see also chap. 6). Furthermore, the subfacets of Openness seem to represent not only aspects of ability, but also (and particularly) fantasy, aesthetics, values, and feelings. In any case, this personality factor seems to be associated with Gc rather than Gf (Ackerman & Heggestad, 1997; Austin et al., 2002).

However, there has been much speculation about the nature and meaning of this association. It has even been argued (Ferguson & Patterson, 1998; McCrae, 1994) that Openness to Experience should be interpreted as an ability rather than a personality factor. This argument has been discussed thoroughly by Brand (1994; see also Goldberg, 1994; Saucier, 1994a, 1994b; Trapnell, 1994), who proposed an alternative psychometric approach to the Five Factor model of personality. According to Brand and following Cattell, the Big Five should be replaced by Neuroticism, Extraversion, Conscientiousness, Pathemia/Affection (instead of Agreeableness), Will or Independence (instead of Openness to Experience), and the inclusion of psychometric intelligence ($g$)—traditionally considered a separate domain—as a sixth factor.

As observed (Section 2.4), the inclusion of an intelligence factor in self-assessed measures of personality was anticipated by some of the work of Cattell, specifically the 16 Personality Factor Questionnaire (16PF; Cattell, Eber, & Tatsuoka, 1970). Further, research supporting the conceptualization of a Six rather than a Five Factor model of personality is not rare (Birenbaum & Montag, 1989; Brand, 1984; Cattell, 1973; Deary & Matthews, 1993). In a recent study, Fergusson and Patterson (1998) suggested that the Five Factor model should be interpreted as a Two Factor model, with Neuroticism, Extraversion, Agreeableness, and Conscientiousness items all loading on a single factor, and Openness to Experience items loading on a separate one, which the authors interpreted as ability. However, the sample used may be regarded as too small ($N = 101$), particularly if one considers the large validation studies of Costa and McCrae (1985, 1988, 1992), who identified a five factor solution across a diverse and very large sample.

Brand (1994) argued that about 40% of the true variance of Openness to Experience in the general population could be attributed to $g$. Support for

Brand's hypothesis about the overlap between Openness to Experience and intelligence can be found in McCrae (1987, but not McCrae & Costa, 1997a). In addition, Openness to Experience has also been reported to correlate highly with the Intuition scale of the Myers–Briggs Type Indicator (McCrae & Costa, 1989), which has been consistently associated with IQ (Brand, Egan, & Deary, 1993). Although Brand's (1994) claims are theoretically sound, psychometric research has yet to provide consistent evidence for the overlap between Openness to Experience and intelligence as measured by objective tests rather than self-report inventories.

On the contrary, several researchers have provided evidence for the psychometric differentiation between intelligence and Openness to Experience (Ashton, Lee, Vernon, & Jang, 2000; Costa & McCrae, 1992; Goff & Ackerman, 1992; McCrae, 1987; 1993; 1994). Further, McCrae and Costa (1997a) emphasized that, even when Openness may tap aspects of intelligence, this personality factor also (and perhaps mainly) accounts for noncognitive individual differences such as need for variety, mood variability, and tolerance of ambiguity. Figure 4.4 (adapted from McCrae & Costa, 1997a) presents a schematic conceptualization of the relationship among Openness, psychometric intelligence, and *intellect* (a term employed to refer to the latent and nonmeasurable variable of actual intelligence). However, it should be noted that intellect can be partly measured not only by psychometric intelligence, but also by Openness. Thus, psychometric intelligence and Openness are related variables because they represent measures of the same (latent) construct—namely, intellect (or what we would refer to as *intellectual competence*). Nevertheless, it is clear from the Venn diagram in Fig. 4.4 that an important part of Openness (perhaps aesthetic sensitivity, fantasy life, and feelings) is unrelated to psychometric intelligence, whereas an equally important aspect of psychometric intelligence (particularly Gf) may be orthogonal to Openness.

The differentiation between Openness and intelligence has also been explained in terms of differences in measurement approach. Thus, Openness is correlated with psychometric intelligence, but it is measured (i.e., *assessed*) as a personality factor. Cronbach's (1984) division between maximal and typical performance illustrates the different approaches that differentiate the measurement of intelligence (*maximal* performance) from that of personality assessment (*typical* performance). It is likely that this division may account for the separate factorial constitution of intelligence with regard to Openness to Experience (Hofstee, 2001). That is, even if Openness to Experience may, to some extent, be a measure of intellectual competence, it would be different from psychometric intelligence in the sense of being self-report and typical, rather than objective and maximal.

Despite the methodological distinctiveness between Openness to Experience and psychometric intelligence, several researchers have shown that the two variables are significantly correlated and therefore not

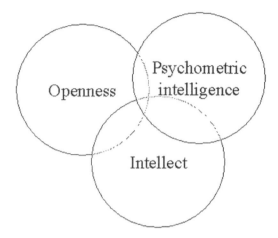

FIG. 4.4.   A schematic representation of the relations among Openness, psychometric intelligence, and intellect (actual intelligence).

independent. McCrae and Costa (1985) reported a correlation of $r = .32$ between Openness to Experience and the vocabulary subtest of the *WAIS*—a highly reliable and valid measure of intellectual ability. Furthermore, McCrae (1993, 1994) and Holland, Dollinger, Holland, and McDonald (1995) later found that Openness to Experience factor was also related ($r = .42$) to the full IQ scale from the *WAIS–R* (Wechsler, 1944).

Studies on authoritarianism or conservatism (Wilson & Patterson, 1978)—in some sense the opposite of Openness to Experience—may also provide evidence for a link between Openness to Experience and intelligence because authoritarianism has been found to be negatively correlated with both Openness ($r = -.57$, Trapnell, 1994), and intelligence (up to $r = -.50$; Zeidner & Matthews, 2000). Further, Trapnell (1994) regarded liberalism as an aspect of Openness. Likewise, Zeidner and Matthews (2000) suggested that open individuals would be more willing to question moral, political, and religious values to adopt less conservative views. Thus, conservative attitudinal systems involving prejudice, antidemocratic sentiments, and right-wing authoritarianism would be more common in less open individuals (see also Adorno, Frenkel-Brunswick, Levinson, & Sanford, 1950). Negative correlations between Openness and authoritarianism may thus be indicative of the positive relationship between Openness and intellectual competence. Furthermore, one may hypothesize, specifically, that high Openness may lead to both low authoritarianism and high intellectual competence.

Although it is often not possible to fully explain the relationship between Openness to Experience and psychometric intelligence

(Zeidner, 1995), it is important to point out that not all aspects of intelligence may be associated with Openness to Experience. There is vast research indicating that Openness to Experience may only be related to the crystallized or *knowledge*—as opposed to the fluid or *reasoning*— aspects of human intellectual ability (Ackerman & Rolfhus, 1999; Brand, 1994). These results may reflect the importance of Openness in knowledge acquisition as well as its relative independence from the more biologically based processes underlying Gf.

Jackson (1984b) found Openness to Experience to be moderately and significantly correlated with the crystallized (specifically verbal) subtest of the Multidimensional Aptitude Battery (Jackson, 1984a), but only weakly with the fluid subtest and in the near-zero order when the test stimuli were not pictures. Likewise, Goff and Ackerman (1992) reported Openness to Experience to correlate moderately ($r = .32$) with Gc, but only modestly ($r = .13$) with Gf. In a recent study involving more than 500 Canadian sibling pairs, Ashton, Lee, Vernon, and Jang (2000) replicated both the moderate ($r = .37$) correlation between Openness to Experience and Gc, and the modest ($r = .18$) correlation between Openness to Experience and Gf, using Jackson's (1984b) Multidimensional Aptitude Battery. Hence, the authors concluded that Openness is relatively orthogonal to the ability to reason and process information.

Theoretically, the significant correlation between Openness to Experience and psychometric intelligence may be interpreted in several ways.

First, it may be possible that people who are more open to experiences (e.g., intellectually curious, liberal, imaginative) tend to engage in activities that are likely to develop and strengthen their intelligence. This is consistent with Cattell's (1971) ideas on the historical effects of interests (i.e., investment) on the development of Gc (see also Ackerman, 1996). An open personality would thus lead to high levels of intellectual competence. It should be noted, however, that the development of intellectual competence may depend not only on the Openness of one's personality, but also on the intellectual richness (or Openness) of the environment. Therefore, one should bear in mind that education may moderate the relationship between Openness and intellectual competence (as it has in fact been shown with authoritarianism; see Christie, 1954).

Second, intellectual curiosity, vivid imagination, artistic sensitivity, and other characteristics of highly open people could be a consequence (rather than a cause) of their high intelligence. In this case, high intellectual ability would pre-exist (and to some extent cause) the development of a highly open personality. That is, the need for cognition and rich intellectual experience would be prompted in more able and handicapped in less able individuals. However, correlational evidence (specifically correlations between Gf and Openness) in support of this interpretation is poor (Ackerman & Rolfhus, 1999; Brand, 1994; Jackson, 1984a).

A third option would be that of an interaction between high intelligence (specifically Gf) and Openness to Experience—in terms of highly intelligent people engaging in (intellectual, artistic, or nonconservative) activities that would lead to high intellectual competence (Goff & Ackerman, 1992) and vice versa. As Matthews et al. (2000) pointed out, objective competence support interests as much as interests may enhance competence.

A fourth option also considered by Goff and Ackerman (1992) is that of Openness to Experience as a self-report measure of intelligence, specifically Gc. This hypothesis is based on Cronbach's (1984) methodological distinction between maximal and typical performance, as well as the conceptual similarities between subjectively assessed intelligence and several self-report items in the Openness scale. However, there is a variation in the way Openness items address subjectively assessed intelligence—namely, indirectly. Items such as "I often enjoy playing with theories and abstract ideas," "I found philosophical arguments boring," "I often lose interest when people talk about very abstract, theoretical matters," and "I enjoy working on mind-twister-type puzzles," all taken from the Openness scale of the NEO–PI–R (Costa & McCrae, 1992), are directed to interests, rather than proficiency. Hence, Openness differs from subjectively assessed intelligence in that it assesses estimates of *preferences* rather than skills. The conceptual relationship between Openness and self-estimates of intelligence may thus be compared to that of skills and interests (see Matthews et al., 2000).

Finally, yet without being conclusive, a fifth interpretation for the significant correlation between the Openness to Experience factor and measures of intellectual ability would be that intelligence may also comprise the *ability* to score higher on Openness to Experience. In a general way, this hypothesis has been proposed by Sternberg and Wagner (1993) and Hofstee (2001) and assumes that personality inventory items, albeit bipolar, can arguably be scored as correct or incorrect, and that respondents (particularly highly intelligent ones) are able to identify the logic behind the scoring of items. For instance, items that tend to disclose a social desirable response (e.g., "I have a very active imagination," "Aesthetics and artistic concerns aren't very important to me," "I consider myself broad-minded and tolerant of other people's lifestyles") are more likely to be affected by the respondents' ability to identify the correct answer, and can therefore result in significant correlations between psychometric intelligence and the Openness trait.

However, several studies have indicated that the relationship between psychometric intelligence and socially desirable responses is negative rather than positive (Austin et al., 2002; see also Ackerman & Heggestad, 1997). A possible explanation for this may be that highly competent individuals would be more confident and thus find little need to conform to others when choosing the responses of a personality questionnaire. In any case, socially desirable responding may be more related to social than to general or academic intellectual competence (see Kihlstrom & Cantor, 2000).

Although several possible interpretations to explain the relationship between psychometric intelligence and Openness have been examined, most of these hypotheses have specific weaknesses. The idea that Openness may increase (and even result from) high Gf, in the sense that intellectual interests would support native abilities, has not been supported by correlational evidence (for Openness correlates significantly with Gc, rather than Gf). For the same reason, an interaction between ability and Openness cannot be considered a valid explanation. Arguments in support of a purely psychometric (methodological) relationship between Openness and intelligence could also be rejected (at least partly) because Openness refers to estimates of preference (interests) rather than abilities (skills). Further, it has been argued that even if Openness would overlap with (and be compared to) subjectively assessed intelligence, this personality scale comprises more and mostly items referred to conventionality, experience seeking, and fantasy life (McCrae & Costa, 1997a, 1997b). The hypothesis that the relationship between Openness and psychometric intelligence may be an artifact of the ability to score high on a socially desirable trait may also be rejected on the basis of negative correlations between socially desirable responding and psychological intelligence. Thus, the idea that Openness may determine intellectual investment through interests and curiosity seems the best explanation to understand correlations between Openness and psychological intelligence. This argument has been thoroughly considered and further conceptualized in the construct of Typical Intellectual Engagement (Goff & Ackerman, 1992).

## 4.8  TYPICAL INTELLECTUAL ENGAGEMENT (TIE)

Among studies attempting to clarify the nature of the Openness to Experience factor, as well as its relationship to intellectual ability, an interesting approach is that of Goff and Ackerman (1992) and Ackerman and Goff (1994), who examined the association among Gc, Openness to Experience, and TIE (a construct put forward by these authors). TIE refers to an individual's tendency to engage in intellectual activities; explore philosophical, scientific, and artistic interests; and further develop these interests in the form of knowledge. When compared to personality measures, TIE—a self-reported inventory—showed to be highly correlated with Openness ($r = .65$; Ackerman & Goff, 1994). Moreover, after correcting for attenuation, Goff and Ackerman (1992) found that the correlation between Openness to Experience and the "abstract thinking" subscale of the TIE inventory was $r = .72$; after adding Conscientiousness, Neuroticism, and Agreeableness as predictors, the attenuation-corrected multiple correlation was nearly $r = .90$.

As we could expect, the authors (Goff & Ackerman, 1992) found that Gc was positively and significantly related to TIE, Openness, absorption (in tasks), hard work, and interests in art and technology. However, when the TIE inventory was examined against high school and university performance, its predictive validity was zero, whereas (maximal performance) intelligence test had validities as high as $r = .40$. Thus, it is important to bear in mind that personality traits like TIE and Openness may be influential in the processes of knowledge acquisition in terms of motivation and interests, without necessarily leading to excellence in performance. Furthermore, TIE may be more related to self-report than to actual knowledge, and only in certain areas such as arts and humanities (Rolfhus & Ackerman, 1996).

The prior sections have discussed the relationship between intellectual ability and three of the Big Five personality traits (although it should be noted that two of these traits—namely, Neuroticism and Extraversion—are also part of the Eysenckian Gigantic Three taxonomy). The remaining two personality factors of the Big Five (i.e., Agreeableness and Conscientiousness) have not been found to be significantly associated with $g$ (Ackerman & Heggestad, 1997; Kyllonen, 1997). However, as is discussed later (see Sections 4.9 and 4.10), Agreeableness may have an impact on test-taking motivation, and Conscientiousness may be negatively related to actual intelligence. Further, it has often been argued that traits classifiable as *adaptive* (i.e., help to achieve personal and social adjustment) should be positively related to general intelligence (Ackerman & Heggestad, 1997; Austin et al., 2002; Thorndike, 1940).

## 4.9 AGREEABLENESS, MODESTY, AND TEST-TAKING ATTITUDES

Among the Big Five personality factors, Agreeableness seems to be the least related to ability. This runs counter to Thorndike's (1940) idea that "intelligence is in general correlated with virtue and good will toward men" (p. 274). Ackerman and Heggestad's (1997) and Kyllonen's (1997) articles revealed positive, but modest and nonsignificant, correlations between ability measures and Agreeableness. These results confirm the theoretical independence of Agreeableness from intellectual competence because none of its primary factor scales (i.e., trust, straightforwardness, altruism, compliance, modesty, tender-mindedness) appear to be conceptually related to intellectual competence. Nevertheless, there may be at least three reasons to expect some significant correlations between Agreeableness and ability measures.

First, in situations where test results have relatively little important consequences for the examinee (unlike in work or university recruitment/applicant samples), agreeable people would have more positive attitudes toward taking the test and would be more collaborative with the examiner. Conversely, less agreeable individuals may be unwilling to concentrate and perform at the highest level. In such cases, Agreeableness may be positively related to ability test results. Given that most research on personality and intelligence is conducted on opportunity samples (such as university students), this effect is not trivial.

Second, it may be hypothesized that intelligence can influence responses on the NEO–PI–R—that is, through socially desirable responding. This possibility applies primarily to situations were both personality and ability scores have decisive consequences for the examinee. Thus, respondents higher on intelligence may be more able to identify the more "correct" (socially desirable) answers, many of which could involve agreeable items. However, recent studies (notably Austin et al., 2002) found negative associations between psychometric intelligence and socially desirable responding. Furthermore, several circumstances in which low Agreeableness is preferable (e.g., in competitive jobs) may require the respondents to do just the opposite and attempt to score low on the scale. Hence, intelligent individuals may be more likely to manage their impression and score in the direction of the desired profile.

Third, the modesty subfacet included in the Agreeableness scale may indirectly reflect people's intellectual competence. Because people are, to some extent, able to judge their own intellectual abilities (Furnham & Rawles, 1999; Paulhus, Lysy, & Yik, 1998), highly intelligent people could be expected to have a higher opinion of themselves. Likewise, less bright individuals would be more likely to be modest in their judgments about themselves. Further, modesty may be regarded as conceptually related to (low) self-confidence and self-concept, which have been associated with performance on a variety of cognitive/ability tests (Crawford & Stankov, 1996). Being modest about one's ability may thus have a negative impact on test-performance (as a self-fulfilling prophecy effect). Accordingly, the relationship between modesty and intellectual ability may be reflected in a negative correlation between ability test results and Agreeableness.

Although the prior arguments may lead to small but significant correlations between Agreeableness and psychometric intelligence, the direction of the correlation appears to vary from positive to negative. Moreover, previous research has failed to identify significant correlations between psychometric intelligence and Agreeableness.

In any case, it seems unlikely that Agreeableness has any significant impact on the development of intellectual competence or adult skill acquisition. Further, even in experimentally weak or organizational settings, when the Agreeableness trait may be expected to be modestly associated with test performance or results, it has been pointed out that faking and sociably desirable responding is only a minor problem (with minor negative consequences) for both industry and academia, and that other traits such as Conscientiousness or (low) Neuroticism would be more relevant in these situations (Ones, Viswesvaran, & Reiss, 1996; see chap. 5).

## 4.10  CONSCIENTIOUSNESS (NEED FOR ACHIEVEMENT)

Conscientiousness is associated with persistence, self-discipline, and achievement striving (Busato, Prins, Elshout, & Hamaker, 2000). However, large-scale studies seem to indicate that Conscientiousness, like Agreeableness, may only be weakly related to psychometric intelligence (Ackerman & Heggestad, 1997; Kyllonen, 1997; Zeidner & Matthews, 2000). When examined in more detail, evidence on the relationship between Conscientiousness and psychometric intelligence is characterized by a lack of consistency.

On the one hand, Eysenck's Psychoticism factor (Eysenck & Eysenck, 1985), a negative correlate and subordinate of Conscientiousness (Digman, 1990; Eysenck, 1991, 1992a, 1992b, 1992c), may be sufficient to expect positive associations between Conscientiousness and psychometric intelligence. Psychoticism reflects an increased tendency to express aggressive behavior, generally as a reaction of frustration or unconditioned punishment (Eysenck, 1981b). Like anxiety, this type of behavior is also likely to impair test performance. Indeed Eysenck (1971) showed that Psychoticism was significantly and negatively correlated with psychometric intelligence.

On the other hand, two recent studies have found negative associations between Conscientiousness and psychometric intelligence. Moutafi, Furnham, and Crump (2003) analyzed data from approximately 900 job applicants and found that individuals high on Conscientiousness tended to score lower in several cognitive ability tests. The authors explained the negative relationship between Conscientiousness and psychometric intelligence in terms of *compensation*. Specifically, less able individuals would become more conscientious as a result of attempting to compensate for their low intellectual ability. Conversely, more able people would be less likely to become conscientious because their high intellectual ability may be enough to excel or at least perform acceptably in a variety of settings. The results and hypothesis of this study were confirmed shortly after by the analyses of a large-scale sample ($N = 4,859$) of applicants. Conscientiousness was significantly correlated with measures of numerical ($r = -.17$), verbal ($r = -.23$), abstract ($r = -.16$) and general ($r = -.22$) ability more so than the rest of the Big Five traits (see Moutafi, Furnham, & Paltiel, 2005).

Further support for the compensation hypothesis can be found in the numerous studies looking at the relationship between Conscientiousness and performance, both work and academic (Barrick & Mount, 1991; Blickle, 1996; De Raad, 1996; De Raad & Schowenburg, 1996; Geisler-Brenstein & Schmeck, 1996; Goff & Ackerman, 1992; McHenry, Hough, Toquam, Hanson, & Ashworth, 1990; Rothstein, Paunonen, Rush, & King, 1994; Wiggins, Blackburn, & Hackman, 1969). Because these studies have shown there is a positive relationship between Conscientiousness and performance, compensation may be a valid explanation for the differential relationship between Conscientiousness and psychometric intelligence, on the one hand, and performance on the other hand. Further, correlational evidence, particularly significant correlations between Conscientiousness and Gf, may be needed to support the compensation hypothesis.

## 4.11 SUMMARY AND CONCLUSIONS

This chapter explored the relationship between personality and intellectual ability. In doing so, it attempted to overcome the frequent problem of lack of theoretical rationale to understand or interpret associations between personality and intelligence at the psychometric level. Accordingly, it attempted to introduce the major conceptual frameworks for understanding interactions between personality and intelligence/ability (arousability, top–down approaches, test performance, and investment) to install some order in the relatively recent but prolific body of empirical findings on personality and ability correlations.

Following top–down approaches (and the two-level model proposed by Chamorro-Premuzic and Furnham, 2004), we have divided the interpretation of personality–ability correlations according to whether they referred to either the impact of personality traits (mediated by states) on IQ test performance or the long-term effects of personality traits on the development of actual intellectual ability. This rationale was based on the simple idea that IQ test performance is (mainly, but) not only influenced by a person's intelligence. This would imply that (a) psychometric intelligence is (a valid and accurate, but) not a pure measure of intelligence, and (b) nonability variables that affect IQ test performance may not necessarily relate to actual (pure) intellectual ability or intelligence as capacity.

Correlations between intelligence and the personality traits of Neuroticism and Extraversion are usually interpreted in terms of testing effects or the influence of personality on an individual's test performance. We examined several examples of how these two traits may affect a person's performance on an intelligence test and how specific methodological issues (particularly in the case of Extraversion) may result in associations between Extraversion/Introversion and psychometric intelligence.

Another question, however, is whether personality traits may genuinely affect an individual's reasoning and learning skills—that is, not whether his or her performance on tests may be distorted by nonability factors confounded in the test scores, but whether certain non-ability traits may have long-term effects, albeit modest, on the development of intellectual competence, knowledge, or skills. Rephrased, this is a question referring to whether personality traits may to some extent determine individual differences in intelligence or whether one individual becomes more intelligent than others.

This question has been addressed in depth from the conceptual perspective of investment theories originated by Cattell (1978, 1987) and followed up by the work of Ackerman and his colleagues (Ackerman, 1996, 1999; Ackerman & Heggestad, 1997; Ackerman & Goff, 1994; Goff & Ackerman, 1992). Psychometric evidence in support of the investment hypotheses, which posits that certain personality characteristics related to intellectual curiosity, imagination, creativity, and achievement motivation would drive some individuals to *invest* in the development of skills and knowledge more than others, is derived from the significant correlations of psychometric intelligence and both Openness and Typical Intellectual Engagement. However, the self-report nature of these two inventories and the obscure conceptual overlap between what ability tests measure and what these personality inventories assess make any interpretation difficult (and proof of this has been the variety of possible interpretations discussed in this chapter). Thus, to some, correlations between Openness and psychometric intelligence may be indicative of the relationship between self-assessed and objectively assessed intellectual competence, whereas to others these correlations may be indicative of the genuine long-standing effects of personality on crystallized intelligence. It is not surprising then that the association of intellectual ability with both Openness and Typical Intellectual Engagement has been the focus of most research on personality and intellectual ability, and that it has been located at the crossroads of the personality—intelligence interface.

Regardless of the different approaches to the relationship between personality and intellectual ability (some of which, but not all, have been examined throughout this chapter), the three common aims for any future research in the area seem to be: (a) the integration of theories and findings, (b) the need for experimental studies on personality and intelligence, and (c) the examination of the concept of intelligence beyond psychometric test performance. The integration of theories and findings facilitate focus-oriented research and avoid free-association-like studies, which attempt to correlate everything with everything and add nothing but confusion to the area. Experimental studies would facilitate insight into the processes underlying the relationship between individual differences in both personality and intelligence and shed light into the causal paths that constitute this relationship. Finally, the examination of intelligence beyond psychometric test performance may broaden our understanding of individual differences in intellectual competence in terms of integrating both cognitive and noncognitive predictors of future achievement; this is the aim of the final three chapters of this book (5, 6, and 7).

# 5

# Personality and Intelligence as Predictors of Academic and Work Performance

The previous chapter examined the salient literature on the relationship between personality traits and psychometric intelligence. This section examines the relationship of personality traits and psychometric intelligence with academic performance (AP), as well as performance in the workplace (WP).

Although psychologists have rarely presented definitions of AP (this may be due to the familiarity with the concept), it can be simply defined as performance in academic settings—that is, formal education such as elementary and secondary school, undergraduate, and postgraduate levels. There are several ways to measure individual differences in AP; most commonly these would include written examinations (essay type or multiple choice) designed to assess students' understanding and knowledge of curricular content. Other (perhaps less frequent) methods may include oral examinations (viva), dissertations (supervised long-term production), group work (long-term production with coworkers), and continuous assessment (coursework, essays, attendance, participation in class; see Furnham & Chamorro-Premuzic, in press).

Like psychometric intelligence, AP may be regarded as an indicator of intellectual competence. In fact AP has always been the criterion par excellence for the validity of ability measures, which originated as an attempt to distinguish between competent and noncompetent students (Binet & Simon, 1905/1961a, 1908/1961b, 1908/1961c; see also Cronbach, 1984; Rolfhus & Ackerman, 1996). One of the aims of this book is to examine the relationship between personality and intellectual competence beyond psychometric intelligence. The concept of AP seems to be an obvious starting point because the development of IQ measures was prompted by the desire to predict individual differences in school performance (see Section 3.1). In this sense, the relationship between psychometric intelligence and AP may be compared to that of a weather forecast and actual weather: An evaluation of the variables that may determine weather (e.g., temperature, pressure, wind, etc.) results in a forecast, but it is only when contrasted with actual weather that we have an idea of the validity of a weather forecast (see Fig. 5.1).

Therefore, the validity of this technique depends on the predictability of actual weather in a specific place. Likewise the measurement of certain mental operations (speed of response, reasoning ability) is only effective (valid) to the extent that it successfully predicts longitudinal performance in academic settings. Whereas psychometric intelligence may be more indicative of a person's capacity, AP may reflect not only intellectual capacity, but also its actual manifestation in real life. As such AP can be considered a measure of long-term intellectual competence, and its relationship to personality traits may provide important information about noncognitive individual differences underlying real-world performance. The same logic applies to WP, although it is seen that the effects of cognitive ability on AP are considerably stronger, especially at elementary and secondary school levels. Before focusing on the link between AP and per-

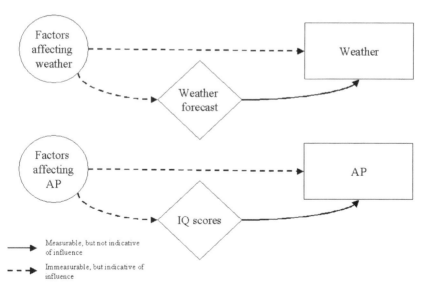

Note: Factors affecting weather may include latitude, humidity, atmospheric pressure and land/sea distribution. Factors affecting AP may include intellectual ability and personality traits.

FIG. 5.1.   Academic performance (AP) as a measure of intellectual competence.

sonality traits, it may be useful to briefly review the literature on AP and psychometric intelligence.

## 5.1 PSYCHOMETRIC INTELLIGENCE AND THE PREDICTION OF AP

For more than a century, psychological and educational researchers have attempted to effectively predict AP (e.g., Binet, 1903; Binet & Simon, 1905/ 1961a; Busato, Prins, Elshout, & Hamaker, 2000; Ebbinghaus, 1897; Elshout & Veenman, 1992; Galton, 1883; Goh & Moore, 1987; Harris, 1940; Neisser et al., 1996; Savage, 1962; Terman, 1916; Thurstone, 1919; Willingham, 1974). As seen throughout chapter 3, these attempts have prompted the development of psychometric measures and, more specifically, modern ability tests (see Cronbach, 1984; Robinson, 1999). Since their design, and particularly since the 1930s, ability tests have been widely employed in school performance prediction and college placement selection (Brody, 2000; Jensen, 1980; Zeidner & Matthews, 2000). Terms such as *underachievement* and *overachievement*, usually used to refer to discrepancies between ability test results (potential) and AP (outcome), may reflect the prestige of these measures (Boyle, 1990), and several studies have presented long-standing evidence for the predictive validity of psychometric intelligence.

Bright (1930) reported high correlations between ability measures and both academic and citizenship grades in public schools. Ten years later, Springsteen (1940) replicated these correlations in a sample of mentally handicapped school pupils. Tenopyr (1967) examined the predictive validity of cognitive (SCAT) and social ability and found that the former was a powerful predictor of academic achievement (these findings were partially replicated in a more recent study by Riggio, Messamer, & Throckmorton, 1991). In a larger sample ($N = 230$) of Hindi female school students, Sharma and Rao (1983) reported high correlations between AP and nonverbal intellectual ability (Raven's Progressive Matrixes). Bachman, Sines, Watson, Lauer, and Clarke (1986) compared the criterion validity of IQ and pathological behavior with regard to AP in a large sample ($N = 873$) of primary school students; IQ test results accounted for most of the variance in academic success. The relationship between psychometric intelligence and AP in school has been thoroughly reviewed by Walberg, Strykowski, Rovai, and Hung (1984), who meta-analyzed more than 3,000 studies and reported an impressive correlation of up to $r = .71$ between the two constructs. More recent studies have replicated this correlation (e.g., Gagne & St. Pere, 2001).

Research has also provided evidence for the predictive power of cognitive ability tests with regard to AP in higher levels of education. Willingham (1974) reported on the significant criterion validity for the graduate record examination (GRE) test (like IQ tests, this is a standardized measure of verbal, mathematical, and logical ability), particularly its advanced version. In a more recent large-scale meta-analysis ($N$ = 82,659), Kuncel, Hezlett, and Ones (2001) tested the validity of the GRE and undergraduate grade point average (UGPA) as predictors of AP at a postgraduate level. It was found that both GRE and UGPA were consistently and significantly related to grade point average in the first postgraduate year of education, overall examination scores, publication citation index, as well as faculty ratings. However, it is noticeable that both predictors, albeit measures of ability, were also indicative of previous knowledge (as assessed by specific subtests in the case of the GRE and content-based examination in the case of the underlying exams of UGPA). Thus, the extent to which a student directs his or her efforts to study, revise, and carefully prepare a specific topic may have been confounded in both GRE and UGPA scores.

Although it would exceed the aims of this chapter to include an exhaustive review of studies reporting significant (and moderate to high) correlations between ability tests and AP, the literature seems to indicate that psychometric intelligence is the most established predictor of AP (Elshout & Veenman, 1992; Gagne & St. Pere, 2001; Neisser et al., 1996; Sternberg & Kaufman, 1998). Ability tests are not only the most significant predictors of AP, but educational level in general (Brand, 1994). Furthermore, psychometric intelligence has been shown to be stable across time (Deary, 2001; Schaie, 1996), which would explain why it has often been found to be the most significant predictor—not just of educational level, but of marital choice, occupational success, moral values, law abidingness, and liberalism in political attitudes (Burtt & Arps, 1943; Brand, 1994; Gottfredson, 1996, 1997; Hernstein & Murray, 1994; Jensen, 1998).

However, there is a considerable amount of research suggesting that the relationship between psychometric intelligence and AP may often be weaker than expected and even fail to reach statistical significance levels (e.g., Metha & Kumar, 1985; Sanders, Osborne, & Greene, 1955; Seth & Pratap, 1971; Singh & Varma, 1995; Thompson, 1934). This is especially true at higher levels of formal education. In fact some researchers have shown that in higher levels of education (after 1, 2, or 3 years of college), the predictive power of psychometric intelligence declines (see Ackerman, 1994). For example, Jensen (1980) reported correlations ranging from $r = .60$ to $r = .70$ between psychometric intelligence and AP in elementary school, dropping to $r = .50$ in secondary school and $r = .40$ in college (see also Boekaerts, 1995). Likewise Hunter (1986) argued that measures of $g$, as well as verbal and quantitative abilities, have only been found to be modest predictors of academic success for adults (see Fig. 5.2).

This has led both theoretical and applied researchers to examine the predictive validity of other constructs that may account for unique variance in AP. Perhaps noncognitive variables, such as interests, motivation, and personality traits, start to play a relevant role as individuals grow older and progress through the formal educational system. These variables

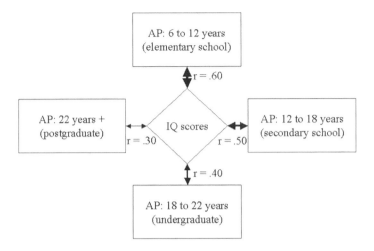

*Note:* All r values are approximate. Based on Ackerman (1994), Boekaerts (1995), Hunter (1986), and Jensen (1980)

FIG. 5.2.    Correlations between intelligence and academic performance (AP) at different levels of education.

could interact with cognitive ability and even direct it toward the development of adult intellectual competence (see Ackerman & Beier, 2003; Ackerman & Heggestad, 1997). Thus, the decrease of the predictive validity of psychometric intelligence with regard to AP at more advanced stages of education may have its counterpart in the increase of the predictive validity of noncognitive traits. No wonder, then, that noncognitive individual differences have received increased attention with regard to AP, particularly in the last 6 years. As Ackerman and Rolfhus (1999) argued, "abilities are only one part of the complex causal framework that determines whether a student pursues the acquisition of knowledge and skills within a particular domain. Two other components of the equation are interests and personality traits" (p. 176).

## 5.2  PERSONALITY TRAITS
## AND THE PREDICTION OF AP

It ought to be clear at the outset that no psychologist is foolish enough to suppose that native intelligence is the sole factor in academic success. (Whipple, 1922, p. 262)

The interest in the relationship between personality traits and AP is not new. Webb (1915) put forward a construct that he labeled *persistence of motives* (a modern version of this factor was developed by Digman, 1990) and considered it of great relevance for intellectual performance. Likewise other noncognitive but performance-related variables can be identified in Alexander's (1935) "factor X," which was believed to determine interests and learning efforts. Hence, Ryans (1938) emphasized the importance of assessing persistence to improve the predictability of academic attainment by IQ tests alone.

Even when ability tests have been found to be significantly correlated with grades, it has been noted that it may not be effective to predict academic success from intelligence scores mostly because "the energy output of the individual student varies independently of ability" (Stanger, 1933, p. 648). Thus, several researchers have emphasized the need to include other variables than intelligence in the prediction of AP, suggesting that academic achievement involves other factors apart from intellectual ability. Attending class, doing the homework, participating in discussions, getting along with other students and teachers, and stressing out during an exam are all (nonintellectual) variables that could be expected to influence AP. Individual differences in personality can therefore play an important role in academic achievement (Chamorro-Premuzic & Furnham, 2002, 2003a, 2003b; Furnham, Chamorro-Premuzic, & McDougall, 2004; Petrides, Chamorro-Premuzic, Frederickson, & Furnham, in press).

The next sections examine the salient literature on personality and AP. To this extent, several empirical studies looking at the relationship between different indicators of AP (notably exam grades) and well-established personality traits (Big Five and Gigantic Three; Costa & McCrae, 1992; Eysenck & Eysenck, 1985) are reviewed.

## 5.3  THE GIGANTIC THREE AND AP

Studies looking at the relationship between personality and AP attracted a considerable amount of research in the 1950s, but it was not until the development of Eysenck's (1947, 1970) and Eysenck and Eysenck's (1985) personality model that researchers could examine the same personality traits, which would of course provide a better means to establish comparisons between studies. As described (see Section 2.3), Eysenckian-based personality inventories assess either two (Extraversion and Neuroticism) (MPI, EPI) or three (Extraversion, Neuroticism, and Psychoticism) (EPQ, EPQ–R) main personality traits that are components of a psychobiological model of personality (Cloninger, 1987; Eysenck, 1967b; Matthews & Gilliand, 1999; Zuckerman, 1991).

We observed that Eysenck identified the physiological basis for personality, located in the cortico-reticular loop (thalamus, ascending reticular activating system, and cerebral cortex) and the viscero-cortical loop that connects the cerebral cortex with the visceral brain. Variability levels in the first of these two neural circuits determine individual differences in Extraversion (introverts are more easily aroused than extroverts), whereas variability in the second neural circuit (which comprises the lymbic system) determines differences in Neuroticism.

Neuroticism and Extraversion are also included in the Five Factor models of personality and are thus well established. In conjunction with the Big Five (Costa & McCrae, 1992), the Eysenckian three personality super factors represent the two predominant conceptual frames to the approach and assessment of personality (see Jackson, Furnham, Forde, & Cotter, 2000, for a comparative study and review).

Several studies have provided evidence for the significant relationship between the Gigantic Three (i.e., Neuroticism, Extraversion, and Psychoticism) and AP. Given that Neuroticism and Extraversion are present in both Eysenck's (Eysenck & Eysenck, 1985) and Costa and McCrae's (1988, 1992) models, Sections 5.4 and 5.5 also review studies where Neuroticism and Extraversion were assessed through the NEO–PI–R.

## 5.4  NEUROTICISM, WORRY, AND EXAM STRESS

Neuroticism has often been associated with AP—largely negatively (Cattell & Kline, 1977; De Barbenza & Montoya, 1974; Furnham & Medhurst, 1995; Furnham & Mitchell, 1991; Goh & Moore, 1987; Lathey, 1991; Rindermann & Neubauer, 2001; Sanchez-Marin, Rejano-Infante, & Rodriguez-Troyano, 2001; Savage, 1962; Weiss, 1998). Two large-scale studies by Hembree (1988) and Siepp (1991) reported a correlation of $r = -.20$ between Neuroticism and AP. This correlation is consistent with the modest, but negative, relationship between Neuroticism and psychometric intelligence (see Section 4.4). Because AP and psychometric intelligence are both measured through maximal performance tests (examinations or ability measures), there is a considerable theoretical overlap for the negative correlation between Neuroticism and both indicators of intellectual competence. One would thus expect that stress, impulsiveness, and anxiety under test/exam conditions may account for the negative correlations between Neuroticism and AP, in the same way they may account for the negative association between Neuroticism and psychometric intelligence.

It has even been suggested that, in heightened emotional situations, Neuroticism may moderate the relationship between AP and intellectual ability. In this respect, Boyle (1983) observed that the correlation between AP and psychometric intelligence drops from $r = .35$ under neutral conditions to $r = .21$ under arousing conditions. However, it is also likely that Neuroticism may affect AP in a more general way (i.e., not merely in stressful environments; Halamandaris & Power, 1999). This may involve study habits and even attendance because Neuroticism has been showed to have negative physical consequences such as racing heart, perspiration, gastric disturbances, and muscle tension (Matthews, Davies, Westerman, & Stammers, 2000). Accordingly, Chamorro-Premuzic and Furnham (2002) found that neurotic students were more likely to be ill during the exam period and request "special treatment" for their exam completion. With regard to take-home assignments, evidence is more ambiguous (Boyle, 1983; Halamandaris & Power, 1999).

Several authors have concluded that evaluation—particularly on demanding tasks—may be overarousing for neurotics and thus exceed optimal arousal levels for performance (Corcoran, 1965; Humphreys & Revelle, 1984), leading to cognitive processing impairment (Eysenck, 1982; Spielberger, 1972). Thus, it is noteworthy that Neuroticism differences in arousal and cognitive performance may only be evident under stressful conditions (Eysenck, 1992a; Stelmack, 1981). Furthermore, whereas Neuroticism may attenuate AP in less able/proficient students or under stressful conditions, it may even facilitate AP in more able/proficient students or under nonarousing situations. Accordingly, Geen (1985) and Zeidner (1998) suggested that, under nonobserved and more relaxed conditions anxiety may be positively related to performance—possibly because it can increase motivation, serving as a drive (Spielberger, 1962). However, several studies have failed to find evidence for the positive effects of Neuroticism on performance under nonarousing conditions (Szymura & Wodnjecka, 2003). Besides AP usually involves intellectual competence under pressure, which would undermine the applied relevance of the relationship between Neuroticism on nondemanding tasks.

As discussed (see Section 4.4), the tendency to worry is an inherent characteristic of high Neuroticism. The processes underlying the relationship between worry and stress have been thoroughly described by Matthews et al. (2000), who emphasized the subjective components of stress: A stressful situation depends more on the individual's perception than on the stressor (see also Lazarus & Folkman, 1984). Likewise Selye (1976) argued that stress reactions depend on the person's appraisals of his or her competence to cope with environmental demands. Thus, worrying about one's performance or fearing to fail an examination may lead to the experience of stress, which would result in poor exam performance (Halamandaris & Power, 1999). Wine (1982) and Sarason et al. (1995; see also Matthews et al., 2000) also pointed out that anxious individuals tend to waste time on self-evaluative conditions that would divert their attention from the actual test. This may lead to difficulties in understanding exam/test instructions (Tobias, 1977).

In the case of neurotics, worry is likely to emerge frequently as a consequence of their lack of confidence in their abilities (Wells & Matthews, 1994). Whether this lack of confidence is merely irrational or a true reflection of neurotics' intellectual competence is difficult to address, but it is certainly possible that "fear of failure" or low "hope of success" (characteristics of Neuroticism) may be a consequence of learning difficulties and poor study habits (and even low intellectual ability). In any case, it is likely that both actual and perceived competencies interact to create a "neurotic feedback," leading to low AP (see Fig. 5.3). As Busato, Prins, Elshout, and Hamaker (1999) observed, "unsuccessful studying may result in more neurotic feelings and an increasing sense of failure, which results in a less conscientious working method, less openness studying and less achievement motivation in general" (p. 138).

Most research between Neuroticism/anxiety and AP has examined university rather than school students. However, Rindermann and Neubauer (2001) provided recent evidence for the negative relationship between AP in secondary school and a German scale of anxiety (Angstfragebogen fur Schuler; Wieczerkowski, Nickel, Janowski, Fittkau, & Rauer, 1986). In university settings, correlations between AP and Neuroticism seem to vary, with some studies reporting negative (Chamorro-Premuzic & Furnham, 2003a, 2003b), some positive (De Barbenza & Montoya, 1974; De Raad & Schowenberg, 1996), and other nonsignificant or variable (Busato et al., 2000; De Fruyt & Mervielde, 1996; Furnham & Mitchell, 1991; Halamandaris & Power, 1999; Kline & Gale, 1971) correlations. However, some order was installed in the literature by Ackerman and Heggestad's (1997) meta-analysis, in which the authors

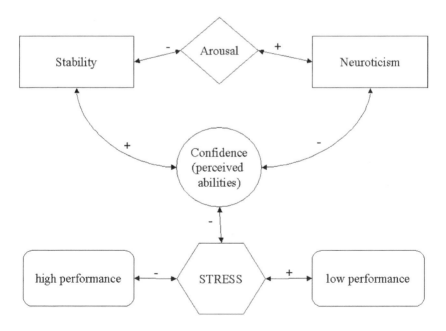

*Note:* positive signs refer to a positive, and negative to a negative, correlation between variables

FIG. 5.3. A graphical depiction of the relationship among Neuroticism, arousal, confidence, stress, and performance (the "neurotic feedback").

found that stable students outperformed neurotics in university, with Neuroticism being negatively correlated to knowledge and achievement in 11 samples. In any case, it is important to bear in mind that the influence of Neuroticism on AP may almost certainly be moderated by a number of variables—from Gc and Gf to assessment methods and stress.

## 5.5   EXTRAVERSION AND STUDY HABITS

There is also some evidence for the significant correlations between AP and Extraversion, although the literature seems to indicate that other variables such as age, level of education, and type of assessment may play a crucial role and even determine the sign (i.e., positive or negative) of this correlation. With regard to age, Eysenck and Cookson (1969) suggested that the correlation between AP and Extraversion changes from positive to negative around the ages of 13 to 14 (see also Entwistle, 1972). In an earlier manual to the EPI Junior, Eysenck (1965) also specified gender differences for this change—namely, 14 for females and 15 for males. Eysenck (1994a, 1994b) attributed the change of sign in the correlation between Extraversion and AP to the replacement of the social and easy atmosphere of primary school by the rather formal atmosphere of secondary school. Alternatively, Anthony (1973) argued that age may merely reflect the fact that the less able individuals become extraverted and vice versa. In this sense, study habits would be a consequence of introverts' investment strategies, whereas socializing may be regarded as a result of extraverts' low intellectual investment.

It is generally accepted that introverts may have an advantage over extraverts with respect to the ability to consolidate learning, as well as lower distractability and better study habits (Entwistle & Entwistle, 1970; Eysenck & Cookson, 1969; Sanchez-Marin et al., 2001). It would appear that introverts condition faster and have slower decay of their conditioned behavior. Accordingly, a recent study by Sanchez-Marin, Rejano-Infante, and Rodriguez-Troyano (2001) showed that extraverts tend to fail their courses more often than introverts (see also Busato et al., 2000). Rolfhus and Ackerman (1999) found negative relations between Extraversion and several knowledge tests, suggesting that these relations may be related to differences in knowledge acquisition time between introverts (spend more time studying) and extraverts (spend more time socializing). Further, Goff and Ackerman (1992) found introverts to outperform extroverts in two levels of formal education (i.e., high school and undergraduate). A recent study by Petrides, Chamorro-Premuzic, Frederickson, and Furnham (in press) replicated the negative association between Extraversion even when IQ was taken into account. This is also consistent with the findings of Goh and Moore (1987), Humphreys and Revelle (1984), and Amelang and Ulwer (1991; see also Furnham, 1995).

Yet some studies have also reported higher AP by extraverts, specifically in school settings (Anthony, 1973; Entwistle, 1972), suggesting that introversion may be an advantage only under highly intellectually demanding tasks. De Barbenza and Montoya (1974) also reported positive correlations between Extraversion and academic success in university students. This correlation was replicated not only in undergraduate (Chamorro-Premuzic & Furnham, 2003b; De Fruyt & Mervielde, 1996) but also in postgraduate (Rothstein, Rush, Pannonen, & King, 1994) students.

In one of the rare studies to examine not only grades but also coursework, Furnham and Medhurst (1995) found that extraverts were rated higher for their seminar performance, albeit receiving lower marks in their exams. This may alert researchers (as well as educators) about the possibility that assessment methods may be differentially related to personality traits. In particular, differences between oral and written assessment methods are likely to be associated with individual differences in Extraversion (see Robinson, Gabriel, & Katchan, 1993). Figure 5.4 represents the relationships between Extraversion and several assessment methods of AP. As can be seen, it may be hypothesized that short multiple-choice exams, oral examinations, and continuous assessment based on participation in class may all favor extraverts, whereas long, untimed, essay-type exams and coursework based on homework assignments may both be beneficial for introverts.

Further inconsistencies concerning the psychometric relationship between Extraversion and AP were added by the results of several studies

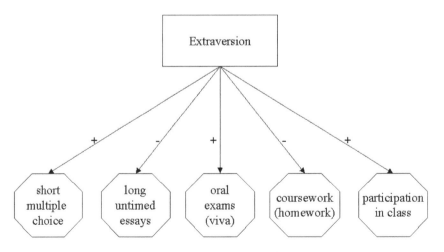

*Note:* positive signs refer to a positive, and negative to a negative, correlation between variables

FIG. 5.4.   How extraverts' academic performance may vary depending on the method of assessment.

that failed to reach significance levels (in either directions). Heaven et al. (2002) found Extraversion to be unrelated to performance in school. Halamandaris and Power (1999) replicated these results on a university sample (see also Furnham & Mitchell, 1991). In Ackerman and Heggestad's (1997) meta-analysis, Extraversion was virtually unrelated to knowledge and achievement.

Research on Extraversion and AP was also conducted at the primary trait (or subfacet) level. In a recent study, Chamorro-Premuzic and Furnham (2003b) found that two subfacets of Extraversion—namely, gregariousness and activity—were negatively and significantly correlated with academic exam performance (in the range of $r = -.21$ to $-.27$) in a sample of 247 university undergraduates. It was suggested that extraverts' greater tendency to socialize (as reflected in these subfacets) may be counterproductive for their AP.

## 5.5  PSYCHOTICISM AND POOR AP

With regard to Psychoticism, the literature is less ambiguous and seems to indicate that this personality trait is significantly and negatively related to academic attainment (Aluja-Fabregat & Torrubia-Beltri, 1998; Furnham & Medhurst, 1995; Goh & Moore, 1987; Maqsud, 1993; Sanchez-Marin et al., 2001). It has been suggested that Psychoticism may affect responsibility and interests in studies, therefore limiting academic success (Aluja-Fabregat & Torrubia-Beltri, 1998). Accordingly, Furnham and Medhurst found that Psychoticism was negatively correlated not only with grades, but also with coursework (seminar reports). This pattern of results was replicated in Chamorro-Premuzic and Furnham (2003a), where Psychoticism was also the most significant predictor of coursework. Additional evidence was recently provided by Petrides, Chamorro-Premuzic, Frederickson, and Furnham (in press), who found that Psychoticism was a negative predictor of AP in school, accounting for unique variance in AP even when cognitive ability was taken into account.

Several studies have also shown that Conscientiousness—a strong negative correlate of Psychoticism (Digman, 1990; Eysenck, 1991, 1992a, 1992b, 1992c)—is a consistent positive predictor of academic success (Blickle, 1996; Busato, Prins, Elshout, & Hamaker, 2000; De Raad, 1996). Studies have replicated this relationship in school (Wolfe & Johnson, 1995) as well as in undergraduate (Busato et al., 2000; Goff & Ackerman, 1992) and postgraduate (Hirschberg & Itkin, 1978; Rothstein et al., 1994) education (see Section 5.8).

Haun (1965) was among the first to provide correlational evidence for the idea that academic excellence is negatively associated with indicators of pathology. This association may be explained by the fact that Psychoticism is linked to poor overall adjustment (Halamandaris & Power, 1999; Hussain & Kumari, 1995). People high on Psychoticism are more likely to be solitary, insensitive, and uncaring with others and tend to reject implicit and explicit social norms that are indispensable for interaction with others (Pervin & John, 1997). Thus, one can expect Psychoticism to have negative (maladaptive) consequences not only in educational, but all, settings.

Maqsud (1993) found negative correlations between Psychoticism and academic attainment, and positive correlations between academic attainment and academic self-concept. These correlations suggest that Psychoticism (like Neuroticism) could affect students' self-conceptions of AP. As is discussed (see Section 6.9), negative self-judgments may impair performance, especially when combined with low or intermediate levels of intellectual ability.

Interestingly, not all characteristics of Psychoticism seem to be problematic for academic achievement. Besides low responsibility, low self-concept, lack of interests and lack of cooperation, Psychoticism is also positively associated with creativity (Eysenck, 1995b). Further, one of the positive correlates of Psychoticism is Openness to Experience, which has often been regarded as beneficial for education (De Raad, 1996). Although Psychoticism and Openness are positively intercorrelated, Psychoticism is associated with low AP, whereas Openness has often been associated with high AP. In this sense, it is important to examine how other correlates of Psychoticism, such as Agreeableness and Conscientiousness (and intellectual competence), may moderate the relationship between Psychoticism and AP. Eysenck (1995b) stressed the fact that creativity should be conceived as a function or byproduct of both Psychoticism and intellectual ability. Further, the author's distinction between *trait creativity* and *productive talent* may denote the importance of traits such as Agreeableness and Conscientiousness, which may provide the necessary order and sociability to obtain productivity (this idea was already present in Freud's concept of sublimation).

## 5.6   OPENNESS AND AP

As mentioned earlier, Openness to Experience has been found to be positively associated with AP (see also Blickle, 1996; De Raad & Schowenburg, 1996; Geisler-Brenstein & Schmeck, 1996). This association has been replicated in studies involving both undergraduate (De Fruyt & Mervielde, 1996) and postgraduate (Rothstein et al., 1994) students.

The positive relationship between AP and Openness has often been interpreted in terms of the fact that Openness seems correlated with psychometric intelligence in the range of $r = .20$ to $r = .40$ (see McCrae & Costa, 1985; also see Section 4.7). Particularly, the use of vocabulary and general knowledge is likely to be more proficient in open personalities (Ackerman & Heggestad, 1997; Ashton, Lee, Vernon, & Jang, 2000; Goff & Ackerman, 1992). Blickle (1996) suggested that Openness to Experience would enable individuals with a wider use of strategies and learning techniques (e.g., critical evaluation, in-depth analysis, open-mindness), which would positively influence their performance in academic settings (see also Mumford & Gustafson, 1988). Accordingly Sneed, Carlson, and Little (1994) found that Openness to Experience (along with Conscientiousness) was considered the most important personality trait by teachers (when it comes to predicting academic excellence). However, Goff and Ackerman (1992) found that TIE, a scale correlated with Openness in the range of $r = .60$ to $r = .80$ (see Rocklin, 1994), was a poor predictor of high school and university GPA. Further, in one of their studies, Rothstein et al. (1994) failed to replicate significant correlations between Openness and AP in a sample of postgraduate students.

Although it may seem surprising that some studies have failed to find evidence for the predictive validity of AP by Openness, there are theoretical reasons to explain this; specifically, the conceptual similarities between some of the aspects of Openness and Psychoticism. Openness and Psychoticism may both be related to low inhibition of attention to task-irrelevant stimuli (Beech & Williams, 1997). Hence, as much as the positive and significant correlation between Openness and AP may be understood in terms of the ability loadings of Openness, the fact that this personality trait is positively correlated with Psychoticism would make it equally possible to expect negative associations between Openness and AP (see Fig. 5.5). In the words of McCrae and Costa (1997a): "very open people appear to have some of the characteristics of schizotypal thinking; whether these are adaptive or maladaptive will probably depend on other aspects of personality and on the individual's social environment" (p. 24). It is, however, important to emphasize the differences—rather than the similarities—between Openness and Psychoticism. These differences can be represented in terms of adaptability. Hence, McCrae and Costa (1997a) argued that the relationship between Openness and personality disorders may be dependent on other variables such as Agreeableness and Conscientiousness.

## 5.7  AGREEABLENESS AND AP

Although research has generally failed to find any significant relationship between AP and Agreeableness (see Ackerman & Heggestad, 1997; De Fruyt & Mervielde, 1996; Rothstein et al., 1994), one may expect high Agreeableness to be beneficial for AP. Specifically, one may expect agreeable students to be more helpful with other students and, moreover, to make a positive impression on teachers (but not in anonymous exams). These two aspects may contribute to higher AP particularly when coursework involves working in groups and when students are not "blindly" assessed. This hypothesis can be supported by the findings of a recent study by Farsides and Woodfield (2003), who found positive and significant cor-

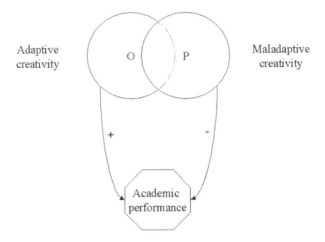

Adaptive
creativity

O    P

Maladaptive
creativity

+        -

Academic
performance

*Note:* positive signs refer to a positive, and negative to a negative, correlation between variables

FIG. 5.5.   Openness to Experience, Psychoticism, and academic performance.

relations between Agreeableness and AP. Furthermore, it was shown that Agreeableness was significantly related to several indicators of application (e.g., attendance, coursework).

It is likely that Agreeableness is more related to academic behavior than exam performance (Farsides & Woodfield, 2003). However, studies on personality and AP have predominantly examined grades. To this extent, it would be interesting to examine whether personality traits in general (not just Agreeableness) play any important role in students' behavior beyond examination performance. Specifically, it would be interesting to test whether individual differences in personality and intellectual ability are likely to influence academic behavioral variables such as truancy, exclusions, and absenteeism.

Although there appears to be a lack of psychological research on the relationship between undesirable school behavior and individual differences, there is some evidence in the literature that links truancy to other, more severe antisocial behaviors (e.g., juvenile offending, substance abuse). Fergusson, Lynskey, and Horwood (1995) found that truancy was frequent (almost 40%) in 12- to 16-year-old school children. Results also indicate that truancy was significantly related to dysfunctional (disadvantaged) home environments as well as early conduct problems. Other studies (notably Williamson & Cullingford, 1998) also provided evidence for the negative association between self-esteem and truancy (as well as exclusions and other disruptive school behaviors). Furthermore, undesirable academic behavior has been negatively related to empathy (particularly in males; Cohen & Strayer, 1996; Roberts & Strayer, 1996).

The literature on truancy and exclusions suggests that these variables could be positively related to Neuroticism (low self-esteem) and Psychoticism (lack of empathy). Hence, it could also be expected that undesirable academic behavior would be negatively correlated with the Big Five traits of Agreeableness and Conscientiousness. Further, to the extent that truancy and exclusions are negatively associated with academic exam performance, these variables could also be expected to be negatively related to intellectual ability.

## 5.8   CONSCIENTIOUSNESS AND AP

It seems that the personality factor more consistently associated with AP is Conscientiousness (Blickle, 1996; Busato, Prins, Elshout, & Hamaker, 2000; Costa & McCrae, 1992a, 1992b, 1992c; De Raad, 1996; De Raad & Schowenburg, 1996; Goff & Ackerman, 1992; Kling, 2001). Researchers have shown that this association is present at school (Wolfe & Johnson, 1995) in undergraduate (Busato et al., 2000; Goff & Ackerman, 1992) and postgraduate (Hirschberg & Itkin, 1978; Rothstein et al., 1994) levels. Further, Conscientiousness appears to be a solid predictor of WP throughout a variety of settings (Barrick & Mount, 1991, 1993; Matthews, 1997). Early studies (notably Smith, 1969) attributed the relationship between Conscientiousness and performance to the so-called *strength of character* factor.

Another explanation has been that Conscientiousness is conceptually related to motivation, a variable of considerable importance with regard to all types of performance (Anderson & Keith, 1997; Boekaerts, 1996; Busato et al., 2000; Furnham, 1995; Hamilton & Freeman, 1971; Harris, 1940; Heaven, 1990; Pelechano, 1972). According to Campbell (1990), motivation can be understood as the choice of (a) expending effort, (b) the level of effort, and (c) persisting at that level of effort. It is noteworthy that one of the subfacets of Conscientiousness is achievement striving, which is likely to affect goal settings and achievement. Therefore, it has been suggested that Conscientiousness is closely related to motivation, and that this personality trait is a significant predictor of performance, particularly when extrinsic determinants of motivation are held constant (Barrick, Mount, & Strauss, 1993; Sackett, Gruys, & Ellingson, 1998). Furthermore, other subfacets such as competence, order, dutifulness, self-discipline, and deliberation were found to be significant predictors of AP in university as measured by examination grades (De Raad & Schowenburg, 1996).

Recent research has confirmed the importance of Conscientiousness in academic settings, showing that this personality dimension is consistently correlated with exam grades, continuous assessment, and final dissertation marks even when previous AP or intellectual ability are taken into consideration (Chamorro-Premuzic & Furnham, 2003a, 2003b; Furnham & Chamorro-Premuzic, 2004c; Furnham, Chamorro-Premuzic, & McDougall, 2003).

An interesting point was recently made by Kling (2001), who observed that Conscientiousness is differentially related to AP and intellectual ability. The author argued that Conscientiousness may be a better predictor of academic achievement than psychometric intelligence. This would explain why females score lower on ability test, but obtain higher grades than males. Because females are usually more conscientious than males, Conscientiousness may be considered as important as intellectual ability in the prediction of students' performance. In other words, careful, organized, hard-working, persevering, and achievement-oriented students may succeed in academic settings despite their low intellectual ability. Personality (notably Conscientiousness) may thus moderate the relationship between intellectual capacity and AP. Hence, a higher score on either psychometric intelligence or Conscientiousness may compensate for a low score on the other as well as predict high AP.

## 5.9   CURRENT DIRECTIONS ON PERSONALITY TRAITS AND AP RESEARCH

Much of the current interest in personality and AP is due to Ackerman's (1996, 1999; Ackerman & Beier, 2003; Ackerman & Heggestad, 1997) recovery of the work by Snow. Snow (1992, 1995) suggested that personal variables such as abilities, attitudes, personality traits, and prior knowledge interact to affect learning and AP. He was particularly interested in identifying which aspects and levels of these personal variables would result in the best combination for achieving efficient learning. Snow concluded that nonanxious learners with low IQ and able learners who are highly anxious are equally handicapped in academic settings. However, it was not until the work of Ackerman and his colleagues that systematic and robust research begun to explore the possible combinations (i.e., trait complexes) of cognitive and noncognitive traits for the prediction of learning and knowledge acquisition.

In line with Snow's (1992, 1995) proposition, Ackerman and Heggestad's (1997) (see also Ackerman, 1999; Ackerman & Beier, 2003; Goff & Ackerman, 1992) psychometric meta-analyses identified four main trait complexes: *social, clerical/conventional, science/mathematical*, and *intellectual/cultural*. The social trait complex (which does not comprise any ability traits) represents Extraversion and social (interpersonal) skills. The clerical/conventional trait complex includes both Conscientiousness and a predisposition for traditional/conventional interests (in a sense, the negative expression of Openness to Experience). Like the social trait complex, the traditional/conventional trait does not represent individual differences in ability. On the contrary, the science/mathematical trait complex is mainly defined by intellectual abilities, particularly visual and spatial. Finally, the intellectual/cultural trait combines Gc, Openness, TIE, as well as art interests. As such this trait complex comprises a mix among interests, personality, and ability, representing a clear example of integration between noncognitive and cognitive individual differences. Trait complexes may thus be regarded as a fundamental contribution to understanding the development of expertise as an interaction between individual differences and the environment as jointly influencing human performance (Snow, 1992, 1995).

## 5.10  SUCCESS IN THE WORKPLACE

Although intelligence tests were created to predict academic success in children (Binet, 1903; see also chap. 3), their popularity and accuracy quickly transformed them into effective business tools. In essence, the prediction of an individual's success in the workplace is not substantially different from that in academic settings. If there are differences in performance (and few people would claim there are not), the prediction of these differences would be based on a standardized exercise that required similar skills from an individual than those required to succeed in the real world. Moreover, if academic success has frequently been regarded as a predictor of future achievement in the workplace, intellectual ability tests could be used to predict not merely scholastic achievement, but also the ability to perform in the workplace.

The economic consequences of the ineffective prediction of future achievement in the workplace and implications for personnel selection have been calculated by Hunter and Hunter (1984), who estimated the profit of successful test administration in recruitment to be worth more than $15 billion (at 1980 prices). This figure represented up to 20% of the U.S. federal budget; even when compared with interviewing techniques and other instruments, intelligence testing appeared to be the most effective and profitable tool to select employees. In a meta-analytic study, the authors reviewed over 80 years of psychological research and confirmed that hiring decisions may have fundamental economical consequences.

Fourteen years later, a second large review article by Schmidt and Hunter (1998) looked at the comparison between different criteria for selection and hiring, from age to graphology and psychometric testing. Table 5.1 presents the results from their meta-analysis. As can be seen, the highest predictor of WP was scores on the work sample test ($r = .54$), followed closely by both IQ test scores ($r = .51$) and structured interviews ($r = .51$). It is noteworthy that work sample tests require all applicants to perform on some of the job tasks for a specific period of time—that is, they refer to the employers' or recruiters' assessment of how well the applicants perform the actual job. In that sense, the predictive power of both structured interviews and psychometric intelligence scores show impressive validity. Further, because psychometric intelligence scores can be obtained quickly and simultaneously from all applicants, their advantages with regard to the rather time-consuming work sample test procedure seem evident (especially now that global recruitment and online selection have become essential resources).

In addition, psychometric intelligence can predict WP even when job-related skills are yet to be learned by the candidate because it is a consistent predictor of learning ability, whereas the work sample test is only useful when differences in WP are determined by previous knowledge and job-related skills. Not shown in Table 5.1, but also reported in Smith and Hunter's (1998) review, were correlations between WP and years of previous job experience ($r = .18$), education ($r = .10$), interests ($r = .10$), graphology ($r = .02$), and age ($r = -.01$). Although these results refer to the analyses of individual relationships between (pairs of) variables—that is, correlations between WP and each of the predictors independently (rather than standardized beta coefficients to show incremental validities of each of these variables with regard to the others[1])—they provide a sound overall perspective of the predictive power of psychometric intelligence compared with other frequently used variables. It should also be noted that the assessment (and let us use the term *assessment* instead of *measurement*) of WP is often associated with several difficulties—in particular, lack of objective criteria. On the contrary, most of the data on WP are composed of managerial reports or subjective appraisals, which make it frequently unreliable. However, it is likely that if WP would be measured objectively, independently of subjective evaluations of the

**TABLE 5.1**
**The Prediction of Work Performance (WP)**

| Predictor | Correlation With WP |
|---|---|
| Work sample test | $r = .54$ |
| Intelligence tests | $r = .51$ |
| Interview (structured) | $r = .51$ |
| Integrity tests | $r = .41$ |
| Interview (unstructured) | $r = .38$ |
| Conscientiousness | $r = .31$ |
| References | $r = .26$ |

*Note.*   Table is adapted from Schmidt and Hunter (1998). Only $r > .20$ are reported here.

---

[1]Nevertheless, in a follow-up analysis of a smaller set of subsamples, it was shown that the best predictor of job performance was psychometric intelligence, and that integrity and work sample test had the most significant incremental validity.

employer on the employee, the predictive power of psychometric intelligence would increase (as both cognitive ability and WP would be measured through power tests with objectively correct responses).

Thus, psychometric intelligence is a well-documented predictor of WP, accounting for an average 25% of the variance of individual differences in the work success. Moreover, standardized ability tests represent a cheap, quick, and reliable instrument for personnel selection, and there are extensive databases reporting the relationship between IQ tests and several outcomes of WP. The selection and use of other methods for recruitment seem far more dependent on personal experience and subjective decision making than on a reliable source of systematic research. It is also noteworthy that the predictive power of psychometric intelligence tends to increase with the intellectual demands of the job—to the point of being an irrelevant predictor of totally unskilled jobs, but an extremely accurate predictor of professional, highly skilled jobs.

In the famous Task Force report commissioned by the APA in 1996 (this was a revision directed by Neisser and conducted by many eminent differential psychologists), consensus about the correlates of intelligence and the importance of psychometric testing was confirmed. It was concluded that IQ scores are significantly related to school performance, years of education, WP, and wider social constructs with observable every-day manifestations, such as crime and delinquency, not to mention individual differences in clinical aspects of psychology (see Neisser et al., 1996).

## 5.11   EVIDENCE VERSUS BELIEF

For many decades, the concept of intelligence has been the target of heavy criticism and attack, both inside and outside the academic forum. It is especially the lay public that has continuously protested against the notion of measurable intelligence, a fact perhaps due to cultural, sociological, and religious constrains to attempt to understand scientific evidence. As Gottfredson (2000), a passionate yet rational advocate of psychometric intelligence who has devoted much of her research career to persuade academic and lay people about the importance of intellectual ability in everyday life noted, this "spasm of denial" over the controversies of IQ research may be a struggle "over how to reconcile our visions of political and social equality with the implications of biological inequality" (p. 80).

As early as 1922, the popular dislike of the concept of *intelligence* was reflected in Lippmann's journalistic critic to the "pretentious" and "abusive scientific methods" of IQ enthusiasts. Although lay people believe that the results of an IQ test are of little, if any, significance, and would at best constitute a narrow measure of human capabilities, evidence for the predictive power of psychometric intelligence can hardly be dismissed. However, there is often the belief that an individual's IQ can change over time, but there is vast empirical evidence indicating that, between adolescence and late adulthood, IQ remains largely stable over time. Even evidence that there are large individual differences in IQ test performance has been questioned, but the normal distribution emerges in any representative sample, showing that there are major differences in cognitive performance between individuals, even in short standardized tasks.

Although the *knowns* and *unknowns* of intelligence have now been summarized in a variety of forms (Deary, 2001; Gottfredson, 2000; Hernstein & Murray, 1994; Neisser et al., 1996), providing evidence for the consensus on the inheritability, variability, stability, and importance of psychometric intelligence, lay beliefs about intelligence are still confounded in the public's negative attitude toward psychometric research and testing. Furthermore, the media and press seem more concerned with the distortion of this evidence than the communication of consensual information, generating unjustifiable controversies and neglecting solid facts. In the end, the nature of the debate can be best described not in terms of conflicting scientific evidence, but in terms of the struggle between evidence and beliefs, which is unfortunately dominated by the neglect of evidence and probably influenced by political fears and sociological anxiety (see Gottfredson, 2000, for a remarkable discussion on the struggle between evidence and beliefs on intelligence and its consequences).

## 5.12  PERSONALITY TRAITS AND WP

The predictive validity of personality traits with regard to WP, as opposed to AP, has been relatively low, although there are some well-documented predictors among the Big Five personality factors (Guion & Gottier, 1965; Hunter & Hunter, 1984; Robertson & Kinder, 1993; Schmitt et al., 1984). On average, correlations between personality and WP were found to be modest ($r = 21$), according to a meta-analysis by Schmitt et al. (1984). However, it is noteworthy that only a few studies have looked at reliable and valid measures of both personality and WP—a fact that probably eclipses the real importance of personality traits in occupational settings (Furnham, 1992a, 1992b).

Furthermore, the lack of a common personality taxonomy/framework for organizing the traits used as predictors made it difficult to compare findings (see chap. 2). The increasing consensus on the reliability and validity of the Five Factor model has thus had a fundamental beneficial impact on research exploring personality correlates of WP. This transformed the preliminary pessimistic views into a widespread optimism within the occupational community concerning the use of personality inventories in personnel selection and development (Fletcher, 1991; Hogan & Holland, 2003; Jackson & Corr, 1998). Indeed four robust meta-analyses in just over a decade (Barrick & Mount, 1991; Judge, Heller, & Mount, 2002; Judge & Illies, 2002; Tett, Jackson, & Rothstein, 1991) encouraged both academic and applied researchers to use personality inventories for employee selection and management.

Studies looking at the relationship of the Big Five personality factors and WP show that Conscientiousness and Neuroticism (the same factors identified as significant predictors of AP) are consistently correlated with WP, the former positively, the latter negatively (Barrick, Mount, & Judge, 1999; Judge & Illies, 2002). This indicates that individuals who are calm, self-confident, and resilient (low Neuroticism), as well as responsible, ambitious, and organized (high Conscientiousness), tend to perform better at work, which is of little surprise.

The major trait of Conscientiousness with its subfacets (competence, order, dutifulness, achievement striving, self-discipline, deliberation) has been cited as the most valid personality predictor of performance, second only to psychometric intelligence. Conscientiousness and Need for Achievement have been correlated with salary (Barrick & Mount, 1991; Orpen, 1983), promotions (Jones & Whitemore, 1995), and supervisor ratings of performance in the military (Hough, Eton, Dunnette, Kamp, & McCloy, 1990; Jones & Whitemore, 1995). Judge, Higgins, Thoresen, and Barrick (1999) found that Conscientiousness was not only significantly correlated with performance (as measured by job status and income), but also job satisfaction (which emphasizes important motivational aspects of this trait). As Mount, Barrick, and Strauss (1999) noted, the idea that thorough, organized, responsible, ambitious, and hard-working individuals do well in their jobs is almost common sense. However, perhaps because the prediction of success and performance has been traditionally confined to psychometric intelligence, self-reports such as those assessing Conscientiousness (or any of its primary traits) have been considered of dubious benefit for the prediction of WP. Thus, although most employers (and employees) were probably aware that the characteristics represented by the Conscientiousness trait are desirable for almost every job, these were assessed through interviews or past achievement records, rather than standardized psychometric self-reports.

Despite the growing body of evidence in support of the predictive validity of Conscientiousness in occupational settings, some recent studies suggested that certain subfactors of Conscientiousness may be detrimental for specific jobs. Moon (2001) measured performance as de-escalation of commitment in a losing situation and found that achievement striving was detrimental, rather than beneficial, whereas duty had a beneficial effect (with the broad Conscientiousness trait being uncorrelated with WP).

Job performance was also negatively correlated with achievement striving (Hough, 1992) and dependability (Hough, Ones, & Viswesvaran, 1998) for certain occupations, such as health care workers. It has further been proposed that Conscientiousness may result in an individual performing fewer tasks as well as taking longer time to complete them, which may be detrimental for certain jobs, in particular at the managerial level (Driskell, Hogan, Sales, & Hoskins, 1994; Robertson, Baron, Gibbons, MacIver, & Nyfield, 2000). Accordingly, one could also expect that in certain jobs that require individuals to take risks and, to some extent, be unaware of the negative consequences of their actions, such as stockbrokers, low Conscientiousness would be more beneficial than high Conscientiousness (at least in the short term).

As mentioned, another personality trait often examined with regard to WP is Neuroticism/Emotional Stability. Studies report that this trait is negatively correlated with salary (Harrell, 1969; Rawls & Rawls, 1968) and occupational status (Melamed, 1996a, 1996b). Conversely, optimism, self-confidence, and self-assurance (typical of emotionally stable individuals) have been found to correlate positively with managerial advancement, executive pay, and job success (Goldberg, 1990; Howard & Bray, 1988; Mount & Barrick, 1995).

The relationship between Neuroticism and work performance may also be mediated by job satisfaction, with emotionally stable individuals more likely to be satisfied with their jobs (Furnham & Zacherl, 1986; Smith, Organ, & Near, 1983; Tokar & Subich, 1997). It has also been pointed that Extraversion may moderate the relationship between Neuroticism and WP, with neurotic introverts performing worse than neurotic extraverts (particularly in trainee jobs; Bartram & Dale, 1982; Jessup & Jessup, 1971). This may reflect the fact that low confidence may be a function of both high Neuroticism and low Extraversion, and it is widely accepted that confidence has an impact on various types of performance (see chap. 6).

In a more recent meta-analysis, Salgado (1997) provided additional empirical evidence for the negative effects of Neuroticism on WP, showing that all facets of this trait—namely, anxiety, angry hostility, depression, self-consciousness, impulsiveness, and vulnerability—are, to some extent, detrimental for WP, perhaps with the exception of artistic professions such as fine arts, where creative painters and sculptures tend to be neurotic and introverted (Götz & Götz, 1973).

Another personality factor frequently linked to WP is Extraversion (Judge, Higgins, Thoresen, & Barrick, 1999). This trait (present in most taxonomies, as seen in chap. 2) has been reported to be a positive predictor of salary, job level (Melamed, 1996a, 1996b), and managerial potential (Craik, Ware, Kamp, O'Reilly, Staw, & Zedeck, 2002). Specific characteristics of Extraversion, like dominance and sociability, have been identified as positive predictors of salary, job title, and level of managerial promotions (Caspi, Elder & Bem, 1988; Rawls & Rawls, 1968). Friendliness has also been modestly correlated with job performance, although measured by supervisor and peer ratings (Borman, White, & Dorsey, 1995). Like Conscientiousness, Extraversion can further be indirectly linked to WP because it has been consistently correlated with job satisfaction (Furnham & Zacherl, 1986; Watson & Slack, 1993).

However, the relationship between WP and Extraversion is less consistent than with Neuroticism and Conscientiousness, such that several studies have failed to replicate the correlations between Extraversion and WP. Barrick and Mount (1993) found Extraversion to be uncorrelated with WP in sales representatives, although Hurtz and Donovan (2000) found a significant, albeit small, positive correlation between these measures. More confusion was brought by Stewart and Carson's (1995) results, in which Extraversion was reported to be negatively correlated with performance in service jobs. However, one limitation to compare these findings is that these three studies used different measures for job performance. Some have suggested that introverts are better at handling routine work activities than extraverts (Cooper & Payne, 1967; Matthews et al., 2000).

The other two Big Five personality factors of Openness and Agreeableness have yet to be consistently examined with regard to WP. At least theoretically, one would expect open individuals to excel in the workplace thanks to their higher flexibility, creativity, and intellectual curiosity, as has been proposed by Judge et al. (1999), although it is clear that this depends on the type of job. Some studies have indeed found Openness to be a valid predictor of training proficiency (Barrick & Mount, 1991) and effectiveness (Judge & Bono, 2000), with open individuals doing better in customer service jobs (Hurtz & Donovan, 2000) and in jobs that require creative behavior (George & Zhou, 2001). It would seem that open individuals would have a greater tendency to learn from experiences, which has been identified as a key trait in successful managers (Montigliani & Giacalone, 1998). However, other characteristics of Openness, such as need for cognition or novel experiences, could well be detrimental for performance in less exciting than in more conventional jobs (Judge et al., 1999). Further, when there are rigid job demands such as attaining to prescribed rules, open individuals may somehow suffer from excess of creativity, as it has been suggested by the negative correlation between Openness and performance of sports referees. Thus, the need to maintain discipline and ensure that rules are followed are conditions that open individuals may find difficult to attain to. Probably for the same reasons, Openness has also been found to correlate negatively with job satisfaction (Boudreau et al., 2001).

Finally, with regard to Agreeableness, it has also been argued that there is no consistent evidence to suggest either positive or negative correlations between this trait and WP. Judge et al. (1999) suggested that the cooperative nature of agreeable individuals may allow them to perform better in many jobs, particularly when teamwork is required. In fact there is evidence indicating that Agreeableness is positively correlated with overall job performance (Tett et al., 1991), notably measures of interpersonal facilitation (Hurtz & Donovan, 2000), even in the army (Hough et al., 1990). It appears that being likeable, cooperative, and good natured has a positive impact on job performance—probably not just one's own, but also that of others. However, agreeable individuals—characterized by their altruism—could sacrifice their success for pleasing others, a hypothesis underlying Hogan and Hogan's (2002) theory of personality. This theory (a socio-analytic model) is based on two generalizations of organizational behavior, derived from the fact that individuals always work in groups. Accordingly, they are (a) motivated to *get along* (with other members of the group), and (b) *get ahead* (achieve status). However, some individuals are more motivated to get along, whereas other prefer to get ahead. Based on this theory, Barrick, Stewart, Neubert, and Mount (1998) proposed that the relationship of WP with Neuroticism and Conscientiousness may be explained in terms of getting ahead, whereas the relationship of WP with Extraversion and Agreeableness may be explained in terms of getting along. Accordingly, Agreeableness has been found to negatively correlate with management potential (Howard & Bray, 1988), with intrinsic measures of executive career success, and with salary (Boudreau et al., 2001).

## 5.12  SUMMARY AND CONCLUSIONS

Throughout this chapter, we examined how established individual differences in personality and intelligence are related to AP and performance and performance in the workplace. Although lay beliefs reflect considerable skepticism with regard to the accuracy of psychometric instruments in the prediction of both academic and WP, there is long-standing evidence for the predictive power of psychometric intelligence.

There is also a noticeable trend that, as individuals progress through the academic levels of formal education (from elementary school to postgraduate education), the impact of cognitive ability on AP decreases, and other nonability traits such as Neuroticism, Extraversion, Openness to Experience, Psychoticism, and, in particular, Conscientiousness become more and more important (Chamorro-Premuzic & Furnham, 2002, 2003a, 2003b; Furnham & Chamorro-Premuzic, in press; Furnham, Chamorro-Premuzic, & McDougall, 2003).

Because personality traits are indicators of an individual's *typical* behavior (rather than *maximal* performance), they can also be expected to show incremental validity in the prediction of both AP and WP. Thus, psychometric intelligence may reflect what a person *can* do, whereas personality traits (notably Conscientiousness) predict what a person *is likely* to do.

It is clear from this chapter that individual differences in intellectual competence cannot be entirely explained in terms of cognitive ability or psychometric intelligence (which is merely a proxy measure of academic achievement and a standardized performance exercise to predict future accomplishments), and personality traits are likely to play an active role in the everyday process determining not only future achievement, but also the development and acquisition of adult skills and knowledge.

# Self-Concepts and Subjectively Assessed Intelligence (SAI)

In the previous two chapters, we discussed the relationship between personality and intellectual competence as conceptualized through standardized ability tests (psychometric intelligence; chap. 4) or academic examinations (AP; chap. 5). In both cases, an individual's capacity was measured through more or less objective parameters and according to competition (against other individuals) in tasks that require intellectual performance. Although this approach is considered to be the predominant paradigm for the study of the relationship between personality and intellectual competence (Hofstee, 2001; Zeidner & Matthews, 2000), it has been noted that nonpsychometric methods may also be examined to broaden our understanding of intellectual competence as a comprehensive aspect of individual differences (Chamorro-Premuzic & Furnham, 2004c). Within these assessment approaches, a particularly interesting and promising field is that of subjective—as opposed to objective—indicators of ability such as self-estimated or subjectively assessed intelligence (SAI; Chamorro-Premuzic, Furnham, & Moutafi, 2004; Furnham, 2001b; Stankov, 1999; Sternberg, 1985).

As observed throughout chapter 3, academic (in particular, differential) psychologists have preferred to measure intelligence through standardized ability tests. However, intelligence can also be assessed in different ways. Lay people, for instance, assess their own and others' intelligence on a regular basis without employing psychometric instruments or academic examinations, relying on different informational cues such as income, academic performance, life and job success, social skills, and so on. Although standardized tests are regarded as an objective method (in particular for the prediction of performance in educational settings), self and others' estimations represent a subjective form of assessment (Fig. 6.1). Although SAI[1] may therefore be considered a different *type* of intelligence than psychometric, its inclusion within the realm of individual differences has not been a central concern for differential psychologists—a fact reflected in the uncertain taxonomic nature of SAI with regard to both personality and intelligence.

Almost 20 years ago, Eysenck and Eysenck (1985) suggested that SAI (self/other assessed in the authors' terminology) should be considered part of personality rather than intelligence mainly because it is assessed through self/other reports (preferences), rather than objective power measures (performance). This is in line with Cronbach's (1984) conceptualization of *maximal* and *typical* performance, as well as the tradition in individual differences to assess personality through self-reports, but measure intelligence through cognitive ability tests. Nevertheless, several studies have indicated that SAI (and related constructs) are significantly related to IQ test performance (e.g., Furnham & Chamorro-Premuzic,

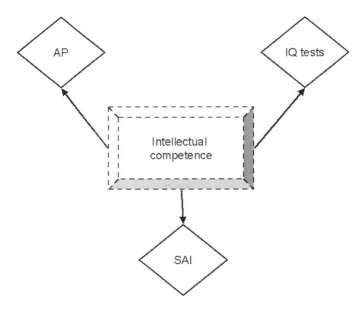

FIG. 6.1.    SAI, AP, and IQ as three measures of intellectual competence.

---

[1]Although the terms SAI and self-estimates of intelligence may be treated as interchangeable, SAI may also be used to refer to estimations of others' (as opposed to one's own) intellectual abilities.

2004a, 2004c; Furnham & Rawles, 1995, 1999; see Section 6.8). Furthermore, there is recent evidence for a significant relationship between SAI and established personality traits (findings are presented in Section 6.10). Accordingly, SAI represents another approach to the relationship between personality and intellectual competence.

Although SAI may have been an implicit concept in differential psychology for many decades (indirectly conceptualized by the higher order constructs of self-concept, self-efficacy, or even in major theoretical paradigm such as social cognition), it was not until Eysenck that researchers considered it an alternative approach to the assessment of intelligence. Eysenck and Eysenck (1985) conceptualized three types (or approaches to the measurement) of intelligence—namely, *genotypic*, *psychometric*, and *self/other-assessed* intelligence. These three types of intelligence or "dimensions of the structure of intellect" (Eysenck, 1979; see also Strelau et al., 2001) can be differentiated on the basis of their assessment methods.

*Genotypic* (also known as biological because it is influenced by biological factors) intelligence cannot be measured directly, but only through elementary and cognitive tasks (e.g., inspection time, reaction time, etc.; see Rindermann & Neubauer, 2001). However, such tasks can only provide a partial indicator of genotypic intelligence. *Psychometric* intelligence, as observed in chapter 3, can be measured through IQ/ability tests, which usually refer to hierarchical models (Carroll, 1993; Deary, 2001). This type of intelligence is not only influenced by biological, but also cultural factors (think of Gc). Finally, *self/other-assessed* (which we group together under the label of SAI) intelligence, as its name indicates, is judged and measured by one self or others. Researchers have argued that this type of intelligence is influenced not only by biological and cultural, but also by personality factors (Eysenck, 1986; Rinderman & Neubauer, 2001). Hence, SAI seems a relevant concept in the relationship between personality and intellectual competence. Figure 6.2 depicts Eysenck and Eysenck's (1985) three-level conceptualization of the structure of intellect.

The importance of examining SAI may be given not only by the fact that this variable may be significantly related to both personality traits and psychometric intelligence, but also because SAI may have direct paths to an individual's performance (regardless of actual intelligence and other personality traits). Further, indicators of SAI (such as single self-estimates of intelligence) are easy to obtain and may therefore be added to personality inventories or ability measures without resulting in time-consuming or costly procedures. Therefore, the study of SAI may provide important information on the relationship between personality and intellectual competence beyond psychometric intelligence and AP, as well as useful practical implications for the assessment of intellectual competence in everyday life.

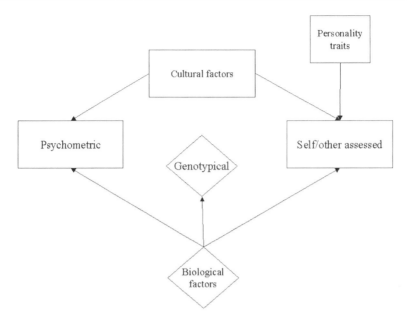

FIG. 6.2.    A graphical depiction of Eysenck's three-conceptual model of intelligence.

## 6.1    INTELLIGENCE FROM A LAY PERSPECTIVE

As observed in chapter 3, the theory and measurement of intelligence have often been the target of academic controversy, in particular the idea that intelligence may be genetically predetermined and that socio-economic differences between groups (especially sex and race) are a reflection of innate individual differences in intellectual ability (Flynn, 1987; Lynn, 1998, 1999; Mackintosh, 1998). Furthermore, the applied implications of these matters have caused the debate to expand beyond the academic forum and concern lay people as well (Hernstein & Murray, 1994).

Yet several academic psychologists such as Sternberg (1997), Goleman (1995), and Gardner (1983, 1999) have published theoretical and applied books on intelligence for lay people—a tradition that started with Eysenck's (1981a) book on how to "know" one's own IQ. There are also several books written for parents, attempting to improve their accuracy in the estimation of their children's IQ (Schoenthaler, 1991). These books reflect the popularity of the concept of intellectual ability. As a consequence, lay people are relatively in touch with the topic of intelligence and able to elaborate their own theories (more or less explicitly) about intellectual ability.

Several researchers have emphasized the importance of examining lay theories of intelligence (Beyer, 1998; Beyer & Bowden, 1999), which have been simply defined as implicit theories or beliefs constructed by individuals, but not on the basis of academic research or scientific empirical evidence (Sternberg, 1990). These theories are "constructions of people (psychologists or lay person or others) that reside in the minds of these individuals, whether as definition or otherwise" (Sternberg, 1990, p. 54). There are at least four reasons that psychologists have considered it relevant to investigate implicit theories/subjective beliefs about intelligence.

*First*, the nature of beliefs or knowledge about intelligence is likely to influence self-judgements on ability, in the sense of providing a framework or comparative basis for the evaluation of one's skills. Thus, if one believes intelligence is defined, say, as the capacity to solve mathematical problems, one will base his or her estimations on that specific capacity, and so on. Further, lay conceptions of intelligence may also determine people's assessment of others' intellectual competence (Sternberg, 1990).

*Second*, conceptions about intelligence may have significant educational and social consequences. Particularly, beliefs or attitudes related to the measurement of intelligence (psychometric intelligence) may be of special importance. If, say, one believes ability tests to be biased or flawed, he or she will be more likely to discourage their use in many settings such as school and job recruitment (Furnham, 2001b).

*Third*, it is likely that lay conceptions of intelligence may affect not only SAI, but also actual performance (Pommerantz & Ruble, 1997). As Beyer (1999) observed, "self-perceptions that are out of touch with reality not only reveal a lack of self-knowledge but may also impede effective self-regulation and goal setting in academic, professional and interpersonal situations" (p. 280). However, it is not clear under what specific circumstances self-beliefs may be positive or negatively correlated with performance because both negative and positive self-beliefs may result in poor performance through either self-fulfillment of prophecies or complacency, respectively (Furnham, 2001b).

A *fourth* reason could also be added—namely, that lay conceptions may be precursors of academic hypotheses (Sternberg, 1985). Thus, exploring people's beliefs about intelligence may inspire researchers to test new hypotheses and help develop further theories. As Sternberg (1985) noted, lay conceptions may expand and change academic theories, "as we come to realize those aspects of cognition or affect which the current explicit theories of intelligence, creativity, and wisdom do not encompass, but possibly, should encompass" (p. 625).

Therefore, it is important to have a well-informed and critical public (in particular participants or testees) when it comes to representations of the concept and measurement of intelligence. In this chapter, we attempt to examine the studies of lay theories of intelligence that have dominated this area for over 50 years, as well as the concept of SAI—that is, the variables that influenced (and are influenced by) a person's estimation of her or his or other's intelligence.

## 6.2    HISTORY OF LAY CONCEPTIONS OF INTELLIGENCE RESEARCH

Studies on lay conceptions of intelligence date back 50 years (Flugel, 1947; Shafer, 1999). According to Goodnow (1980), there are several ways one can investigate people's beliefs about intelligence and their underlying implicit definitions—from simply asking them to define intelligence, to analyzing local proverbs, examining the connotations of a term (via semantic differential techniques), or looking at the differences between positively and negatively rated test answers (within a specific culture).

As seen in chapter 3, academic/scientific research on intellectual ability long predates that of lay conceptions of intelligence, dating back more than 100 years. To some, however, psychological theories about intelligence may also be regarded as constructions of equally subjective nature, albeit more systematic and empirically based. Further, the idea that some men are more virtuous/able/talented/wiser than others is probably ubiquitous to any form of human society. Thus, Sternberg (1990) distinguished between *explicit* theories defined as "constructions of psychologists or other scientists that are based on, or at least tested, on data collected from people performing tasks presumed to measure intellectual functioning" (p. 53) and *implicit* theories, which are "constructions of people (psychologists or lay persons or others) that reside in the minds of these individuals, whether as definition or otherwise" (p. 54). Sternberg argued that implicit and explicit theories are often related. Accordingly, understanding implicit theories is not only important to understand the determinants of lay people's evaluations of their own and others' intelligence, but also commonsense beliefs that may give origin to preliminary psychological hypotheses and consequent academic theories on intellectual ability.

In an article entitled, "An Inquiry as to Popular Views on Intelligence and Related Topics" (the first formal account of looking at implicit or lay theories of intelligence), Flugel (1947) designed a 16-item inventory to assess people's beliefs on intellectual ability and tested it on 302 respondents. He concluded that lay people are generally less aware of the distinction between intelligence and knowledge (often confusing both concepts or taking them as synonyms). This would reflect their beliefs that intellectual ability is, to a great extent, determined by education and is consistent with their idea that intelligence would continue to increase after adolescence (a belief contrary to scientific evidence). Another difference between lay people and experts is that the former ones are generally less aware of the distinction between intelligence and achievement (although experts would not normally use them as interchangeable terms, significant correlations between these measures are usually interpreted in terms of the predictive validity of psychometric intelligence).

However, lay theories of intelligence tend to be associated with the belief that intellectual ability is somehow learned or the result of experience, rather than affected by genetic factors. Interestingly, Flugel's results also show that lay persons are less likely to conceptualize differences between intelligence and personality (which, as observed throughout this book, has often been a discussed topic within differential psychology; see chap. 4). In addition, lay people are more likely to associate intelligence with verbal (crystallized) than nonverbal (fluid) abilities, this of course at an implicit level. Flugel also reported that, although inclined on the whole to accepting the general view of intelligence, the lay person has a tendency to overrate in some respects the importance of specific ability factors and is not aware of the multiple intercorrelations among different ability factors. With regard to psychometric intelligence (i.e., the measurement of intelligence through standardized performance tests), it was concluded that lay people generally believe that:

1. Tests can to some extent measure intelligence apart from the effect of education.
2. Tests are better than examinations for measuring intelligence.
3. Superior intelligence is desirable or necessary for higher education.
4. There is not appreciable sex difference as regards intelligence (though he is often inclined to think there may be some relevant qualitative difference, while men are more liable than women to think that the male sex is the more intelligent one). (p. 152)

A replication of Flugel's findings was attempted 25 years later in a study by Shipstone and Burt (1973), who looked at 575 British adults. The authors compared each of the 16 original questions by Flugel and found significant differences in 12 of the items, thus arguing that lay perceptions of intelligence had changed over that period of time. Specifically, they found that both lay and psychological views have moved closer to the idea of multiple intelligences (opposing the theory of a single, general intelligence factor). No wonder then that a number of differential psychologists began to publish books on hot intelligence in the years to follow (Gardner, 1983; Sternberg, 1985, 1990). People were also more likely to believe that there were no significant gender differences in intelligence and question the validity of intelligence tests as predictors of WP.

Studies on lay concepts of intelligence have not been confined to English-speaking samples or to studies of adults. Keehn and Prothero (1958) examined lay conceptions of intelligence in Lebanon and found teachers' implicit theories to be related to Conscientiousness (thoughtfulness and persistence) as well as Neuroticism (emotional stability), but relatively independent of Agreeableness. Serpell (1976) found Zambian village children had criteria for judgments of intelligence quite unrelated to Western notions (see also Irvine, 1966, 1969). Wober (1972, 1973), examining East African attitudes toward intelligence, found that quickness of reasoning was not regarded as an essential aspect of intellectual ability (particularly among Ugandans).

Additional cross-cultural evidence for the cultural determinants of lay theories of intelligence derived from Asian studies (Gill & Keats, 1980; Keats, 1982). Nevo and Khader (1995) found subtle but significant differences among Chinese, Indian, and Malayan Singaporean mothers' conceptions of their childrens' intelligence. However, all groups distinguished clearly among three major underlying factors: *cognitive/ academic ability, appropriate behavior*, and *socially interactive behavior*.

In a Japanese study, males and females from a college sample, as well as their mothers, were asked to rate 67 descriptors of intelligence (Azuma & Kashiwagi, 1987). "Being a quick thinker," "having good memory," and "quick judgment" were rated as fundamental aspects of intelligence by all groups. Moreover, highly rated qualities (descriptors) related to receptive social competence tended to be associated with high intelligence, particularly in comparison with American studies. The authors concluded that Japanese conceptions of intelligence are heavily influenced by gender stereotypes, more so than in other societies.

Studies on lay theories of intelligence have also examined aspects of intellectual development in children (Siegler & Richards, 1982) and children's theories (Crocker & Cheeseman, 1988; Dweck & Elliot, 1983; Yussen & Kane, 1985). Siegler and Richards (1982) found intelligence in babies (6 months) and toddlers (12 months) was largely conceived of in perceptual motor terms, but became more cognitive as children got older. This is consistent with Piaget's developmental theory (as discussed in Section 3.5). With regard to school children, Fry (1984) showed that teachers of primary school pupils tended to emphasize social variables (e.g., popularity, interest in the environment), whereas secondary school teachers were more likely to focus on verbal variables as the most relevant aspects of intelligence at that age level. In contrast, university teachers were likely to define intelligence of university students in terms of cognitive variables such as reasoning ability and general knowledge.

Yussen and Kane (1985) found that older children tended to have a more differentiated conception (less global view) and to stress less overt signs of intelligence than did younger children. Chen, Holman, Francis-Jones, and Burmester (1988) found three major dimensions or factors underlying primary, high school, and college students' beliefs about intelligence (after participants rated 26 items taken from four well-known intelligence tests). These factors were *non-verbal reasoning, verbal reasoning,* and *retrieval of information,* and there were significant group differences in these factors. Primary school children considered verbal reasoning skills the most important aspect of intelligence, high school pupils considered all three factors to be equally important, and university students tended to consider nonverbal reasoning skill as the most relevant aspect of intellectual ability.

## 6.3   STERNBERG'S RESEARCH ON LAY CONCEPTIONS OF INTELLIGENCE

In the 1980s, the study of implicit theories of intelligence gained momentum, mainly thanks to the research of Sternberg and his colleagues. The starting point was a fairly large study by Sternberg, Conway, Ketron and Bernstein (1981), in which the authors asked nearly 500 lay people and 150 experts to list representative behaviors of intelligence, academic intelligence, everyday intelligence, and nonintelligent behaviors. Generally, a great variety of responses (behaviors) were listed by the participants, although certain characteristics such as logical reasoning, reading widely, being open minded, and having common sense were frequently quoted. Sternberg (1982) noted:

> On the whole, the informal theories of intelligence that laymen carry around in their heads—without even realizing that their ideas constitute theories—conform fairly closely to the most widely accepted formal theories of intelligence that scientists have constructed. That is, what psychologists study as intelligence seems to correspond, in general, to what people untrained in psychology mean by intelligence. On the other hand, what psychologists study corresponds to only part of what people mean by intelligence in our society, which includes a lot more than IQ test measures. (p. 35)

In a second series of studies, Sternberg (1985) looked at implicit theories of intelligence in relation to creativity and wisdom (two important yet widely unexplored variables in individual differences research). Results show that, when rating attributes of all three qualities, both academic *and* lay people believe intelligence and wisdom to be closely related, whereas creativity and wisdom are usually regarded as relatively unrelated concepts. The same year, Berg and Sternberg (1985) examined implicit theories in a wide age range of individuals (20—83 years old) and found older people were more likely to understand everyday competence as a function of intelligence (distinguishing between exceptionally able and average individuals). Middle-aged (approximately 50 years old) and older (70 years) participants did not distinguish clearly between problem-solving ability (Gf) and acquired knowledge (Gc; see chap. 3 for a scientific account of these aspects of intellectual ability). Overall, the importance of everyday competence was found to increase as a function of the age of the rater and ratee.

As mentioned earlier, Sternberg argued that, although there is a considerable overlap between experts' and lay men's theories of intelligence, implicit theories usually comprise aspects not included in the formal theories of intelligence, certainly not in terms of psychometric intelligence (or what is measured through standardized ability tests). Thus, a variety of skills not measured through well-established IQ tests may be considered a fundamental aspect of intelligence by the lay person. Like experts, lay persons believe that bright individuals are able to solve problems well, reason clearly, think logically, and have a good store of information. Unlike most experts, however, lay people also emphasize an intelligent person's ability to balance information and act wisely beyond academic settings. Lay theories of creativity overlap with those of intelligence, but tend to downplay analytic abilities, stressing rather unconventional/original ways of thinking and acting. In addition, aesthetic taste, imagination, inquisitiveness, and intuitiveness are also part of lay theories of intelligence, yet clearly absent in experts' definitions and certainly not measured by most standardized psychological tests. However, it has been seen that the Openness personality trait assessed through self-report inventory taps directly on these aspects and is significantly correlated with psychometric intelligence (see Section 4.7).

Thus, Sternberg believed that lay theories are predecessors of formal intelligence theories (in the same way that intuition or common sense may give birth to scientific hypotheses or theories). However, he argued that lay theories are an important topic in psychology regardless of their relationship to scientific theories of intellectual ability. Hence, their validity should not be judged against experts' theories of intelligence, but in terms of their use and effect in everyday life.

In later research, Sternberg (1990) identified seven academic metaphors of intelligence. He argued scientific research on intelligence is often determined and specified as a function of these initial metaphors or conceptual perspectives. Thus, scientists may often be unaware of other metaphors and limited by certain paradigms that somehow predetermine their objects of study. In the words of Sternberg, "It is important to understand the metaphor or metaphors underlying one's theory so as to understand the questions one is likely to ask and why one is likely to ask them" (p. 18). The metaphors he described were:

1. *Geographic*, which seeks to map the mind and understand the structure of intelligence.
2. *Computational*, which seeks to understand information-processing programs and processes underlying intelligence.
3. *Biological*, which attempts to understand how the anatomy, physiology, and chemistry of the brain and CNS accounts for intelli-

gence thought through hemispheric localization and neural transmission.

4. *Epistemological*, which attempts to answer the fundamental question of what are the structures of the mind through which all knowledge and mental processes are organized.
5. *Anthropological*, which asks what form intelligence takes as a cultural invention and may be comparative and relativistic.
6. *Sociological*, which examines how social pressure (mediated learning experiences) in development is internalized.
7. *Systems*, which is concerned with how we understand the mind as a system that cross-cuts metaphors.

Although this may be regarded as an accurate taxonomic critique of academic theories and research in the field of intelligence, the question remains as to whether lay people think in such metaphors (and why). It also remains an empirical question as to what extent these metaphors may be more or less explicitly held by nonexperts in the field of intelligence. It would not be surprising, for instance, if people today thought of intelligence in terms of computer analogies like hardware and software, although others may prefer older mechanical models or even Dickensian models of empty vessels filled up with education and experience.

To summarize, Sternberg's research has highlighted some major *knowns* in the study of implicit theories of intelligence (as well as the fundamental reasons that one should explore these theories). It is now widely accepted that lay theories of intelligence get more sophisticated with age and are, to a great extent, culture and group determined. Further, lay theories tend to be more inclusive than formal theories (perhaps for being less determined by, and limited to, certain methodological aspects, particularly with regard to assessment or measurement). Yet let us focus on the specific issue of subjectively assessed (as opposed to psychometrically measured) intellectual ability and how it may relate to gender, personality, and intellectual competence.

## 6.4  GENDER DIFFERENCES IN SAI

The study of SAI has a relatively short history in differential psychology and has been mostly related to the issue of gender differences in estimates of intelligence. Thus, it is appropriate to review the salient literature on gender and SAI.

In one of the first articles reviewing empirical evidence on indicators of SAI, Hogan (1978) reported the results of 11 different studies of American university students. These studies assessed participants' estimations of their own and their parents' intelligence, as well as their estimates of males' and females' intellectual ability in general. In comparison to males, females were found to underestimate their intelligence (give lower indicators of SAI) and that of their mothers' (in comparison to that of their fathers'). A later study by Beloff (1992) replicated these results on a Scottish sample and further specified and quantified the differences in estimation between gender—namely, 1 *SD* higher for males (see also Byrd & Stacey, 1994). The author concluded that, "young women students see themselves as intellectually inferior compared to young men ... women see equality with their mothers, men with their fathers. Women see themselves as inferior to their fathers and men superior to their mothers. Mothers therefore come out as inferior to their fathers. The pattern has been consistent each year" (Beloff, 1992, p. 310).

Reilly and Mulhern (1995) compared SAI and psychometric intelligence in a sample of students who completed subtests of the *WAIS* IQ and estimated their scores (after taking the test). It was found that males tended to give significantly higher estimations than their actual scores, whereas the opposite applied to females (although this pattern was reflected in a mere numerical trend rather than a statistically significant difference).

Most of the research on SAI has been directed by Furnham and colleagues (Furnham, 2000b; Furnham & Baguma, 1999; Furnham, Clark, & Bailey, 1999; Furnham, Fong, & Martin, 1999; Furnham, Hosoe, & Tang, 2003; Furnham & Rawles, 1995; Furnham, Shahidi, & Baluch, 2003), who paid particular attention to gender differences in self-estimates of intelligence.

Furnham and Rawles (1995) replicated the results of Beloff (1992) and Byrd and Stacey (1994), confirming that males tend to estimate their intelligence significantly higher than females and that both tend to think of their fathers as more intellectually able than their mothers. Their study also looked at gender differences in estimations of grandparents' intelligence, and results show the effect was also present here because both males and females rated their grandfathers' intelligence higher than their grandmothers'. In another article, Furnham and Gasson (1998) reported that males' overestimations were also present when participants were asked to estimate their children's intelligence.

A central question to interpret the systematic overestimation of males' intelligence compared with that of females' is whether gender differences in SAI correspond to gender differences in actual intellectual competence or whether, on the contrary (perhaps due to stereotypes), they are merely the reflection of inaccurate perceptions. Accordingly, Furnham and Rawles (1999) examined the relationship between SAI and psychometric intelligence (in this case, a measure of spatial ability). The authors found that, although males tended to estimate their ability significantly higher than females, these differences were also present in psychometric intelligence. That is, males outperformed females in the cognitive ability test. However, the correlation between SAI and psychometric intelligence was rather modest ($r = .16$) and would have probably been even lower if different abilities had been assessed (as gender differences in psychometric intelligence are especially noticeable on spatial ability tests).

Research variations on the study of gender differences in SAI have included estimations of multiple—as opposed to general or single—intelligences. Studies in this area are usually based on Gardner's (1983, 1999) theoretical framework. Although academics in the field of individual differences tend to support a single (or dual), rather than a multidimensional, theory of intelligence, it is possible that lay people have differential evaluations (SAI) about their different skills or abilities. Further, they may also believe that men are better in some, but not other, domains of intelligence.

Table 6.1 presents the results of various studies on estimated overall intelligence (in self and others).

This hypothesis was tested by Furnham (2000b), who examined parental beliefs of their own and children's multiple intelligences. Fathers gave significantly higher estimates of mathematical ability for themselves, whereas mothers gave significantly higher estimates of mathematical and spatial ability for their children than fathers. Also parents in general believed their sons to be better in mathematics than their daughters. Because mathematical and logical intelligence are often considered the essence of intellectual competence, Furnham (2000b) speculated that lay conceptions of intelligence may be male normative—that is, based on abilities in which males usually outperform females.

Although the reviewed literature seems to indicate that estimations of males' abilities are consistently higher than that of females', a recent study failed to replicate these results. Furnham, Rakow, and Mak (2003) found that, although fathers tended to estimate their own spatial and mathematical intelligences higher than mothers and children, there were no significant gender differences in parents' estimations of children's intelligences. This led Furnham (2001b) to conclude that, "the results of these studies seem reliant on the simple fact that we still are not clear whether the disparity between male and female IQ estimates is a male overestimation, a female underestimation, a combination of both, or an accurate reflection of reality" (p. 1394).

In another recent study involving more than 600 participants from New Zealand, Furnham and Ward (2001) asked people to estimate their multiple intelligences and found associations between gender and mathematical/logical, spatial, and existential abilities. Hence, it is likely that these types of abilities are indeed male normative. Also noteworthy was that subjects who had previously completed an ability test gave higher SAI on 8 of the 10 types of intelligences. It is thus possible that having taken an IQ test in the past may lead people to give higher estimations of their abilities. Alternatively, however, it may be that people with higher SAI tend to test their abilities more often (perhaps in the search of some feedback or confirmation of their high estimations).

Although the topic of gender differences in intellectual ability has been academically controversial (Flynn, 1987; Furnham, 2001b; Lynn, 1998,

**TABLE 6.1**

**Results of Studies on Overall SAI (*g*):**
**Estimating Themselves and Others**

| Study | Women | Men | Difference |
|---|---|---|---|
| *Beloff (1992) Scotland* | (N = 502) | (N = 265) | |
| self | 120.5 | 126.9 | 6.4 |
| mother | 119.9 | 118.7 | −1.2 |
| father | 127.7 | 125.2 | −2.5 |
| *Byrd & Stacey (1993) New Zealand* | (N = 105) | (N = 112) | |
| self | 121.9 | 121.5 | −0.4 |
| mother | 114.5 | 106.5 | −9.0 |
| father | 127.9 | 122.3 | −5.6 |
| sister | 118.2 | 110.5 | −7.7 |
| brother | 114.1 | 116.0 | 1.9 |
| *Bennett (1996) Scotland* | (N = 96) | (N = 48) | |
| self | 109.4 | 117.1 | 7.7 |
| *Reilly & Mulhern (1995) Ireland* | (N = 80) | (N = 45) | |
| self | 105.3 | 113.9 | 8.6 |
| measured | 106.9 | 106.1 | −0.8 |
| *Furnham & Rawles (1995) England* | (N = 161) | (N = 84) | |
| self | 123.31 | 118.48 | 6.17 |
| mother | 108.7 | 109.42 | 0.72 |
| father | 114.18 | 116.09 | 1.91 |
| *Furnham & Rawles (1998) England* | (N = 140) | (N = 53) | |
| self | 116.64 | 120.50 | 3.9 |
| measured | 4.47 | 6.94 | |
| *Furnham & Gasson (1999) England* | (N = 112) | (N = 72) | |
| self | 103.84 | 107.99 | 4.15 |
| male child (1st child) | 107.69 | 109.70 | 2.01 |
| female child (1st child) | 102.57 | 102.36 | −0.21 |
| *Furnham, Reeves, & Budhani (2002) England* | (N = 84) | (N = 72) | |
| self | 104.84 | 110.15 | 5.31 |
| male child (1st son) | 116.09 | 114.32 | −1.77 |
| female child (1st daughter) | 110.66 | 104.32 | −6.34 |

*Note.* From Furnham (2001a, 2001b).

1999; Mackintosh, 1998), it is usually acknowledged that gender differences in psychometric intelligence are far too small to consider gender a relevant predictor of ability tests performance (Hyde, 1981; Reilly & Mulhern, 1995). Therefore, it is likely that the so-called *gender differences* in SAI may be more precisely understood in terms of lay beliefs or stereotypes about gender, on the one hand, and intelligence, on the other hand (rather than in terms of gender differences in actual intelligence). Hence, the belief that men are more intelligent than women may vary across cultures, age, and even gender (it has been observed that men are more likely to support the belief of male superiority than women; Flugel, 1947; see also Furnham, 2001b). Furthermore, Shipstone and Burt (1973) showed that stereotypes about gender differences in intelligence may suffer changes over time. Thus, gender differences may be stereotype-dependent rather than intrinsic, and lay conceptions of intelligence may determine the extent to which men and women underestimate and overestimate their intellectual ability.

As is discussed in Section 6.9, SAI may influence performance not only in that it affects confidence on specific tasks such as examinations, but also in the sense of determining differences in motivation to invest on intellectual activities or prepare for specific examinations (particularly in academic settings). Beyer (1990, 1998, 1999) also demonstrated that SAI (in terms of expectations and self-beliefs) may affect performance on ability tests. Thus, stereotypes about gender differences in intellectual ability may lead to gender differences in psychometric intelligence, which would imply that SAI may have self-fulfilling effects rather than merely reflect differences in intellectual ability. Hence, it is important to examine specific lay conceptions with regard to SAI.

## 6.5  ESTIMATING RELATIVES' SCORES

Research on SAI has not only examined self, but also other, estimates of intelligence—notably, estimates of relatives' intellectual ability. There have been studies looking at estimates of grandparents' (Furnham & Rawles, 1995), parents' (Byrd & Stacey, 1993; Furnham & Rawles, 1995), siblings' (Byrd & Stacey, 1993; Furnham, Fong, & Martin, 1999; Furnham, Rakow, Sarmany-Schiller, & de Fruyt, 1999), and children's (Furnham, 2000a; Furnham & Gasson, 1998; Furnham, Reeves, & Budhani, 2002) intellectual ability (see Table 6.2).

There are several reasons that researchers have deemed it necessary to examine estimates of others' (such as relatives') intelligence. First, differential psychologists have attempted to identify the factors that may have accounted for the well-documented increase, over the past 50 years or so, of intelligence test scores (the so-called *Flynn-effect*), a much debated topic with no certain causes (Flynn, 1987; Lynn & Pagliari, 1994; Mackintosh, 1998). Thus, looking at SAI, one may expect estimates of dif-

## TABLE 6.2
### Estimated Overall Scores for Parents, Grandparents, and Self

|                      | Male   | Female | Overall | Mean   |
|----------------------|--------|--------|---------|--------|
| Grandfather[1]       | 108.14 | 104.37 | 106.29  | 102.79 |
| Grandmother          | 97.37  | 100.20 | 99.29   |        |
| Father[2]            | 121.20 | 125.96 | 123.55  | 118.25 |
| Mother               | 111.53 | 114.36 | 112.95  |        |
| Son[3]               | 112.01 | 111.89 | 111.95  | 108.34 |
| Daughter             | 103.34 | 106.15 | 104.74  |        |
| Self A[4]            | 117.06 | 113.20 | 115.13  | 115.13 |
| Self B[5]            | 109.07 | 104.34 | 106.70  | 106.70 |

[1]Furnham and Rawles (1995).
[2]Means of the data from Beloff (1992), Byrd and Stacey (1993) and Furnham and Rawles (1995).
[3]Means based on data from estimate of the first child from Furnham and Gasson (1998) and Furnham, Reeves, and Budhani (2002).
[4]Based on the mean of all studies reported—Table 6.1.
[5]Based on the means of the two studies looking at adult parents not students.

ferent generations in the family to increase over time, consistently with the findings that IQ scores have increased over time. In particular, these estimates can also be examined with regard to family members' educational background to test whether there are educational (and cultural) factors influencing the increase of both estimated and psychometric intelligence. Because each generation is better (and longer) educated (at least in terms of years of formal education) than the previous one, it may certainly *appear* as if they are more intelligent.

Another reason that researchers have explored SAI in terms of estimates of relatives' intelligence has been the attempt to further explore gender differences in intelligence (both estimated and pychometric; see Section 6.4). By getting males and females to estimate the intelligence of their parents and siblings, it is possible to test whether the hubris-humility findings (replicated in studies of self-estimates of intelligence) also apply to estimations of others'—that is, looking at the gender of the target and not just the person providing the estimate. This allows one to explore a variety of combinations, such as son estimating father, son estimating mother, daughter estimating father, daughter estimating mother, and, conversely, mother estimating daughter and son, and so on (the same also applies to grandparents, which allows one to test the effects across generations). If males believe their fathers are brighter than mothers, their brothers are brighter than their sisters, and so on, this may be seen as robust evidence for gender difference in SAI and would suggest that stereotypes on gender and IQ are relatively ubiquitous. It is particularly interesting to explore the perceptions of females to discover whether their noted self-depreciation and humility in self-estimates extend to others as well.

Finally, studies on estimations of relatives' intelligence have also been conducted to test the possible self-fulfilling effects of SAI, particularly in the case of parents estimating their children's intellectual ability. Thus, believing that someone (e.g., one's child) is bright may increase the likelihood of that child becoming bright even if the belief is initially not true (it may cause the event to happen). Conversely, the belief that someone has a low IQ may have detrimental effects for the development of that person's intelligence (perhaps because it will affect confidence and self-perception). This is usually referred to as the *Pygmalion* effect; it has been examined in the context of educational settings (looking at the effects of teachers' initial perceptions of their students and how these perceptions may have self-fulfilling effects). It has been suggested that students identified by their teachers as "intellectual bloomers" do better on achievement tests than their counterparts (who were not perceived as intelligent by their teachers), although this issue remains hotly contested (Mackintosh, 1998).

Furnham and Gasson (1998) asked 184 British parents to provide estimates of their overall intellectual ability as well as that of their children. Results show that fathers rated their own IQ significantly higher than mothers (108 vs. 104), whereas both parents rated their sons' (first and second) intelligence higher than their daughters'. The $d$ statistic (the measure of degree of difference between two normal distributions) expressed in $SD$ units was .67, which, according to Cohen (1977), is between moderate and large. The authors also regressed the parents' sex and age and child's sex and age onto the IQ estimates. For parental self-estimates, both sex and age were equally powerful predictors of self-estimated $g$, accounting for 14% of the variance total. Yet for the estimates of the children, sex, much more than age, was the strongest predictor of their parentally estimated IQ.

It was the authors who suggested that, if male children are believed to be more intelligent by their parents and this is explicitly reinforced during childhood, they may be more immune to negative feedback given later in life regardless of the accuracy of this feedback. Further, given that men tend to occupy higher, more prestigious, and better paid jobs in most sectors of society, it may be easy to understand why both sexes believe males to be superior in intellectual ability (this is in line with the finding that lay people tend to regard intelligence and achievement as synonyms; see Section 6.2).

In a different study, Furnham (2000a) looked at parental estimates of children's multiple intelligences (Gardner, 1983) to test whether gender differences in SAI could also be present when parents estimate specific abilities, rather than overall IQ. As before, fathers rated themselves more intelligent on mathematical and spatial intelligence than mothers. Parents estimated their sons' mathematical and spatial abilities higher than their daughters'. Furthermore, fathers' self-estimates on these abilities were significantly higher than that of mothers'. According to Furnham (2000a), results once again confirm that lay conceptions of intelligence are male normative—that is, it is those specific abilities like mathematical and logical intelligence that men are best at, which are considered the essence of intelligence (see Sections 6.2 and 6.3). Musical, interpersonal, and other novel or "hot" intelligences proposed by Gardner were less likely to indicate gender differences in self and other estimates, suggesting that lay people conflate mathematical and spatial intelligence with overall intelligence (see Tables 6.1 and 6.3).

## 6.6 CULTURE DIFFERENCES IN ESTIMATED INTELLIGENCE

As noted in Section 6.4, cross-cultural studies on implicit theories of intelligence and SAI have indicated that there are subtle but significant differences in the way in which cultures tend to conceptualize or define *intelligence*, even at an implicit level. Closely related to the cultural aspects of these theories of intelligence is the question of how SAI (in particular, self-estimates) has been found to vary across cultures—that is, how people from different cultures rate their own intelligence—although this is a rather controversial topic because of its association with the question of differences in actual (psychometric) intelligence.

Particularly after the publication of the Bell Curve (Hernstein & Murray, 1994; see also Lynn, 1994; Rushton, 1999), there has been heated debate on the nature of group differences in intelligence—specifically, whether high IQ was a cause or consequence of social inequalities in society. This led experts, in the same year, to compile a definite dossier on the *knowns* and *unknowns* on intelligence as agreed by 50 experts in the field. It was concluded that:

> the bell curve for whites is centered roughly around IQ 100; the bell curve for American blacks roughly around IQ 85; and those for different subgroups of Hispanics roughly midway between those for whites and blacks. The evidence is less definitive for exactly where above IQ 100 the bell curves for Jews and Asians are centered. (Furnham, 1999, p 177)

To test whether these distributions in psychometric intelligence were also reflected in SAI (across cultures), Furnham and colleagues conducted extensive cross-cultural research on SAI, although mostly on university students. They looked at samples in Africa (Uganda), America (the United States), Asia (Japan & Singapore), and Europe (Britain, Belgium, and Slovakia). Most of these studies showed that there are several signifi-

**TABLE 6.3**

**Parents Self-Estimates and Those of Their First Children**

| | Furnham (2000b) | | Furnham et al. (2000b) | | Furnham (2000b) | | | | Furnham et al. (2000b) | | | |
|---|---|---|---|---|---|---|---|---|---|---|---|---|
| | | | | | Father | | Mother | | Father | | Mother | |
| | Father | Mother | Father | Mother | Son | Daughter | Son | Daughter | Son | Daughter | Son | Daughter |
| | N = 46 | N = 66 | N = 72 | N = 84 | | | | | | | | |
| Verbal | 113.91 | 109.12 | 108.97 | 106.61 | 113.68 | 109.76 | 115.97 | 116.57 | 108.00 | 99.77 | 111.09 | 108.10 |
| Mathematical | 110.54 | 102.66** | 109.15 | 96.88** | 113.20 | 106.90 | 119.58 | 107.01 | 110.27 | 97.95 | 109.69 | 103.97 |
| Spatial | 111.84 | 104.81 | 112.92 | 101.25** | 108.60 | 102.14 | 117.64 | 108.93 | 110.68 | 100.00 | 110.01 | 103.10 |
| Musical | 93.80 | 98.33 | 100.72 | 96.52 | 107.32 | 107.62 | 107.31 | 107.40 | 107.57 | 101.36 | 104.84 | 103.34 |
| Body-K | 100.43 | 102.72 | 104.04 | 101.79 | 103.80 | 108.81 | 110.22 | 105.57 | 104.59 | 97.05 | 106.88 | 104.34 |
| Interpersonal | 112.82 | 112.42 | 113.40 | 112.18 | 106.40 | 110.00 | 113.33 | 110.33 | 108.51 | 99.77 | 108.59 | 107.76 |
| Intrapersonal | 110.21 | 109.89 | 111.74 | 111.99 | 108.40 | 103.81 | 112.08 | 106.00 | 106.38 | 100.23 | 105.63 | 105.50 |

* p < .05; ** p < .01.

111

cant cultural differences in SAI. In a three-country (and three-continent) comparison, Furnham and Baguma (1999) found a significant national difference in the average SAI for estimates of Gardner's (1999) seven intelligences as well as on three factor scores: verbal (verbal, interpersonal, intrapersonal), numerical (mathematical, spatial), and cultural (musical, body kinesthetic). White American students rated themselves as significantly more intelligent on overall, numerical, and cultural intelligence, whereas African students awarded themselves the highest verbal intelligence.

In another study that looked at American, British, and Japanese university students, Furnham, Hosoe, and Tang (2000) obtained similar patterns of results, with most American and British students (mostly White) awarding themselves highest overall IQ ratings (British were slightly lower than Americans), followed by the Japanese. With regard to verbal, numerical, and cultural self-estimates, there were no significant differences between American and British students, although both groups tended to award themselves significantly higher self-estimates than the Japanese (similar results were obtained by Furnham, Fong, & Martin [1999], who found British SAI to be significantly higher than Asian—this time Singaporean—ones).

Nearly all of these studies have been conducted on student populations, which may render them relatively comparable, but clearly unrepresentative of the population from which they are drawn. Hence, more recent research is concentrating on examining whether these differences are noticeable in representative adult populations in different countries.

## 6.7   ESTIMATES OF OTHER AND MULTIPLE INTELLIGENCE

As mentioned earlier, studies on SAI have examined not only estimations of overall or general intelligence (e.g., $g$, IQ), but also multiple abilities, particularly since Gardner (1983, 1999) formulated his theory. Furthermore, several *hot* intelligences (see Sections 3.6 and 3.7), including emotional intelligence (Petrides & Furnham, 2000), have been examined, as well as lay dimensions as discovered by Sternberg et al. (1981). Most of these researchers (Bennett, 1996, 1997, 2000; Furnham, Clark, & Bailey, 1999; Furnham, Fong, & Martin, 1999) were interested in further exploring the gender differences revealed by Beloff (1992).

Furnham (1999) asked 260 students to rate themselves on 12 statements ("speaks clearly and articulately," "is knowledgeable about a particular field," "accepts others for what they are") that made up the underlying dimensions of implicit theories of intelligence identified by Sternberg et al. (1981). Data reduction replicated this solution, and further analyses revealed sex differences in two of the three factors—namely, verbal and practical intelligence (with males awarding themselves higher estimates than females). Particularly surprising and counterintuitive was males' overestimation of their verbal abilities (compared with that of females'), as much of the literature suggests the opposite pattern is usually found in psychometrically measured verbal ability (i.e., females tend to outperform males; Mackintosh, 1998).

With regard to emotional intelligence, sex differences in SAI are relatively less common. Petrides and Furnham (2000) reported sex differences in only 3 of 15 abilities related to emotional intelligence (in a sample of 260 undergraduates). These factors were empathy and self-motivation, and males thought they were more able to cope with (and perform under) pressure, being more able to accept responsibility and motivate themselves. However, regressional analysis demonstrated that those who awarded themselves higher scores on the two estimated factors *did* actually score higher in the actual EQ test.

Finally, several studies have looked at SAI in terms of Gardner's (1983, 1993a, 1993b, 1999) multiple intelligence framework, providing an alternative route for research to the psychometrically measured approached to multiple abilities (because most of the novel intelligences defined by Gardner's can only be assessed subjectively and not objectively tested). This approach was initiated by Bennett (1996, 1997, 2000) and followed up by Furnham's systematic series of studies (Furnham, 2000a, 2000b; Furnham & Baguma, 1999; Furnham, Clark, & Bailey, 1999; Furnham, Fong, & Martin, 1999).

Bennett (1996, 1997) asked students to estimate their scores on Gardner's (1993) six multiple intelligences (intra- and interpersonal were combined into personal) and found that estimates could be collapsed via factor analysis onto two major dimensions, which he argued correspond to Western stereotypes about sex differences in intelligence. This led Bennett (2000) to examine whether males' higher SAI was a mere function of their implicit views of intelligence as male typical (e.g., mathematical, spatial, practical). Accordingly, he asked participants to rate how masculine or feminine each of Gardner's six intelligences were. Results show that three of Gardner's dimensions (kinesthetic, logical-mathematical, and visuospatial) were indeed considered more masculine, suggesting that there is a considerable overlap between ratings of masculinity and overestimations of these dimensions my males. Thus, males' higher SAI may be a function of their implicit theories of intelligence and their definition of intelligence in terms of male-normative abilities.

However, findings have often failed to replicate the consistent pattern of sex difference in estimated multiple intelligences. In one of the first studies to look at SAI as assessed by the full scale of Gardner's seven multiple intelligences, Furnham, Clark, and Bailey (1999) found sex differences only in estimates of the logical/mathematical dimension. Furthermore, factor analysis showed that people's estimates of the multiple intelligences could be simplified in a three-factor solution (accounting for over two thirds of the variance). The two personal and verbal factors loaded on the first factor, musical and body-kinesthetic on the second, and mathematical and spatial on the third. This provides conflicting evidence for the nature of people's implicit theories of intelligence, suggesting that even when asked to estimate seven different abilities their implicit estimates reflect close associations between some abilities and weaker links with others. Results also show that there were significant sex differences in the mathematical and spatial factor, which is consistent with the previous literature.

Furnham, Dixon, Harrison, and O'Connor (2000) asked 209 young people to make estimates of overall ($g$) intelligence as well as Gardner's (1999) new list of 10 multiple intelligences. Participants were also asked to provide their SAI in terms of overall IQ, and estimates for their partners' and three well-known figures (Prince Charles, Tony Blair, and Bill Gates) were also obtained. In accordance with previous research, results show significant sex differences (males rated themselves higher than females) in verbal, logical, and spatial intelligence, whereas females considered themselves higher in verbal and spiritual, but lower in spatial intelligence. A series of multiple regressions indicated that the best predictors of one's overall intelligence estimates were logical, verbal, existential, and spatial ability estimates. Once again, data reduction showed that Gardner's idea of 10 orthogonal (independent) abilities was not supported by people's estimates. This would suggest that, even if these abilities could all be measured psychometrically, there may be several significant intercorrelations between Gardner's multiple intelligence, which is in line with the hierarchical view of intelligence in terms of higher order underlying ability factors (see chap. 3).

## 6.8 CORRELATIONS BETWEEN SELF-ESTIMATED AND PSYCHOMETRICALLY MEASURED IQ

Another important aspect in the study of SAI has been defined by studies looking at the relationship between SAI (notably self-estimates) and psychometrically measured intellectual ability. These studies have often attempted to validate self-estimates against actual (psychometric) IQ scores, although it has been argued that there are several other reasons that one should study SAI and that estimated intelligence may have an effect on confidence and performance regardless of their accuracy (this is discussed further in Section 6.9).

As suggested (see Sections 6.2 and 6.3), theories of intelligence are not radically different from academic (psychometric) ones. Thus, one could expect lay people to have some insight into their intellectual abilities— that is, to assess how bright they are. Studies looking at the relationship between SAI and psychometric intelligence have attempted to test this hypothesis.

Researchers' decision to look at SAI with regard to standardized intelligence tests has usually been driven by attempts of using them as proxy intelligence tests (Paulhus, Lysy, & Yik, 1998). This would enable them to overcome disadvantages of some intelligence tests such as being expensive, time-consuming, and perceived as threatening by respondents. However, it was not until relatively recently that differential psychologists included indicators of SAI as part of their intelligence research (see Furnham, Clark, & Bailey, 1999). Thus, there are little more than 25 published papers on estimated or SAI (Furnham, 2001b).

In one of the first empirical studies to look at the relationship between psychometric and estimated ability scores, De Nisi and Shaw (1977) asked students to predict their scores on 10 different ability tests (including measures of verbal, spatial, and numerical intelligence), and correlations between estimated and psychometrically derived scores were significant in the $r = .30$ order. Although this led the authors to conclude that SAI should not be used as a replacement of psychometric intelligence tests, several researchers began to conduct similar studies in the 1990s.

Borkenau and Liebler (1993) examined the relationship between SAI and psychometric intelligence in a sample of German students. Measures of verbal and nonverbal ability correlated with SAI in the range of $r = .29$ to $r = .32$. These results support both the findings of De Nisi and Shaw (1977) as well as their conclusion that SAI cannot replace psychometric indicators of intelligence. Moreover, Borkenau and Liebler (1993) found that participants' estimations of strangers' intelligence (as shown in a brief video) correlated by $r = .43$ with targets' (i.e., strangers') psychometric intelligence. This (rather surprising) result may suggest that the correlation between self and psychometric intelligence is relatively low (because individuals may be better at judging strangers than themselves).

Reilly and Mulhern (1995) examined students' SAI with regard to the digit and vocabulary subtests of the *WAIS*. Findings reveal significant differences in SAI, with males overestimating their scores and women underestimating their scores (gender differences in SAI were discussed in Section 6.4).

Another study that aimed at examining the relationship between psychometric and estimated intelligence was that of Furnham and Rawles (1995). Although this study replicated the significant correlation between SAI and psychometric intelligence (in this case, a measure of spatial ability), the correlation was rather modest ($r = .16$) and gender dependent ($r = .27$ for men and $r = .09$ for women). A similar, modest, correlation between SAI and psychometric intelligence ($r = .19$) was obtained in a cross-cultural study by Furnham, Fong, and Martin (1999), who compared estimates with scores on the Raven Standard Matrixes, a test of Gf.

Although significant correlations between SAI and psychometric intelligence have been consistently replicated, they have rarely been found to exceed $r = .30$ (Borkenau & Liebler, 1993; Paulhus et al., 1998). As Brand (1994) suggested, this correlation is likely to be even smaller in the general population because most of the studies looking at this relationship involved data from highly educated (usually psychology) university students. This may be expected to have more explicit theories of intelligence and overall insight into their intellectual abilities than the average person. However, if samples are composed of bright students, there may be a restriction of range in both psychometric and estimated intelligence, which may reduce the correlation between these constructs. However, Gabriel, Critelli, and Ee (1994) found that, even when these samples are composed of individuals across which ability levels are not homogeneous (like in students from competitive universities), the correlation between SAI and psychometric intelligence does not exceed $r = .27$ (see also Brand, Egan, & Deary, 1994). Despite these relatively modest sizes in correlation between psychometric intelligence and SAI, it must be emphasized that SAI is important regardless of its accuracy (i.e., whether it correlates highly with psychometric intelligence). People's estimations of their own abilities are important because they can have a significant impact on performance (e.g., academic, work, and even IQ tests). This is discussed in the next section.

In a review of the salient literature, Paulus, Lysy, and Yick (1998) showed that correlations between single-item self-reports of intelligence and IQ scores rarely exceeded $r = .30$ (at least in college students). However, they suggested three ways in which the correlation between SAI and psychometric intelligence may be increased: (a) aggregating both estimates and tests to increase reliability and therefore validity, (b) using a weighting procedure to weighted items before aggregation (according to their individual diagnosticity), and (c) using indirect, rather than direct, questions to assess SAI (this would reduce the influence of self-presentational and social desirability effects). However, in their study, Paulus et al. (1998) used the Wonderlic (1990) test as the dependent measure and collected self-estimates from two large groups of undergraduate students ($N_1 = 310$ and $N_2 = 326$); there was little improvement when indirect item and weightening were used, with both direct and indirect measures correlating with psychometric intelligence in the range of $r = .04$ to $r = .34$ (most of them being $r = .20$). Furthermore, results show that direct items were often more correlated with psychometric intelligence than their indirect variations. Thus, the authors concluded that SAI should not be used to replace psychometric intelligence measures.

From the prior studies, one may conclude that the standard correlation between estimated and psychometric intelligence measures is, at best, only moderate, suggesting that people have a limited insight of their intellectual abilities (regardless of how these estimations are obtained). These correlations, however, may obscure the fact that some people are better and more accurate estimators of their intelligence scores than others. It may prove useful to obtain subsamples of highly accurate versus inaccurate estimators and see on what other criteria they differ (e.g., self-esteem, experience of IQ tests, etc.). In addition, there may well be important motivational factors at play in the self-estimation of intelligence, which may lead to serious distortions in the scores. Because of the correlational nature of these data, it is difficult at arrive to any conclusions regarding the causal direction of the (weak but significant) relationship between psychometric intelligence and SAI. Although, based on the literature, one would be inclined to dismiss the importance of SAI as indicators of intelligence in terms of their relatively weak correlation with actual IQ scores, one should also bear in mind that both SAI and psychometric intelligence are nothing but different indicators of intellectual competence, and that the validity of these measures is ultimately judged against performance indicators such as academic achievement or WP indicators. Moreover, even with regard to the relationship between SAI and intellectual ability, it is uncertain whether correlations should be interpreted as an indicator of people's insight into their intellectual ability or, rather, evidence for the influence of subjective beliefs (in this case, beliefs concerning one's intellectual ability) on psychometric test performance, or both. This remains largely a theoretical issue, although looking at the relationship of SAI and psychometric intelligence with AP indicators may answer important questions regarding the incremental validity of one and other measures, as well as the likelihood that subjective beliefs on one's abilities may have direct paths to performance (regardless of their accuracy, and regardless of a person's actual ability as measured through psychometric tests).

## 6.9   SAI AND AP

The relationship between SAI and AP is representative of a long-standing research area (social cognition), which deals with the effects of subjective beliefs on real-life outcomes. Several variables such as self-concept (Burns, 1982), self-efficacy (Bandura, 1986), success expectations, perceived controllability, attributional style (Metalsky & Abramson, 1981; Ryckman & Peckham, 1987), and specifically internal causes (e.g., ability, effort) have a substantial theoretical overlap with SAI in terms of their relationship and possible effect to real-life outcomes, although this section focuses on SAI and AP.

It has been shown that AP has been the criterion par excellence to examine the validity of psychometric intelligence tests (see chaps. 3 and 5). Thus, a broad conception of intellectual competence should not be based entirely on the notion and measurement of intellectual ability (which is usually limited to standardized cognitive tests), but be inclusive of AP. Further, as much as indicators of AP have been used to design, develop, and validate psychometric (notably IQ) tests, the relationship between SAI and AP may provide useful information on the validity of SAI as measures of intellectual competence in two major theoretical ways. First, they indicate whether lay people have certain insight into their intellectual competence. Second, they suggest whether lay persons' beliefs on their intellectual ability may have positive or negative effects on their AP. Both questions can be addressed if SAI and AP are correlated, although it remains a speculative issue to decide whether this correlation, if significant, is a function of people's insight or the self-fulfilling effects of SAI on AP, or both. In either case, however, it is deemed necessary to examine this relationship, and this section discusses this matter.

Although SAI may be a considerably worse predictor of AP than psychometric intelligence (which, as seen in Sections 3.1 and 5.1, has been a well-documented predictor of scholastic success and failure), there is some evidence suggesting that subjective beliefs are also related to actual AP, although more modestly than objectively measured intelligence. Thus, performance is more dependent on actual intellectual ability than on SAI, and believing one is intelligent, when in fact one is not, will not influence test scores much, whereas the opposite pattern (low SAI and high IQ) might. This phenomenon is usually referred to as *expectancy effect* and has been found in a number of related constructs—self-monitoring (Stankov, 1999), self-handicap (Rhodewalt, 1990), self-evaluation (Flett, Hewitt, Blankstein, & Gray, 1998; Morris & Liebert, 1974), self-motivation (Zeidner, 1995), self-efficacy (Bandura, 1986; Matthews, 1999), self-concept (Rinderman & Neubauer, 2001), self-esteem, and self-confidence (Koivula, Hassmen, & Fallby, 2002).

Although research has yet to examine the relationship between SAI (as given by single or multiple estimations of one's intellectual ability/abilities) and the constructs listed earlier, it is likely that subjective self-beliefs in general affect performance (Zeidner, 1995). Moreover, there is also evidence that others' (as opposed to self) expectations (e.g., parents' estimations of their children's abilities) may also influence objective performance (see Furnham, 2000b; Goodnow, 1980). Hence, it is important to examine not just objective, but also subjective (or perceived) competencies.

Although all of these variables seem to indicate that self-concepts (such as SAI) need not be accurate to affect performance, there are conflicting hypotheses about the direction of this effect. Whereas some have identified and explained the processes by which low SAI may lead to poor performance (Bridgeman, 1974; Stipek & Gralinski, 1996), others have argued (and shown) that beliefs about superior ability may, if erroneous, lead to arrogance, complacency, and equally impair performance. Conversely, self-beliefs of poor intellectual ability may also lead to enhanced efforts and improve performance.

Dweck and her colleagues (e.g., Bempechat, London, & Dweck, 1991; Dweck, 1986) argued that overconfidence or excessively high SAI may lead to the belief that academic success is a natural consequence of native intelligence and therefore undermines motivation and impairs actual performance (Muller & Dweck, 1998). Accordingly Furnham and Ward (2001) noted that, "whilst some researchers seem concerned to study and help females who are seen to be biased in favour of modesty and lower-than-actual estimations (Beloff, 1992; Beyer, 1999), others believe it is more important to examine male biases and the potential negative consequences of hubris in self-estimated intelligence" (p. 58). However, negative concepts may not always lead to improved performance. As Nauta, Epperson, and Wagoner (1999) showed, persistent university students tend to interpret their success as a consequence of their efforts, rather than their ability (this was found even when controlled for intelligence). Thus, the relationship between SAI and AP remains to be examined. Further, given the likelihood that SAI have self-enhancing (or self-defeating) effects on AP, it seems of capital importance to examine other correlates of SAI—notably, gender.

## 6.10   SAI AND PERSONALITY TRAITS

Although there is currently no consensus on whether the SAI dimension should be considered part of intelligence (Stankov, 2000) or personality (Hofstee, 2001), it could be that, as Eysenck and Eysenck (1985) argued, personality is related to SAI rather than psychometric abilities. This is certainly true from a methodological perspective because SAI is essentially a self-report measure. Recent research has provided some evidence for the significant relationship between personality traits, such as the Big Five, and SAI.

Furnham, Kidwai, and Thomas (2001) found Neuroticism (negatively) and Extraversion (positively) to be significantly correlated with SAI (i.e., stable extraverts estimated their intelligence significantly higher than others). These two personality traits were found to account for nearly 20% of the variance in SAI. This relationship may be attributed to the high and low confidence of extraverts and neurotics, respectively.

As discussed (Section 4.7), it is also likely that Openness to Experience is related to SAI because both variables refer to self-report intellectual competence. Regarding the other two Big Five personality super-traits, Agreeableness and Conscientiousness, hypotheses are not so clear. Agreeableness may be expected to be negatively related to SAI because agreeable individuals tend to be more modest than disagreeable ones. However, this may only reflect lower reports of SAI rather than actual beliefs of low SAI. In contrast, Conscientiousness may be expected to relate to high as well as low SAI. On the one hand, it is possible that the fact that Conscientiousness is positively associated with AP may lead conscientious individuals to give higher SAI. On the other hand, recent studies have indicated that Conscientiousness may be negatively related to IQ. Thus (if individuals can accurately estimated their ability), conscientious individuals would be more likely to give lower SAI. Given the lack of evidence on the relationship between well-established personality traits and SAI, and considering the importance of SAI with regard to academic as well as IQ test performance, it is necessary to further explore the link between personality traits and SAI.

## 6.11   SUMMARY AND CONCLUSIONS

The increase of popular books on intelligence (Gardner, 1983, 1999; Goleman, 1995; Herrnstein & Murray, 1994; Howe, 1997; Sternberg, 1997) may be regarded as a reflection of people's interest in the concept of intelligence. Although scientifically complex and linked to sophisticated statistical and psychometric techniques, the applied implications of intelligence in real-world settings have maintained lay interest for decades. In particular, the meaning and measurement of intelligence, group differences in IQ scores, its practical importance, sources and stability of within- and between-group differences, and implications for social policy are all of concern to the lay public.

Research on lay conceptions of intelligence has shown that lay people's ideas of intellectual ability (often referred to as *implicit theories*) are closely related to academic or explicit theories. Psychologists have argued that lay theories may influence the development of academic theories, as well as having consequences for the individual's confidence and performance—notably, in educational settings.

In this chapter, we have seen that lay beliefs on intelligence and intelligence testing are time and culture specific. Moreover, they often go beyond formal/academic/explicit theories to include ideas about social and practical intelligence (Gardner, 1983, 1999; Sternberg, 1985, 1996). Although these theories have been formulated by differential psychologists, there is a lack of psychometric evidence (and power tests of performance) for the existence of individual differences in these domains within the realm of human intellectual competence. However, lay people believe that these aspects of intelligence are important for "success in life," although they cannot be measured psychometrically.

Regardless of whether lay theories of IQ are closely related to academic/formal theories, lay people, like psychologists, assess individual differences in human ability on an everyday basis, although without using standardized psychometric tests. Recent research on SAI has helped highlight some of the important issues in this area (Beloff, 1992; Bennett, 2000; Furnham, 2000a, 2000b). Results demonstrate a widespread sex difference in SAI, which extends from self-estimates to estimates of relative' abilities, particularly parents and children. These differences are present in both estimates of general or multiple abilities. The results also demonstrate cultural differences.

Perhaps the two most interesting findings from the more recent studies on SAI are those on the male normativeness of IQ estimates and correlations between SAI and psychometric test scores. Furnham (2000a, 2000b) suggested that it is abilities like spatial and mathematical that are generally equated to intellectual ability. As noted by Furnham et al. (2000), findings on SAI suggest that intelligence is usually associated with "traditional intelligences (verbal, spatial and mathematical) that are statistically closest to a self-estimate of overall general intelligence. This appears to be the case irrespective of a person's experience of tests. There may be various reasons for this finding. It could be the ideas of emotional, practical or social intelligence are either rejected by many western educated people as not really part of intelligence or else the ideas are too new to have taken hold in the popular imagination. Equally it could be that people have been told in educational settings that certain tasks reflect their IQ and these have not included the wider conceptions of intelligence. What is particularly interesting about theses findings is that they may explain the commonly observed sex difference because IQ tests are seen to be male normative."

Correlations between SAI and psychometric intelligence have been significant and positive, albeit generally modest ($r < .30$). This led researchers to reject SAI as proxy measures of intelligence, although several interpretations could be made. First, the modest correlation between SAI and psychometric intelligence still supports the idea that people have some insight into their intellectual abilities (even if this insight is limited). Second, it is possible that SAI affects IQ test performance in a way that higher SAI may be associated with confidence, which can maximize test scores (and vice versa). Third, theoretically at least, psychometric intelligence and SAI may be regarded as two different indicators of intellectual competence. Although psychometric tests are certainly more objective than SAI (which may be influenced by an array of noncognitive traits such as personality), both variables are measures of the same latent construct—namely, intellectual competence. Thus, the validity of both SAI and psychometric intelligence can be judged against real-world criteria, such as AP (see chap. 5), which nonetheless would represent another measure of intellectual competence. Ultimately, then, all three variables should be considered to improve our understanding of the relationship between personality traits and individual differences underlying intellectual competence.

Thus, the importance of SAI studies lies not only in exploring their relation to lay theories of intelligence, but also of understanding the possible self-fulfilling nature of self-evaluations of ability. In a series of programmatic studies, Beyer (1990, 1998, 1999) demonstrated sex differences in expectations, self-evaluations and performance on ability-related tasks. These results support the male hubris, female humility results of these studies on SAI. Sex differences in self-evaluations affect expectancies of success and failure and, ultimately, performance on those tasks. She noted:

Because of the serious implications of under-estimations for self-confidence and psychological health more attention should be devoted to the investigation of gender differences in the accuracy of self-evaluations. Such research will not only elucidate the underlying processes of self-evaluation biases and therefore use of theoretical interest but will also be of practical value by suggesting ways of eliminating women's under-estimation of performance. (Beyer, 1990, p. 968)

# Individual Differences and Real-Life Outcomes

In the previous three chapters (4, 5, and 6), we examined interactions between personality traits and three different measures of intellectual competence—namely, psychometric intelligence, AP, and SAI. Each of these investigations showed that personality traits such as the Big Five may be significantly related to intellectual competence, suggesting that they may influence performance in the short as well as the long term. Throughout this chapter, we look at three additional constructs referring to latent variables that are commonly believed to determine success in real-life outcomes: leadership, creativity, and art judgment. There are other topics we could have chosen, but selected these to show the diversity of constructs that are determined in part by personality traits and intelligence. To the extent that these constructs may also be indicative of a person's intellectual competence, it is important to look at the possible impact of personality traits on these variables, notably in terms of the Big Five framework previously discussed.

Although most differential psychologists have looked at the relationship between personality and intelligence in terms of correlations between ability tests and personality inventories, an alternative approach to the study of personality and intellectual competence (or noncognitive and cognitive traits in general) consists of identifying mixed constructs (novel or existent); that is, psychometric identification and validation of latent variables that are a mix of both cognitive and noncognitive traits (see Hofstee, 2001; Zeidner & Matthews, 2000). In most cases, these variables have involved new types of intelligence, such as the so-called *hot* intelligences (e.g., emotional intelligence, spiritual intelligence, practical intelligence, interpersonal intelligence;

Gardner, 1999; Goleman, 1996; Mayer & Salovey, 1997; Sternberg, 1997; see chap. 3). These constructs may differ with regard to the specific type of ability they refer to, but they all confound noncognitive characteristics such as motivation, emotional stability, or Extraversion (see Goleman, 1996; Petrides & Furnham, 2001). Indeed there seems to be no end to the discovery of new intelligences.

However, it is often the case that researchers have attempted to validate these novel types of intelligence as ability measures rather than a mix of cognitive and noncognitive traits (for a detailed discussion on this topic, see Petrides & Furnham, 2001). Despite this, practically none of the hot intelligences has been exempted from criticisms with regard to their specific assessment or measurement approaches, as well as providing satisfactory evidence of incremental validity (see Davies, Stankov, & Roberts, 1998). In this section, we focus on another interesting, but less explored, construct that may also refer to the relationship between personality traits and intellectual competence; this construct is art judgment.

## 7.1 LEADERSHIP

There has been a great deal of speculation about the personality of leaders. Historians, political scientists, novelists, and business people as much as psychologists have speculated on the characteristics of great, as well as failed and derailed, leaders. Leadership has also proved difficult to define, although a few published chapters suggested that leadership can be defined in terms of the ability to build, motivate, and maintain high-performing teams, groups, departments, and organizations.

It is possible to classify the major leadership theories into three groups. Leadership *trait* theory assumes there are distinctive physical and psychological characteristics accounting for leadership effectiveness. *Behavioral* leadership theory assumes that there are distinctive styles that effective leaders continually use: These may be variously classified (i.e., autocratic, democratic, laissez faire) or based on grids/models that specify dimensions such as tasks versus person orientated. *Situational* (or contingency) leadership theories assume that leadership style varies from situation to situation.

What is interesting about the trait approach to leadership is that once popular it went out of favor but has reemerged. The trait approach was characterized by the *great person* approach to leadership. Three questions guided the research efforts of the trait theorist before World War II:

- Could specific traits of great leaders be identified?
- Was it possible to select people for leadership positions by identifying those who possess the appropriate traits?
- Could someone learn the trait that characterizes an effective leader?

It was assumed that finite set of individual traits—age, height, social status, fluency of speech, self-confidence, need for achievement, interpersonal skills, attractiveness, and so on—distinguished leaders from nonleaders and successful leaders from unsuccessful leaders. The sorts of traits more frequently investigated have been grouped under different headings: physical characteristics (height, energy), social background (education, social status), intellectual ability (intelligence quotient, verbal fluency), personality (self-confidence, stress tolerance), task orientation (achievement need), and social skills (personal competence, tact). A considerable amount of effort went into identifying traits associated with successful leaders. These traits include personality traits, cognitive abilities, interpersonal styles, and ability factors.

The problem with the approach was that people came up with a list that combined traits like initiative and decisiveness as well as more well-known traits like being self-assured. The list of traits grew swiftly, leading to confusion and dispute, but little insight into the process by which the model worked. Traits included a "rag-bag" of different features like physical characteristics (height, body shape), social background (class), abilities (fluency), social skills, as well as personality.

This tradition continues today. Thus, Locke (1997) identified leadership various "traits" under quite specific headings.

A. Cognitive Ability and Modes of Thinking:

    1. *Reality focus:* They are not susceptible to evasions, rationalizations, and delusions, but faced the actual and often grim reality.

    2. *Honesty:* This applied to the assessment of the market, judgments about the attractiveness of own products and capabilities of employees, and how to deal with suppliers, lenders, and costumers.

    3. *Independence and Self-Confidence:* Being confident to break new ground, think "outside the box," and "borrow" the best ideas from others.

    4. *Active Mind:* Continually searching for new ideas and solutions. It takes constant thought to do constant realistic improvements.

    5. *Competence and Ability:* In a sense this is simply intelligent: to make valid generalizations from data, to grasp causal connections, and to see actionable principles from overwhelmingly complex data.

    6. *Vision:* A detailed, innovative, long-term plan for the future of companies' products and services.

B. Motivation, Values, and Actions:

    1. *Egoistic Passion for the Work:* A sort of intrinsically motivated workaholism. The passion is a source of energy.

    2. *Commitment to Action:* This means doing after thinking, getting on with it.

    3. *Ambition:* Personal drive and desire to achieve expertise and a level of responsibility.

4. *Effort and Tenacity:* Being hard working and resilient, and not easily discouraged by failure.
C. Attitude Toward Employees:
1. *Respect for Ability:* Hiring and developing people with drive, talent, and the right attitude.
2. *Commitment to Justice:* Rewarding people appropriately.

Locke (1997) argued that these traits are timeless and universal—not just applying to successful Americans in the 20th century. He did raise and answer two central questions:

> Would quantitative analysis support 12 distinct traits, or could they be grouped into a smaller number without loss of important information? My prediction is that they can be combined into a smaller number. Do the traits operate independently (e.g. in additive fashion) or are there interactions between them? I have one prediction here: I think dishonesty negates all a person's other virtues in that it divorces a person from reality in principle. … A complicating factor, however, is that people are not always consistent in their honest and dishonesty. (p. 22)

Many writers seem to echo the same themes that good/great leaders have/need integrity, competencies, decisiveness, vision, people skills, and business skills.

For most researchers in the area, the trait approach failed for four reasons. First, the list of traits was not *grouped, rank-ordered,* or *parsimoniously described,* and it was impossible to see how they did or did not relate to each other. Second, the trait approach tended to be *retrospective* so it was unclear whether traits were a cause or consequence of leadership. Third, it was uncertain whether all the traits on the list were either or both *necessary and sufficient.* Finally, trait theory ignored the role of *situational/organizational/context* factors as well as the role of subordinates.

However, there has been a strong re-emergence of the trait approach. This has happened essentially for three reasons. As noted, there has been considerable taxonomic consensus around the Five Factor model, allowing researchers to compare their work. Advances in measurement has helped describe behaviors and understand process and mechanisms of behavior. Third, and equally important, meta-analyses of many good studies have demonstrated the predictive power of personality traits at work.

Furnham (1994) speculated about the role of the Big Five personality traits at work (see Table 7.1). He argued that leaders are likely to be open, conscientious, stable, agreeable, and extraverts.

More recently, Judge and Bono (2000) looked at 14 samples of leaders in 200 organizations to see which of the Big Five traits predicted transformational leadership. They hypothesized that Extraversion, Openness, and Agreeableness would be positively and Neuroticism negatively related to ratings of transformational leadership behaviors. They partially

### TABLE 7.1
#### Probable Relationships Between Personality and Work Variables

| Work Variables | N | E | O | A | C |
|---|---|---|---|---|---|
| Absenteeism | +++ | + | | | ++ |
| Accidents | + | + | | | |
| Creativity | | | +++ | | ++ |
| Derailment | +++ | | +++ | | +++ |
| **Leadership** | + | ++ | +++ | + | +++ |
| Motivation | +++ | +++ | ++ | + | +++ |
| Productivity | ++ | ++ | | | +++ |
| Sales | | ++ | | | + |
| Vocational choice | ++ | ++ | ++ | + | ++ |
| Satisfaction | +++ | +++ | | + | ++ |

Note. The + sign indicates the strength, not the direction, of the association.

confirmed results: Extraversion and Agreeableness were related, but Neuroticism and Conscientiousness were unrelated to leadership.

Judge, Bono, Illies, and Gerhordt (2002) reviewed the extant literature on personality and leadership. Ten writers, mainly from the 1990s listed what they thought to be the essential traits of effective or emergent leaders. They noticed considerable overlap such that most writers listed such things as self-confidence, adjustment, sociability, and integrity, but that others like persistence and masculinity were unique to specific reviewers. However, in their meta-analysis, they considered the possible linkages between personality and leadership. Results that Neuroticism was negatively and Extraversion, Openness, and Consciousness were positively correlated with both leadership emergence and effectiveness.

Using 222 correlations from 73 studies and classifying the personality variables in the Big Five framework, Judge, Bono et al. (2002) concluded that Extraversion/Surgency is the most consistent predictor of both leadership emergence and effectiveness criteria. The estimated true validities for leadership emergence and effectiveness, respectively, are: Extraversion/Surgency (.33; .24); Agreeableness (.05; .21); Conscientiousness (.33; .24); Emotional Stability (.24; .22); and Intellect/Openness to Experience (.24; .24). Regressing all Big Five personality measures on overall leadership yielded a multiple correlation of .48 with Extraversion/Surgency and Intellect/Openness to Experience, Extraversion/Surgency, Intellect/ Openness to Experience, and Conscientiousness were the best predictors when using the Big Five as a test battery.

Results show strong support for the personality approach to leadership once the traits are organized according to the Big Five model. Extraversion was the most consistent correlate no doubt because of the assertiveness, dominance, and sociability of extraverts. However, Judge, Bono et al. (2002) accepted that the research does not always explain why these traits related to leadership:

> Is Neuroticism negatively related to leadership because neurotic individuals are less likely to attempt leadership, because they are less inspirational, or because they have lower expectations of themselves or others? Similarly, Extraversion may be related to leadership because extraverts talk more, and talking is strongly related to emergent leadership. Alternatively, it may be that individuals implicitly expect leaders to be extraverted. Implicit views of leaders include aspects of both sociability ("outgoing") and assertiveness ("aggressive," "forceful"), or extraverts could be better leaders due to their expressive nature or the contagion of their positive emotionality. Open individuals may be better leaders because they are more creative and are divergent thinkers, because they are risk-takers, or because their tendencies for esoteric thinking and fantasy make them more likely to be visionary leaders. Agreeableness may be weakly correlated with leadership because it is both a hindrance (agreeable individuals tend to be passive and compliant) and a help (agreeable individuals are likeable and empathetic) to leaders. Finally, is Conscientiousness related to leadership because conscientious individuals have integrity and engender trust because they excel at process aspects of leadership, such as setting goals, or because they are more likely to have initiative and persist in the face of obstacles? Our study cannot address these process oriented issues, but future research should attempt to explain the linkages between the Big Five traits and leadership. (p. 774)

Hogan and Hogan (2002) argued that leadership can only be defined vis-à-vis team followers who rate the reputation of a leader. They pointed out that the recent literature looks at charismatic leadership, particularly the distinction between *transactional* and *transformational* leaders. It is the transformational leaders who attract the most attention. They argued that charismatic/transformational leaders are agreeable, open, and extraverts. Leaders need acceptance and status; they achieve this by being generous and sensitive. This reflects their Agreeableness score. They also need to be expressive, dominant, and persuasive, which the role of extraversion openness helps is their vision and imagination to do things differently.

Spangler, House, and Palrecha (2004) agreed that the Five Factor model has substantially helped our understanding of leadership, but they pointed out its various limitations. The Five Factor model fails to provide causal explanations for much human behavior at work. Most important, the model does not deal enough with *motivation* to become a leader. Next, there always remains a debate as to the *comprehensiveness* of the Five Factor model to fully describe behavior at work. Also the old argument is that the model does not list specific *combinations*, *contexts*, and *situations* under which specific traits operate. Last, the model does not explain the *mechanisms* by which traits interact with environmental characteristics to produce leader behavior and outcomes. They argued their leadership effectiveness is best seen in terms of both natures and traits. Most theorists would be happy to add the dimension of implicit nature to account for the variance in explaining leadership behavior.

The bottom line from current work, however, is this: Stable individual differences (i.e., traits) predict who becomes, stays, and derails as a leader. Different data sets, from different countries, different perspectives, and different historical periods, yield similar results. Great leaders are also bright, open, conscientious, extraverted, and stable. Trait profiles show clear patterns, but trait extreme scores are often an indicator of trouble.

## 7.2  CREATIVITY

The early psychological study of creativity was traditionally closely aligned to the study of intelligence. That is, creativity was seen more as a power than a preference trait. Gardner (1993a, 1993b) suggested this is because early researchers in creativity had already established careers as intelligence psychometricians. Terman (1925) insisted on an entry-level IQ score of 140 for participants in his *Genetic Studies of Genius*.

More recent research has indicated that, with an IQ above 115, the amount of variance in creative achievement explained by IQ is negligible (Getzels & Jackson, 1962). What these avenues of research did make clear was that the study of intellectual factors of creativity did not provide a comprehensive picture of the creativity complex. Instead researchers began to look at the influence of personality traits on creative achievement, believing that they would explain more variance than intelligence.

Guilford's (1967) pioneering work resulted in a flourish of new research in the 1950s and 1960s. Torrance (1979) suggested in a review of this wave of research that attempts to divine creativity could be dichotomized thus:

> Creativity tests tend to be of two types—those that involve cognitive-affective skills such as the *Torrance Tests of Creative Thinking* … and those that attempt to tap a personality syndrome. … Some educators and psychologists have tried to make an issue of whether creativity is essentially a personality syndrome that includes openness to experience, adventuresomeness, and self-confidence. (Torrance, 1979, p. 360)

There has been a sustained, if sporadic, attempt to investigate trait correlates of creativity however defined and measured. Because both variables have been measured in different ways, it is difficult to succinctly summarize the literature. Feist (1998) suggested that personality research with regard to creativity has taken two forms. The first is the *between-groups* comparison. Here two groups of people are compared (e.g., artists compared with scientists). If differences are significant and meaningful between the two groups, it is generally concluded that personality variables can be used to distinguish between artists and scientists. The second form of creativity research with regard to personality has sought to analyze *within-group* differences. In these cases, highly creative individuals from a domain are compared with their less creative peers. Feist (1998) suggested such analyses are essential because the within-group variance in creativity is markedly different for artists and scientists. Scientists were posited to have more pronounced variation in ratings of creativity because they may be involved in "very routine, rote, and prescribed" research, in addition to the few scientists engaged in "revolutionary" work. Alternatively, although artists can be employed in routine work, "anyone who makes a living at Art has to be more than one step above a technician" (Feist, 1998, p. 291).

The early studies of creativity and personality were characterized by a lack of convergence in the personality measures used. This continues, but may change with a gradual acceptance of the Five Factor model.

For instance, MacKinnon (1965), using expert ratings and the California Personality Inventory (CPI; Gough, 1957), investigated architects' creativity. To ascertain within-group differences, creative architects were compared with their less creative peers. MacKinnon stressed the importance of comparing similarly talented groups. A comparison of creative architects versus *normal* people would have failed to take into account that architects have, on average, IQs 2 standard deviations higher than normal people. The key findings from MacKinnon's work is that the highly creative architects, in comparison with the noncreative architects, were less deferent and team oriented; more aggressive, dominant, and autonomous; and less socialized (Responsible, Self-Controlled, Tolerant, Concerned With Good Impressions, and Communal in Attitude).

At much the same time, Heston (1966) studied 47 children of American schizophrenic mothers who were raised by foster parents and 50 controls. Heston found that half of the experimental sample exhibited psychosocial disability. They possessed artistic talents and demonstrated imaginative adaptations to life that were uncommon in the control group.

Domino (1974) used the CPI, the Edwards Personal Preference Schedule (Edwards, 1959), the ACL scored for creativity (Domino, 1970), the Barron–Welsh Art Scale (Welsh, 1959), and the Remote Associates Test (RAT; Mednick & Mednick, 1967) to assess the creativity of cinematographers versus matched controls. The results show that cinematographers, in comparison with matched controls, exhibited a greater desire for status, need for achievement, self-acceptance, and need for change. The cinematographers scored lower than the controls on the scales for Need for Deference and Need for Order. The scores for ACL, when scored for creativity, differentiated the two groups, with the cinematographers scoring higher. There were no differences revealed between the two groups on the Barron–Welsh Art Scale or the RAT.

Woody and Claridge's (1977) study of Psychoticism and Thinking demonstrated the link between psychoticism and trait creativity. One hundred undergraduates were administered the EPQ (Eysenck & Eysenck, 1975) and slightly modified versions of the five tests that make up the Wallach–Kogan (1965) "creativity tests." The creativity tests yielded scores for fluency and originality. Fluency scores for the five tests were all significantly correlated with P, with a range of correlation coefficients between $r = 0.32$ and $r = 0.45$. Originality scores were also significantly correlated with P, with a range of correlation coefficients between $r = 0.61$ and $r = 0.68$. There were no significant correlations between the scores for the creativity tests and E or N.

Götz and Götz (1973, 1979a, 1979b), studied artists. Their investigations revealed that in the domain of the Visual Arts, Neuroticism as measured by the Maudsley Personality Inventory and the EPQ is an important predictor of talent. Their 1973 study indicated that 50 gifted art students were more predisposed toward Neuroticism and Introversion than 50 less gifted art students. Götz and Götz (1979a) studied professional artists and found them to have higher scores on P than a group of controls. In a follow-up study, Götz and Götz (1979b) compared the scores of highly successful and less successful professional artists. They found that successful artists scored significantly higher on the P scale than less successful artists. No differences were found between the two groups on the E, N, or L scales.

Kline and Cooper (1986), however, published research that cast doubt on the generality of the link between creativity and P (Psychoticism). They wished to test the supposition that P was more predictive of originality than fluency scores on DT tests (Eysenck & Eysenck, 1976; Woody & Claridge, 1977). Thus, 173 undergraduates were given the EPQ and the Comprehensive Ability Battery (CAB; Hakstian & Cattell, 1976). The CAB consisted of several measures of primary ability factors, including several used to measure creativity: Flexibility of Closure, Spontaneous Flexibility, Ideational Fluency, Word Fluency, and Originality. The results show only one significant correlation between the CAB and P—this was for males only on the Word Fluency measure. There were no significant correlations between P scores and CAB measures for the females sampled ($n = 96$). These findings "[run] counter to the claim that of all the creativity variables, P is most closely related to originality" (Kline & Cooper, 1986, p. 186). To explain why the results from this study were incongruent with the findings of Woody and Claridge (1977), the authors suggested that, unlike the untimed tests of creativity used by Woody and Claridge, the CAB was timed. Wallach and Kogan's (1965) assertion that timed tests produce less creative responses may be at the heart of these discrepant findings on the nature of P and creativity. It was also noted that the variance in IQ scores for the Kline and Cooper sample was greater than the students used in the Woody and Claridge experiment.

Eysenck and Furnham (1993) tested the relationship between personality and creativity using the EPQ and Barron–Welsh Art Scale. The number of simple items disliked correlated significantly with P, and the number of complex drawings liked did not demonstrate a statistically significant relationship with P. The total score for the Barron–Welsh Art Scale was "just shy" of a significant correlation with P. Extraversion and Neuroticism scores did not correlate with P.

In a study of adolescents (mean age 15.8, $n$ = 300), Sen and Hagtvet (1993) administered a battery of tests that included measures of personality (MPI; Eysenck, 1960), Creative Thinking (Torrance, 1966), Intelligence (Raven, 1963), and a Study of Values (Allport, Vernon, & Lindzey, 1960). Examination marks were also taken as a measure of academic achievement. Of the personality variables, only Extraversion correlated significantly with the composite creativity score ($r$ = .14, $p$ < .05). When the sample was split to compare the scores of high scorers and low scorers on the creativity tests, the high creatives were significantly more extraverted.

Upmanyu, Bhardwaj, and Singh (1996) tested 250 male graduate students in India. They were interested in testing a finding of Gough's (1976) that moderately unusual responses on a Word Association Test were more predictive of creativity than extremely unusual responses. Gough did not control for psychic disturbance in his study; because unusualness of response is a characteristic of schizophrenia, Upmanyu et al. (1996) wished to test the relationships among unusualness of response, creativity scores, personality variables, and measures of psychic disturbance. Among other measures, they used the EPQ (Eysenck & Eysenck, 1975), the Word Association Test (K-R WAT; Kent & Rosanoff, 1910), and figural and verbal tests of creative thinking (Torrance, 1966). To assess schizotypical tendencies, they utilized the *MMPI*–Psychopathic Deviate subscale (Hathaway & McKinley, 1967).

They found that extremely unique word associations were positively associated with verbal creativity. However, atypical or moderately unusual responses were substantially related to verbal creativity. Extremely unique word associations were positively associated with P and psychopathic deviation. The authors suggested that the P scale contributes toward creativity, in that it predisposes individuals to social anhedonia, social deviance, unconventionality, and mild antisocial behavior. The authors concluded that the findings seem to support "a link between psychoticism, mild antisocial behaviour, and lack of conformity/ unconventionality rather than the more specific clinical entity of psychopathic behaviour" (Upmanyu et al., 1996).

Martindale and Dailey (1996) used measures of personality (EPQ; Eysenck & Eysenck, 1975; NEO–PI; Costa & McCrae, 1985) and several measures of creativity (Fantasy Story Composition, Alternate Uses Test, and Remoteness of Association). The experiment failed to find any correlation between the measures of creativity and the P scale. The correlations between NEO Openness and creativity scores all failed to reach significance. Significant correlations were demonstrated between the EPQ–E scores and creativity scores at the .05 level. Significant correlations were observed for the NEO–E scores and creativity scores, but only at the 0.1 level of significance.

Using a slightly different approach, Merten and Fischer (1999) selected creatives on the basis of occupation: 40 actors and writers were compared with 40 schizophrenics and 40 unselected subjects. A Word Association Test requiring common and uncommon responses (Merten, 1993, 1995), two tests of verbal creativity (Schoppe, 1975), and two story-writing tasks were used as measures of creativity. The EPQ (Eysenck & Eysenck, 1975) was used as well as a short multiple-choice vocabulary test, Raven's (1956) Standard Progressive Matrices, and a measure of basic cognitive functioning (Reitan, 1992). The creatives' sample scored higher on the P scale than the nonpatient group controls. The creatives also produced the most original word associations of the three groups. The creatives did not produce any response repetitions in the common or unusual response conditions. This was taken to be an indication of the creative group's mental health.

> Most importantly, however, they [the creatives] produce the most original associations in the individual response condition, which schizophrenics do not. All this seems to be a good reason for conceiving the specific associative behaviour of the creatives as controlled weirdness, to borrow a term employed by Barron (1993), rather than interpreting it as an indicator of thought disorders. In contrast to studies in which only free associations are used, a combination of different methodological approaches clearly shows that the associative behaviour of creative individuals does *not*, after all, resemble that of mental patients. (Merten & Fischer, 1999, p. 941)

An innovative study by Dollinger and Clancy (1993) required participants to create autobiographical story essays using 12 photographs (Ziller, 1990). The instructions were that the "photographs should describe who you are as you see yourself." Participants were also given NEO–PI (Costa & McCrae, 1985). The pictorial autobiographical stories were extensively coded, with a main rating of "richness of self-depiction." A multiple regression to predict richness rating revealed that Openness to Experience had a significant beta weight. Neuroticism and Extraversion fell just short of significance. When the analyses were conducted to analyze gender differences, the richness of men's essays was predicted by Openness ($r = .28$), with the only significant facet being aesthetic openness ($r = .42$). These results were also replicated for women. However, the Openness facet *ideas* was also a significant predictor. The richness ratings for women were significantly correlated with the Neuroticism (high) and Extraversion (low) domains.

King, Walker, and Broyles (1996) examined the relations among creative ability, creative accomplishments, and the Five Factor model of personality. Seventy-five participants were given verbal DT tests (Torrance, 1990), asked to list their creative accomplishments over the previous 2 years and took the 44-item Big Five Inventory (BFI; John, Donahue, & Kentle, 1991). The Pearson correlations indicated that verbal creativity was significantly correlated with Extraversion ($r = .26, p < .05$) and Openness to Experience ($r = .38, p < .01$). There were significant correlations between creative accomplishments and Openness ($r = .47, p < .01$) and negative Agreeableness ($r = -.23, p < .05$). A regression plotting all five personality factors against verbal creative ability revealed a significant prediction for Openness alone. A second regression plotting the personality variables against creative accomplishments again yielded a significant prediction for Openness only.

Furnham (1999) replicated an earlier study (Eysenck & Furnham, 1993), but with a different personality measure. Participants were administered the Barron–Welsh Art Scale (Welsh, 1975) and Form S of the NEO Five Factor Inventory (Costa & McCrae, 1991). Participants were also requested to provide three self-ratings of creativity (estimate of Barron–Welsh score, a rating of how creative they thought they were, and a rating of the frequency of creative hobbies). Four regressions were performed, each using a different criterion of creativity. When the criterion was the Barron–Welsh score, none of the Five Factor model factors was a significant predictor. Openness to Experience was a significant predictor of the participant's estimate of their Barron–Welsh score, the self-rating of how creative they thought they were, and the rating of creative hobbies.

George and Zhou (2001) adopted an interactional approach, investigating the roles of Openness and Conscientiousness and the work environment on creative behavior. They demonstrated that the application of creative potential depends on several factors. They found rated creative behavior was highest when individuals with high Openness were set to tasks that had unclear demands or unclear means of achieving ends and were given positive feedback. Their analyses of the role of Conscientiousness also yielded clear findings. They found that if an individual's supervisor monitors his or her work closely and coworkers were unsupportive of creative endeavour, then high Conscientiousness inhibited creative behavior.

In a study using three measures of creativity, Wolfradt and Pretz (2001) investigated the relationship between creativity and personality. The measures of creativity deployed were the Creative Personality Scale (CPS; Gough, 1979) for the Adjective Checklist, a story-writing exercise for which the stimulus was a picture and a list of hobbies. The story exercise and list of hobbies were rated using the Consensual Assessment Technique (CAT; Amabile, 1982, 1996). A German 60-item version of the NEO–FFI was used to assess personality (Borkenau & Ostendorf, 1993; Costa & McCrae, 1989). Participants were 204 students from diverse academic fields. The CPS was predicted by high scores on Openness and Extraversion. The best predictor of "hobby creativity" was Openness. Creative story writing was predicted by Openness and low scores on Conscientiousness. The results were also analyzed by field of study, with "scientists" scoring significantly lower on the three measures of creativity and Openness to Experience than subjects studying Psychology or Art and Design. There were also gender effects, with females scoring higher on story and hobby creativity.

Wuthrich and Bates (2001) gave 54 subjects the NEO–PI–R (Costa & McCrae, 1992) and the P scale of the EPQ-R (Eysenck et al., 1985), in addition to the Pattern Meaning (Wallach & Kogan, 1965) and Unusual Uses Test (Torrance, 1974). Tests of Latent Inhibition (LI) were administered (Ginton et al., 1975), as well as a priming test involving a word-stem completion and recognition task (Rajaram & Roediger, 1993). The results of the experiment indicate that the creativity measures were related to N, E, and O, but not P, LI, or priming.

In a study with similar research interests, Peterson, Smith, and Carson (2002) administered a Latent Inhibition (LI) task (Lubow et al., 1992), the NEO–FFI Form S (Costa & McCrae, 1992), the Creative Personality Scale (CPS; Gough, 1979), and two tests of Intelligence (Vocabulary and Block Design; *WAIS–R*; Wechsler, 1981). The results indicate that decreased LI is associated with creative personality. The authors found that individuals with low LI scored higher on the CPS. The study also confirmed an earlier finding that decreased LI is correlated with Openness and Extraversion (Peterson & Carson, 2000). These results seem to contradict the findings of Wuthrich and Bates (2001), one explanation being that quite different measures of creativity were used.

In what is possibly the first comprehensive meta-analysis of the creativity literature, Feist (1998) investigated creativity personality in the Arts and Sciences. To analyze the disparate collection of personality data, the data from 83 experiments were converted so that the different personality scores were all in the Five Factor model format, and effect sizes were measured using Cohen's *d* (Cohen, 1988). Subsequent analyses were conducted investigating three main comparisons: (a) scientists versus nonscientists, (b) creative versus less creative scientists, and (c) artists versus nonartists.

For the scientists versus nonscientists, 26 studies were analyzed. The results indicate that Openness, Extraversion, and Conscientiousness differentiated scientists from non-scientists. The confidence-dominance subcomponent was found to be more important than the sociability subcomponent of Extraversion. With regards to Conscientiousness, relative to nonscientists, scientists were roughly half a standard deviation higher on conscientiousness and controlling of impulses.

For creative scientists compared with less creative scientists, 28 studies were meta-analyzed. The traits that most strongly distinguished the creative from less creative scientists were Extraversion and Openness. Similar to the results from the comparison of scientists compared to nonscientists, the confidence-dominant subcomponent of E contributed to the effect size, with no effect derived from the sociability subcomponent. A moderate effect size was noted for the direct expression of needs and psychopathic deviance subcomponents of Conscientiousness.

For the artists compared with nonartists sample, 29 studies were scrutinized. The traits that most clearly differentiated artists from nonartists were Conscientiousness and Openness; artists were roughly half a standard deviation lower on C and half a standard deviation higher on O.

Soldz and Vaillant (1999) reported the results of a 45-year study of 163 males. Participants were regularly assessed to measure factors as diverse as health, career functioning, social relations, mental health, political attitudes, childhood characteristics, and creative achievement. Participants were given the NEO–PI at a mean age of 67. NEO scores were then calculated for the men at the end of their college careers. The procedure for the calculations involved trait ratings taken while the participants were enrolled in college study. These ratings were produced by a psychiatrist and psychologist and required the codification of behaviors across 25 domains. Using seven raters, these scores were converted to a Five Factor model format. The results of the study confirm that Openness to Experience was significantly positively related the ratings of creativity. Interestingly, Openness also demonstrated significant relations to Psychiatric Usage and Depression.

Feist (1999) presented a summary of research into the influence of personality on creative achievement in the Arts and in Science. He found that there were some personality variables that occurred in both groups. Creative scientists and artists were found to be open to new experiences, less conventional, less conscientious, but more self-confident, self-accepting, driven, ambitious, dominant hostile, and impulsive. Artists were found to be more affective, emotionally unstable, less socialised and less accepting of group norms than scientists. Scientists were found to be more conscientious than artists. These findings seem to suggest why it is has proved difficult to produce a comprehensive list of the personality characteristics of creative people.

The results of a 55-year longitudinal study were reported in Feist and Barron (2003). The sample consisted of 80 male graduates from 14 different academic departments. Data were collected for the subjects at ages 27 and 72. The nature of the longitudinal data-collation procedures meant that complete sets of data for all of the different measures were unavailable. The range of the frequency of subjects was between 62 and 72 for all but one set of data. Complete personality data were available for only 43 subjects. The primary interest of the study was to report on the prediction of creativity from early to late adulthood utilizing measures of intellect, potential, and personality. The main hypothesis was that personality would predict variance in creative achievement over and above the measures of intellect and potential. Intellect was measured. The results indicate that at age 27 years, personality traits predicted an additional 8% of the variance in a composite originality score over intellect and a rating of potential. Personality trait scores were also predictive of lifetime creative achievement.

The results in this area have begun to show consistent results despite the use of different measures of both personality and creativity. Two factors from the Big Five (+O and –C) and one from the Big Three (+P) seem implicated in creativity, but there remain many caveats. For instance, creativity in the arts may have a slightly different correlation from creativity in the sciences. Also motivational factors need to be considered. However, it does seem that personality traits account for more of the variance than traditional, psychometric measures of intelligence. However, as in other areas, it is no doubt the interaction of the two individual difference factors that best predicts creativity.

## 7.3   ART JUDGMENT

Art judgement refers to appreciative skills or the ability to discern between better and worse artistic works. Over the years, psychologists attempted to construct and validate several tests of artistic judgment (Bryan, 1942; Burkhart, 1958; Burt, 1933; Child, 1965; Furnham & Chamorro-Premuzic, 2004b; Furnham & Walker, 2001). To the extent that there is some consensus, among experts, on the quality of artistic productions (particularly the discrimination between original art products and their imitations), the assessment of art judgment may be based on correct and incorrect responses. These would present the advantage of being measures of maximal performance, and thus more reliable.

The psychometrics of art judgment date back more than seven decades, when Meier and Seashore (1929; see also Seashore, 1929), after 6 years of research, published an "objective measure of art talent." This measure was designed to facilitate the identification of "promising art talents." Although Meier and Seashore conceived of art as a general ability complex (comprising more than 20 different, but related, traits), they regarded aesthetic or artistic judgment as a basic and indispensable component, which all gifted artists should possess in highly developed manner. The test consists of pairs of pictures that differ in one feature. This feature is indicated to the participant in the instructions. One of the pictures is "real" (corresponds to an original work of art and has been rated as such by experts of the arts), whereas the other represents a simple variation of the original. Participants are given the task to identify the better (original) design.

Although early studies have reported on the predictive (Eurich & Carroll, 1931) and cross-cultural (Stolz & Manuel, 1931) validity of Meier and Seashore's (1929) test, researchers expressed concern about its poor relationship to psychometric intelligence (see Carroll, 1932; Farnsworth & Misumi, 1931; see also Stolz & Manuel, 1931). Naturally, if art judgment is to be conceived of as an objective measure of ability, it must bear a certain degree of association with well-established psychometric intelligence tests. This led Carroll (1932, 1933) to question the nature and meaning of the construct of art judgment.

However, Meier presented a modification of this test—the Meier art judgment test (Meier, 1940). This version was believed more reliable and valid than its antecessor, the Meier–Seashore (1929). The Meier art test kept the 100 most discriminating of the 125 original items of the Meier–Seashore. Of these, 25 have been assigned double weight in scoring. Thus, the Meier art judgment also allows for a shorter administration time. Nevertheless, research on the Meier art judgment test has been rather infrequent (e.g., Furnham & Rao, 2002; Hill & Junus, 1979; Karaeng & Sandstroem, 1959). In a recent study, Furnham and Rao (2002) found that art judgment as measured by the Meier test was not significantly related to aesthetic judgments of Mondrians or Hirst (which the authors presented alongside facsimiles). It was suggested that art judgment as measured by the Meier test may only apply to representational art. Interestingly, however, scores on the Meier test were significantly predicted by personality (specifically the Big Five traits of Openness and Conscientiousness).

Another recent study by Furnham and Chamorro-Premuzic (2004b) found that intelligence was a significant predictor of art judgment as measured by the Maitland Graves (1948) art judgment test. Like the Meier–Seashore, this test is based on participants' discrimination/identification of the better designs. The Maitland Graves test has attracted wide attention to determine its validity (Eysenck, 1967a, 1967b, 1970, 1972; Pichot, Volmat, & Wiart, 1960; Uduehi, 1996). Further, Götz and Götz (1974) found that 22 different arts experts (designers, painters, sculptors) had .92 agreement on choice of preferred design, albeit being critical of them.

Furnham and Chamorro-Premuzic (2004b) found intelligence (as measured by the Wonderlic Personnel Test; Wonderlic, 1992) to be significantly associated with art judgment as measured by the Graves (1948) abstract art design test, but not with art interests/background/experience (as defined by the responses of a self-report scale designed by the authors). Further, the authors also looked at the relation between art judgment and personality (Big Five; Costa & McCrae, 1992). Results show that two personality traits—namely, Conscientiousness (negatively) and Extraversion (positively)—were significant predictors of art judgment. The clearest finding in Furnham and Chamorro-Premuzic (2004b) concerned the relationship between personality traits (notably Openness to

Experience) and art interests. In several regressions, Openness was found to account for up to 33% of the variance in art experience.

Although in Furnham and Chamorro-Premuzic (2004b) the correlations between personality traits and art interests seem to suggest, quite clearly, that personality traits (notably Openness) may be relevant to the processes of artistic engagement, it remains questionable whether art judgment should be considered a measure of intelligence or personality. Perhaps the significant correlation of art judgment with *both* personality and intelligence may be indicative that art judgment is a measure of both noncognitive and cognitive traits.

In a second study, Chamorro-Premuzic and Furnham (in press) set to explore the link among personality traits, psychometric intelligence, art interests (self-report artistic background), and art judgment, this time measured by another test (Meier, 1940). Confirming the results of Furnham and Chamorro-Premuzic (2004b), art judgment (in this occasion measured by the Meier art test instead of the Maitland–Graves art test) was significantly related to art interests as assessed through a self-report questionnaire. Specifically, this inventory addressed self-reported art experience (e.g., formal education in the arts, reading habits in arts), art activities (visits to galleries), and art recognition (of different art styles). Intercorrelations among these three measures suggested they could be conceptually combined to provide a single measure of art interests: high scorers being overall interested and education in the visual arts. This factor was a significant (albeit modest) predictor of art judgment scores, accounting for 7% of the variance in the Meier art judgment test. This indicates that participants who reported greater interests in arts tended to score higher in art judgment and vice versa (no doubt due to exposure). Hence, the data suggest a positive and significant relation between interests (in arts) and ability (in art judgment). Although one may only speculate about the causal direction of this relation (whether people tend to be interested in arts because of their natural ability, or whether interests in arts may lead to a more developed art judgment), this association may be indicative of the construct validity of the Meier test. Furthermore, it is clear from this association that the Meier art judgment test is related to noncognitive variables such as interests.

Another unsurprising finding was the significant relationship between art judgment and the two intelligence measures employed (i.e., Wonderlic and Raven). These results confirm those of Furnham and Chamorro-Premuzic's (2004b) study, in which the Wonderlic Personnel test was examined against the Maitland–Graves Design test. It is worth noticing that in Chamorro-Premuzic and Furnham's (in press) study, a measure of Gf (Raven) was also included, although multiple regression showed that Wonderlic accounted for unique variance in art judgment. Hierarchical regression indicated that psychometric intelligence (Wonderlic and Raven combined) had some incremental validity (with regard to art interests) in the prediction of art judgment, accounting for an additional 11% of the variance. The moderate relationship between psychometric intelligence and art judgment suggests that art judgment may be measuring a distinct ability (but certainly *something* of the ability domain). Therefore, the results provide further evidence for the validity of the test, particularly as a measure of maximal performance (see Chamorro-Premuzic & Furnham, 2003; Cronbach, 1984; Meier, 1940; Seashore, 1929). Thus, it seems straightforward to interpret these associations: If art judgment is an ability, it must be significantly related to well-established intelligence tests.

Regarding the relationship between art judgment and personality traits (Big Five and TIE), the analyses indicate that three of the Big Five—namely, Neuroticism, Extraversion, and Conscientiousness—were significantly associated with art judgment scores. According to the initial prediction, the negative relation between art judgment and Conscientiousness may be interpreted in terms of the negative associations between this personality trait and creativity, on the one hand (Eysenck, 1993, 1994a, 1994b, 1995a, 1995b; Furnham, 1999), and intelligence, on the other hand (Furnham, Chamorro-Premuzic, & Moutafi, in press). Further, it is also possible that conscientious individuals are less likely to express interests in arts and creative disciplines.

With regard to the significant association between art judgment and Extraversion, the interpretation appears to be less straightforward, as the initial prediction was of a positive, rather than a negative, relation between these variables. However, and running counter to Furnham and Chamorro-Premuzic's (2004b) results, Extraversion was negatively related to art judgment. One possibility to explain this relation is that introverts may be more likely to invest in art appreciation—for instance, reading more about arts than extroverts. Another possible interpretation would be to attribute these associations to the test characteristics because the Meier art test requires respondents to concentrate for more than 40 minutes and carefully evaluate each set of stimuli. These characteristics are known to favor introverts more than extraverts (see Matthews et al., 2000). However, in Furnham and Chamorro-Premuzic (2004b), a similar measure (roughly the same administration time) of art judgment was employed. It is thus recommended that future research should explore the relationship between art judgment and Extraversion.

Neuroticism was positively related to art judgment. Although no predictions were made with regard to the relationship between Neuroticism and art judgment, it is possible that neurotic participants (like introverts) may have been better at focusing and concentrating on the stimuli of the art test, particularly if one considers that participants were tested under no pressure (Matthews et al., 2000). Thus, the nonthreatening test environment and the attentional demanding nature of the test (which requires concentration and discrimination from the participants) may have interacted, resulting in the positive association between Neurotic and art judgment.

As predicted and confirming previous findings (Furnham & Chamorro-Premuzic, 2004b), Openness was not significantly related to art judgment. Moreover (and also following predictions), TIE was not significantly related to art judgment either. Because both Openness and TIE are significantly and positively related to art interests, it is possible that the relation between Openness and TIE with art judgment may be mediated by interests, such that people high on Openness and TIE would be more likely to engage in artistic activities (and hence score higher on art judgment).

Personality traits showed incremental validity with regard to art interests and psychometric intelligence in the prediction of art judgment. This further indicated that the Meier art test taps both cognitive (intelligence) and noncognitive (personality, interests) items.

Finally, studies have also explored the relation between intelligence and personality with art interests. Results show that Openness and TIE were significantly and positively related to art interests. This confirmed initial predictions. In the case of Openness, the positive associations between this trait and art interests are also consistent with McCrae and Costa's (1997a, 1997b; see also Costa & McCrae, 1992) characterization of open personalities as intrinsically artistic: "as neurotics can be used as examples of high scores on the dimension of Neuroticism, so artists can be considered primer examples of individuals high in Openness to Experience" (McCrae & Costa, 1997a, 1997b, p. 825). Thus, the imaginative and sensitive nature of open individuals may lead them to engage in artistic experiences. Likewise individuals high on TIE seem inclined to get involved in artistic activities. Although this may reflect the reported overlap between TIE and Openness (Rocklin, 1994), it is noteworthy that TIE also comprises aspects of Conscientiousness (which, as shown in the present results, is negatively albeit nonsignificantly related to art interests and negatively and significantly related to art judgment). In addition, it is also noticeable that the TIE scale (unlike Openness) does not include items referring to artistic engagement. Rather this scale assesses the frequency and satisfaction with which individuals engage in philosophical thinking and intellectual reading (Goff & Ackerman, 1992). However, the present results clearly indicate that people high on TIE are more likely to get involved in (and enjoy) artistic activities.

It is thus likely that art judgment comprises both cognitive (intelligence) and noncognitive (interests, personality) individual differences. Given the recent interests in the integration of these individual differences (Ackerman & Heggestad, 1997), art judgment appears to be a promising and rather unexplored area for psychometricians. Further, the theoretical challenge of understanding the processes underlying the development of art judgment may be regarded as an area of interest not only to psychologist, but also to educational and art researchers, as well as artists.

## 7.4  SUMMARY AND CONCLUSIONS

This book is essentially about the relationship between personality and intellectual competence. As such it attempts to go beyond the traditional approaches of focusing exclusively on the relationship between personality inventories and ability measures. This chapter took three diverse areas to illustrate that personality and intelligence together can go a long way to explain the variance in social behavior. Who becomes a leader or who is creative is a function of many things, but it is likely that personality and intelligence will play a significant role in the processes underlying both leadership and creativity.

Further, this research begins to explain the mechanisms and processes that underlie individual performance. By understanding an individual's ability and trait profile, we can understand their preferences and products. More important, these factors (ability/personality) are stable over time and can be used for prediction. Individual differences are stable for three reasons—namely, reactive, evocative, and proactive processes.

First, personality and ability dictate how people see the world differently (people perceive and experience the same thing quite differently). The paranoid see challenges, the neurotic threats, the narcissistic complements, and the adventurous excitement. That is, people react to an identical situation differently as a function of their personality and ability. In this sense, it is impossible to give people the same experience—be it a training course or an appraisal. Personality is a filter of reality: It determines how you react, and therefore people react to different situations similarly or vice versa depending on their personality.

Next, people tend to evoke different responses in others. Neurotics' moodiness tends to lead to different responses in others than do stable individuals, who are less prone to ups and downs. You only have to be in the presence of someone who is very good looking, bright, or extroverted to notice how they evoke quite different responses compared with the average individual. Extroverts put people at their ease more than introverts.

Different children evoke in them very different emotions and parenting styles. Naughtiness evokes spanking, whereas compliance evokes praise. How people respond to you is therefore relatively consistent because abilities and traits tend to lead to responses in similar ways.

The third process is pro-activity. People choose and change situations in accordance with their personality. Extroverts choose noisy situations, introverts quite ones. Consider how people arrange identical furniture in identical offices to reflect their personality. It can be arranged to signal dominance or optimize interaction. It can reflect artistic taste, which has also been shown to be part of personality (and can be assessed partly through the Openness trait).

Thus, through these three processes, people see and create situations to make our world stable. This explains the paradoxical findings or geneticists, who study twins throughout their lives. Twins get more alike over time: If tested at 8, 28, 48, and 88 years of age, they get more alike in their attitudes, beliefs, and behaviors. Most people would believe the opposite because, as they are inevitably exposed to different environments, they should change as a result of this differential experience.

Yet through the process of reaction, evocation, and proaction, people seem to ensure their experience of the world is surprisingly tailored to their personality and ability. So they stay much the same. The fact that people create stable worlds for themselves means that ability and personality tests are useful for long-term prediction. Indeed the last 20 years or so have seen a resurgence of interest in abilities and traits because of their explanatory and predictive power in educational and occupational settings.

# 8

# Overall Summary and Conclusions

This book has attempted to examine and discuss the fundamental links between personality traits (such as the Big Five) and several indicators of intellectual competence, notably psychometric intelligence (chap. 4), AP and WP (chap. 5), and SAI (chap. 6). In addition, we have looked at other latent constructs that may be predicted by, and understood in terms of, a combination of both personality and intelligence (e.g., leadership, creativity, and art judgment; chap. 7). Yet what are the salient points to be summarized from the previous chapters, and what conclusions can be drawn from this book?

It is clear from the first two review chapters (chaps. 2 and 3) that personality and intelligence (as traditionally conceptualized and measured through standardized tests of cognitive ability) are two well-established domains within the realm of individual differences. Further, former controversies—which dominated both fields of research until the late 1950s—have now been replaced with scientific consensus, and the robust empirical methodology of differential psychology has allowed researchers to establish a state-of-the-art technique for the assessment and measurement of these fundamental individual differences.

Not only is it now clear which dimensions of an individual should be assessed and measured to provide the most comprehensive and reliable description of both what a person *can* do (intelligence) and what she or he *is likely* to do (personality). It is also evident that these constructs—albeit latent and psychometrically inferred or deduced—are solid indicators of a surprisingly wide variety of real-life outcomes and the most general, invariable, and culture-free predictors in social psychology. Thus, personality and intelligence as concepts and measures can be used not only in scientific research, but also in applied, real-world settings.

However, it is important (and in fact one of the key aims of this book) to explore links between these two variables: first, to clarify their global taxonomic position with regard to an individual's description in general; second, to gain some insight into the combined effect of both sets of constructs in the prediction of diverse behavioral outcomes; and third, to identify the possible developmental effects of both personality and intelligence. This can only be done by looking at the relationship between both personality and intelligence. Because of the historical independence of one and other research area, the relationship between these constructs has remained a largely unaddressed task for several decades.

In chapter 3, we addressed the question of whether interactions, at the psychometric level, between measures of intelligence and inventories of personality (mainly in terms of the Big Five traits, which represent the predominant and state-of-the-art approach to individual differences in personality) can increase our knowledge on the relationship between the major constructs in differential psychology and, moreover, shed some light into the possible effects of personality on intellectual competence. This has been a salient research question in the area particularly in the last 7 years (Ackerman & Heggestad, 1997; Chamorro-Premuzic & Furnham, 2004; Zeidner & Matthews, 2000).

It has been noted that most findings in this area—dealing specifically with the interaction between personality and intelligence at the psychometric level—could be organized according to a two-level conceptual framework, which proposed a theoretical distinction between actual intellectual ability (a latent construct that does not equal psychometric intelligence) and cognitive performance as output—that is, as measured by standardized psychometric tests. Thus, there has been evidence for the possible effects of certain personality traits on intelligence test performance, such as Neuroticism and Extraversion, as well as other long-term and developmental effects of personality traits on actual intellectual competence (notably Openness to Experience).

Although the correlational evidence for the relationship between psychometric intelligence and personality traits is indicative only of modest links between these constructs, it seems likely that personality traits have a minor but significant effect on both cognitive performance (as measured by a one-off ability test), as well as the longitudinal development of intellectual competence. For instance, anxious individuals are likely to have a disadvantage in IQ test performance (regardless of their ability), and extraverts can be predicted to have an advantage on certain types of psychometric tests (e.g., short, timed, verbal, etc.). This means that, given two individuals with the same actual intelligence (and we need to emphasize, again, that this can only be inferred, but not *purely* measured), the one that is stable and extraverted will benefit from higher confidence and more distraction-free cognitive processing.

However, it would be wrong to assume that either Neuroticism or Extraversion are indicative of a person's actual intellectual competence—that is, her or his ability to reason and learn new things, as well as her or his acquired knowledge. Thus, correlations between these personality traits and psychometric intelligence should be interpreted purely in psychometric terms, not at the level of inferred/latent constructs. This is in line with the literature suggesting that experimentally manipulated variables such as pressure and time can moderate (and, to a great degree, intensify) the relationship of Neuroticism and Extraversion with cognitive ability measures (Furnham, Forde, & Cotter, 1998a, 1998b).

However, it has been suggested that links between personality and actual intelligence can also be investigated empirically and through the same psychometric approach. These claims have emerged as an attempt to interpret the relationship between cognitive ability and its strongest correlate, Openness to Experience. In line with such claims, we have proposed that the relationship between Openness and psychometrically measured intelligence (which usually correlates in the order of $r = .30$ with personality traits from the Big Five framework) may indeed be indicative of links between personality and intelligence at the latent level, such that open individuals would, in general, be more intelligent (and not merely have an advantage for test performance). Further, it is likely that Openness may have beneficial, long-term effects for the development of adult intellectual ability, such that open individuals, more curious, creative, and imaginative, would have a greater likelihood (and desire) to invest in intellectually stimulating activities. Likewise the TIE trait (Goff & Ackerman, 1992) may reflect the fact that both open and conscientious individuals are more willing to develop skills that are beneficial for knowledge acquisition and increase their crystallized intelligence (although other parts of the shared variance among Openness, TIE, and psychometric intelligence may still be accounted for by measurement effects, notably the relationship between self and other—in this case psychometrically—estimated scores).

Bearing in mind the distinction between crystallized and fluid intelligence, it has been argued that the causal paths between personality and intelligence (at the level of latent constructs) can also follow the opposite direction—that is, representing the influence of actual intelligence on personality. This refers to the relationship between Conscientiousness (a trait associated with self-discipline, responsibility, and achievement striving) and cognitive ability, in particular Gf. Negative correlations between these constructs (see Moutafi, Furnham, & Crump, 2003; Moutafi, Furnham, & Patiel, 2005) have been interpreted in terms of the *compensatory* function of Conscientiousness. Thus, in competitive settings, conscientious individuals would compensate for their lower intellectual ability by becoming more organized, responsible, and intrinsically motivated. This implies that Conscientiousness could partly develop (i.e., increase) as a function of (low) intellectual ability. Conversely, very bright, capable individuals (with high Gf) would have little need to develop systematic, consistent, and dutiful work habits because it would somehow suffice with their high intellectual ability to excel in the real world.

In a sense, the major contribution of this book is given by our attempt to understand the relationship between personality traits and intellectual competence beyond psychometric intelligence, which is why it is important to summarize and discuss the other chapters of this book (notably chaps. 5 and 6, which referred to the relationship between personality traits and AP as well as WP, and an examination of the concept of SAI). Thus, whereas the concept of psychometric intelligence may seem a direct approach and solid measure of intellectual competence, other indicators, such as school or university performance (originally the dependent variable and criterion par excellence of individual differences in intellectual ability), should not be neglected when attempting to identify links between noncognitive and cognitive variables.

As seen in chapter 5, personality and psychometric intelligence can (and *should*) be used as different predictors of performance in academic as well as occupational settings precisely because they are extensively measures of different, distinctive individual differences (Hofstee, 2001). Thus, knowing both what a person can do and what a person typically does will increase our accuracy in her or his prediction of AP or WP. Although this may seem unsurprising, few theories (if any) have attempted to understand the possible impact of personality traits on intellectual competence in terms of AP or WP, as if psychometric intelligence were the only indicator of intellectual competence. Although it is also true that psychometric intelligence provides an excellent indication, a priori, of what a person is likely to achieve in school, university, or in the workplace, the relationship between personality traits and indicators of performance provide further evidence for the importance of nonability traits in the prediction of real-life outcomes, and how these traits may influence an individual's output as well as his or her intellectual competence.

Consistently with the links between personality and psychometric intelligence, the relationship between personality traits and AP show that Neuroticism seems to impair performance on academic as well as organizational settings, and not merely on IQ tests (although this may reflect the fact that academic assessment is based predominantly on exam situations, which are similar to an IQ testing scenario). Again, in line with the literature reviewed in chapter 4 (concerning the relationship between personality traits and psychometric intelligence), we have seen that Extraversion is modestly but significantly related to AP and WP, although dependent on the type of tasks, tests, or method of assessment. In contrast, the effects of Openness to Experience on AP and WP are consistent with investment theories and the likelihood of open individuals to score higher on IQ. As said, it is therefore likely that Openness and intellectual competence are related at the conceptual level, specifically in terms of the long-term intellectual investment (through higher creativity, intellectual curiosity, and imagination) of individuals described as open.

The strongest personality correlate of both job and scholastic achievement is undoubtedly Conscientiousness, which may suggest that, even if this personality trait would develop as a compensatory function for poor intellectual ability (Gf), its effects on real-world performance are not easily undermined. It is of little surprise that a higher sense of responsibility and dutifulness, and more organized, systematic work habits, together with higher achievement striving and intrinsic motivation, are all beneficial for performance across a variety of settings. What should be emphasized, however, is that this is a self-report assessed trait derived not from power tests, but from simple descriptive inventories. Although faking and bias due to sociably desirable responding are possible, the Conscientiousness trait is consistently related to both AP and WP. Once again, drawing on Cattell's classic distinction between Gc and Gf, it can be seen how personality traits may be differentially related to one and another type of intellectual competence. Thus, lower Gf may lead to higher Conscientiousness, which in turn may lead to higher AP or WP, such that both intelligence and personality are important for performance as well as the development of adult intellectual competence.

A third major indicator of intellectual competence, as observed throughout chapter 6 (and following the two-level conceptual framework by Chamorro-Premuzic & Furnham, 2004), is SAI—for instance, self-estimates of intellectual abilities. Increasing research in the past decade has examined the relationship between these estimates and other variables such as gender and psychometric intelligence. However, and despite that Eysenck and Eysenck (1985) conceptualized SAI as another indicator or level of intellectual ability, differential psychologists have largely ignored the possibility of looking at SAI in terms of intellectual competence. Further, the fact that SAI is assessed through self-reports—like personality— but refers to abilities—like psychometric intelligence—makes this a relevant and particularly interesting variable for understanding the relationship between personality traits and intellectual competence.

Although there has been little research into the relationship between established personality traits like the Big Five and indicators of SAI, correlational evidence has indicated that SAI are modestly related to psychometric intelligence, suggesting that (a) people may have some insight into their intellectual abilities, and/or (b) self-estimates may have self-fulfilling effects on performance (self-efficacy or high confidence may prove beneficial for an individual's performance). An alternative theoretical interpretation is simply that SAI constitute a third approach to the study of intellectual competence, and these subjective indicators of ability should be included in any overarching, comprehensive framework attempting to integrate noncognitive and cognitive individual differences. It is also possible that SAI are at least in part self-fulfilling. That is, self-perception affects whether, why, and how people complete psychometric ability tests and how they actually perform on them.

If there are individual differences not only in psychometric intelligence and AP, but also in SAI, and if these differences are stable across situation and time and are related to other, objective indicators of intellectual competence, they should be classified alongside well-established traits such as personality and the long-standing concept of psychometric intelligence. Further, SAI also reflect implicit or lay theories of intelligence, which are useful for many reasons (from generating a new research hypothesis to understanding how self-beliefs and beliefs about intellectual competence in general may shape an individual's goals and actual performance). Thus, the taxonomy of personality and intellectual competence should include SAI, and researchers should further explore how the Big Five factors of personality may relate to individual differences in SAI, expanding the scope for the relationship between personality and intellectual competence beyond psychometric intelligence and indicators of performance (such as AP and WP).

In chapter 7, we also examined the possible effects of personality traits on other real-life, individual differences such as creativity, leadership, and art judgment. The differences between these constructs and the previously examined approach are (a) the fact that these variables have not been systematically scrutinized (at least not empirically) with regard to other psychometrically established taxonomies, and (b) their relative independence, if merely theoretical, from these other established constructs. Thus, we believe that it is probably the case that individual differences in leadership and creativity, for instance, are taxonomically different from other traits. At the same time, however, we have considered the possibility that, not just personality traits (such as Extraversion and Openness), but also intellectual ability may contribute to the development of high creativity and effective leadership. Nonetheless, much of these claims are based on unrelated historical evidence (and, to a great extent, theoretically, rather than empirically, grounded), indicating that future research is deemed necessary to tackle the question of the extent to which personality and intellectual ability may be used as effective predictors of leadership, creativity, or art judgment (although ultimately most of the methodological constraints have derived from the fact that these constructs have rarely been measured reliably and validly).

To conclude, we believe that the field of individual differences has experienced a well-deserved transformation in the past 10 to 20 years based on explicit and successful attempts to establish links between what were once developing theories or instruments, but are now established concepts within scientific psychology. As in every science, it is the progressive and constructive body of evidence that allows our scientific knowledge to expand, and the relationship between theories and concepts is proving a key aspect in the evolution of differential psychology. What started as an attempt to quantify qualitative, latent characteristics of the individual has finally developed into an extensive body of evidence that not only sheds light into the most general, stable, and fundamental aspects of human mind and behavior, but also permits one to predict real-life outcomes more accurately than ever before. The research has been descriptive, then taxonomic, and then psychometric. More important, we are beginning to understand processes and mechanisms that explain the origin of individual differences. Rapid developments in genetics and neuroscience will only add to our knowledge in the area.

It is this prediction that will ultimately determine the importance not only for personality and intellectual competence, but of differential psychology and perhaps psychology in general. Even if individual differences in test performance, AP, or WP could be measured reliably, these differences would be of little interest to both the scientific and lay public unless they related to observable and meaningful acts of behavior. Thus, the aim of future individual differences research shall continue to pursue a two-fold goal—namely, the understanding of the processes and structural patterns underlying behavioral outcomes, as well as the prediction of these behavioral outcomes.

Therefore, there are important applied implications that can be drawn from this book. First, it is likely that the development of comprehensive, broad, and overarching conceptual frameworks on individual differences will improve our prediction of human behavioral outcomes (from specific experimentally observable and manipulated behaviors such as RT to very broad latent constructs such as happiness). Second, it must be said that no such framework could be justifiably considered overarching unless it includes individual differences in both personality as well as intelligence. Third, it has been noted that, because it is the broader concept of intellectual competence (which is not confined merely to psychometrically measured intelligence, but also to measures of AP and SAI) that accounts for the maximum amount of variance in individual differences underlying performance, any comprehensive conceptual model would benefit from the inclusion of several parameters or criteria to conceptualize intellectual competence. Based on these three conclusions, it can be expected that the prediction of human success and failure across a variety of settings could be improved by measuring intelligence as well as assessing personality traits. Most important, it is only after examining the significant links (at both psychometric and conceptual levels) between personality and intellectual competence that we can start having justified hopes—not only on our capacity to predict a wider spectrum of human behaviors, but also to improve our understanding of the most universal, culture-free, and general aspects of human behavior and individuality.

# References

Ackerman, P. L. (1994). Intelligence, attention, and learning: Maximal and typical performance. In D. K. Detterman (Ed.), *Current topics in human intelligence: Theories of intelligence* (pp. 1–27). Norwood: Ablex.

Ackerman, P. L. (1996). A theory of adult intellectual development: Process, personality, interests, and knowledge. *Intelligence, 22,* 227–257.

Ackerman, P. L. (1999). Traits and knowledge as determinants of learning and individual differences: Putting it all together. In P. L. Ackerman & P. Kyllonen (Eds.), *Learning and individual differences: Process, trait, and content determinants* (pp. 437–462). Atlanta: Georgia Institute of Technology.

Ackerman, P. L., & Beier, M. E. (2003). Intelligence, personality, and interests in the career choice process. *Journal of Career Assessment, 11,* 205–218.

Ackerman, P. L., & Goff, M. (1994). Typical intellectual engagement and personality: Reply to Rocklin (1994). *Journal of Educational Psychology, 86,* 150–153.

Ackerman, P. L., & Heggestad, E. D. (1997). Intelligence, personality, and interests: Evidence for overlapping traits. *Psychological Bulletin, 121,* 219–245.

Ackerman, P. L., & Rolfhus, E. L. (1999). The locus of adult intelligence: Knowledge, abilities, and non-ability traits. *Psychology and Aging, 14,* 314–330.

Adorno, T. W., Frenkel-Brunswick, E., Levinson, D. J., & Sanford, R. N. (1950). *The authoritarian personality.* New York: Harper & Row.

Alexander, W. P. (1935). Intelligence, concrete and abstract. *British Journal of Psychology, 19,* (Supplementary Monograph).

Allport, G. W., & Odbert, H. (1936). Trait-names: A psycho-lexical study. *Psychological Review Monographs, 47,* 211.

Allport, G. W., Vernon, P. E., & Lindzey, G. (1960). *Study of values.* Oxford, England: Houghton-Mifflin.

Aluja-Fabregat, A., & Torrubia-Beltri, R. (1998). Viewing of mass media violence, perception of violence, personality and academic achievement. *Personality and Individual Differences, 25,* 973–989.

Amabile, T. M. (1982). Social psychology of creativity: A consensual assessment technique. *Journal of Personality and Social Psychology, 43,* 997–1013.

Amabile, T. M. (1996). *Creativity in context*. New York: Westview.

Amelang, M., & Ullwer, U. (1991). Ansatz und Ergebnisse einer (fast) umfassenden Ueberpruefung von Eysencks Extraversionstheorie (Results of a [nearly] comprehensive study of Eysenck's extraversion theory). *Psychologische Beitrage, 33*, 23–46.

Anastasi, A. (2004). *Psychological testing* (4th ed.). New York: Macmillan.

Anderson, E. S., & Keith, T. Z. (1997). A longitudinal test of a model of academic success for at-risk high school students. *Journal of Educational Research, 90*, 259–268.

Anthony, W. (1973). The development of extraversion, of ability, and of the relation between them. *British Journal of Educational Psychology, 43*, 223–227.

Ashton, M. C., Lee, K., Vernon, P. A., & Jang, K. L. (2000). Fluid intelligence, crystallized intelligence, and the Openness/Intellect factor. *Journal of Research in Personality, 34*, 198–207.

Austin, E. J., Deary, I. J., & Gibson, G. J. (1997). Interactions between intelligence and personality: Three hypotheses tested. *Intelligence, 25*, 49–70.

Austin, E. J., Deary, I. J., Whiteman, M. C., Fowkes, F.-G. R., Pedersen, N. L., & Rabbitt, P., et al. (2002). Relationships between ability and personality: Does intelligence contribute positively to personal and social adjustment? *Personality and Individual Differences, 32*, 1391–1411.

Austin, E. J., Hofer, S. M., Deary, I. J., & Eber, H. W. (2000). Interactions between intelligence and personality: Results from two large samples. *Personality and Individual Differences, 29*, 405–427.

Azuma, H., & Kashiwagi, K. (1987). Descriptors for an intelligent person: A Japanese study. *Japan Psychological Research, 29*, 17–26.

Bachman, E. E., Sines, J. O., Watson, J. A., Laver, R. M., & Clarke, W. R. (1986). The relations between Type A behavior, clinically relevant behavior, academic achievement, and IQ in children. *Journal of Personality Assessment, 50*, 186–192.

Baddeley, A. (1968). A 3 min reasoning test based on grammatical transformation. *Psychonomic Science, 10*, 341–342.

Bandura, A. (1986). The explanatory and predictive scope of self-efficacy theory. *Journal of Social and Clinical Psychology, 4*, 359–373.

Barratt, E. (1995). History of personality and intelligence theory and research: The challenge. In D. Saklofske & M. Zeidner (Eds.), *International handbook of personality and intelligence. Perspectives on individual differences* (pp. 3–13). New York: Plenum.

Barrick, M. R., & Mount, M. K. (1991). The Big Five personality dimensions and job performance: A meta-analysis. *Personnel Psychology, 44*, 1–26.

Barrick, M. R., & Mount, M. K. (1993). Autonomy as a moderator of the relationships between the Big Five personality dimensions and job performance. *Journal of Applied Psychology, 78*, 111–118.

Barrick, M. R., Mount, M. K, & Judge, T. A. (1999). *The FFM personality dimensions and job performance: A meta-analysis of meta-analyses*. Paper presented at the 14th annual conference of the society for industrial and organizational psychology, Atlanta, GA.

Barrick, M. R., Mount, M. K., & Strauss, J. P. (1993). Conscientiousness and performance of sales representatives: Test of the mediating effects of goal setting. *Journal of Applied Psychology, 78*, 715–722.

Barrick, M. R., Stewart, G. L., Neubert, M., & Mount, M. K. (1998). Relating member ability and personality to work team processes and team effectiveness. *Journal of Applied Psychology, 83,* 377–391.

Barron, F. X. (1993). Controllable oddness as a resource in creativity. *Psychological Inquiry, 4,* 182–184.

Bartram, D., & Dale, H. C. A. (1982). The Eysenck Personality Inventory as a selection test for military pilots. *Journal of Occupational Psychology, 55,* 287–296.

Beech, A., & Williams, L. (1997). Investigating cognitive processes in schizotypal personality and schizophrenia. In G. Matthews (Ed.), *Cognitive science perspectives on personality and emotion* (pp. 475–502). London: Elsevier Science.

Beloff, J. (1992). The research with B. D.: A reply to George Hansen. *Journal of Parapsychology, 56,* 363–365.

Bempechat, J., London, P., & Dweck, C. S. (1991). Children's conceptions of ability in major domains: An interview and experimental study. *Child Study Journal, 21,* 11–36.

Bennett, M. (1996). Men's and women's self-estimates of intelligence. *Journal of Social Psychology, 136,* 411–412.

Bennett, M. (1997). Self-estimates of ability in men and women. *Journal of Social Psychology, 137,* 540–541.

Bennett, M. (2000). Gender differences in the self-estimates of ability. *Australian Journal of Psychology, 52,* 23–28.

Berg, C., & Sternberg, R. (1985). Response to novelty: Continuity versus discontinuity in the developmental course of intelligence. In H. Reese (Ed.), *Advances in child development and behaviour* (Vol. 19, pp. 2–47). New York: Academic Press.

Beyer, S. (1990). Gender differences in the accuracy of self-evaluations of performance. *Journal of Personality and Social Psychology, 59,* 960–970.

Beyer, S. (1998). Gender differences in self-perception and negative recall biases. *Sex Roles, 38,* 103–133.

Beyer, S. (1999). The accuracy of academic gender stereotypes. *Sex Roles, 40,* 787–813.

Beyer, S., & Bowden, E. (1999). Gender differences in self-perceptions. *Personality and Social Psychology Bulletin, 23,* 157–171.

Binet, A. (1903). *L'etude experimentale de l'intelligence (Experimental study of intelligence).* Paris: Schleicher.

Binet, A., & Simon, T. (1961a). Methodes nouvelles pour le diagnostique du niveau intellectuel des anormaux (New methods for the diagnosis of the intellectual levels of subnormals) (E. S. Kite, Trans). In J. J. Jenkins & D. G. Paterson (Reprint Eds.), *Studies in individual differences: The search for intelligence* (pp. 90–96). New York: Appleton-Century-Croft. (Original publication 1905)

Binet, A., & Simon, T. (1961b). The development of intelligence in the child (E. S. Kite, Trans.). In J. J. Jenkins & D. G. Paterson (Reprint Eds.), *Studies in individual differences: The search for intelligence* (pp. 96–111). New York: Appleton-Century-Croft. (Original publication 1908)

Binet, A., & Simon, T. (1961c). Upon the necessity of establishing a scientific diagnosis of interior states of intelligence. In J. J. Jenkins & D. G. Paterson (Eds.), *Studies in individual differences: The search for intelligence* (pp. 81–90). East Norwalk, CT: Appleton-Century-Croft. (Original publication 1908)

Birenbaum, M., & Montag, I. (1989). Style and substance in social desirability scales. *European Journal of Personality, 3,* 47–59.

Blickle, G. (1996). Personality traits, learning strategies, and performance. *European Journal of Personality, 10*, 337–352.

Block, J. (1977). Advancing the psychology of personality: Paradigmatic shift or improving the quality of research? In D. Magnusson & N. S. Endler (Eds.), *Personality at the crossroads: Current issues in interactional psychology* (pp. 37–63). Hillsdale: NJ: Lawrence Erlbaum Associates.

Boekaerts, M. (1995). Self-regulated learning: Bridging the gap between metacognitive and metamotivation theories. *Educational Psychologist, 30*, 195–200.

Boekaerts, M. (1996). Self-regulated learning at the junction of cognition and motivation. *European Psychologist, 1*, 100–112.

Boring, E. G. (1923, June 6). Intelligence as the tests test it. *New Republic*, pp. 35–37.

Borkenau, P. (1988). The multiple classification of acts and the Big Five factors of personality. *Journal of Research in Personality, 22*, 337–352.

Borkenau, P., & Liebler, A. (1993). Convergence of stranger ratings of personality and intelligence with self-ratings, partner-ratings and measured intelligence. *Journal of Personality and Social Psychology, 65*, 546–553.

Borkenau, P., & Ostendorf, F. (1993). *NEO-Fünf-Faktoren-Inventar (NEO-FFI) nach Costa und McCrae (NEO-Five-Factor Inventory according to Costa and McCrae).* Göttingen (Germany): Hogrefe.

Borman, W. C., White, L. A., & Dorsey, D. W. (1995). Effects of ratee task performance and interpersonal factors on supervisor and peer performance ratings. *Journal of Applied Psychology, 80*, 168–177.

Boudreau, J. W., Boswell, W. R., & Judge, T. A. (2001). Effects of personality on executive career success in the United States and Europe. *Journal of Vocational Behavior, 58*, 53–81.

Boyle, G. J. (1983). Effects on academic learning of manipulating emotional states and motivational dynamics. *British Journal of Educational Psychology, 53*, 347–357.

Boyle, G. J. (1990). Stanford-Binet IV Intelligence Scale: Is its structure supported by LISREL congeneric factor analyses? *Personality and Individual Differences, 11*, 1175–1181.

Brand, C. R. (1994). Open to experience-closed to intelligence: Why the "Big Five" are really the "Comprehensive Six." *European Journal of Personality, 8*, 299–310.

Brand, C. R., Egan, V., & Deary, I. (1993). Intelligence, personality and society: "Constructivist" versus "essentialist" possibilities. In D. K. Determan (Ed.), *Current topics in human intelligence* (pp. 29–42). Norwood: Ablex.

Bridgeman, B. (1974). Effects of test score feedback on immediately subsequent test performance. *Journal of Educational Psychology, 66*, 62–66.

Bright, I. J. (1930). *A study of the correlation obtaining between academic and citizenship grades and between academic grades and intelligence quotiens.* Oxford: Leavenworth Public Schools.

Brody, N. (1988). *Personality: In search of individuality.* San Diego: Academic Press.

Brody, N. (1992). *Intelligence* (2nd ed.). San Diego: Academic Press.

Brody, N. (2000). History of theories and measurements of intelligence. In R. J. Sternberg (Ed.), *Handbook of intelligence* (pp. 16–33). New York: Cambridge University Press.

Brooks, A., Fulker, D. W., & De Fries, J. C. (1990). Reading performance and general cognitive ability: A multivariate genetic analysis of twin data. *Personality and Individual Differences, 11*, 141–146.

Bryan, A. (1942). Grades, intelligence and personality of art school freshmen. *Journal of Educational Psychology, 33,* 50–64.

Burkhart, R. (1958). The relation of intelligence to art ability. *Journal of Aesthetic and Art Criticism, 14,* 230–241.

Burns, E. (1982). Psychometric deficiencies of the short form version of the Northwestern Syntax Screening Test. *Journal of Speech and Hearing Disorders, 47,* 331–333.

Burt, C. (1933). The psychology of art. In *How the mind works.* London: Allen & Unwin.

Burtt, H. E., & Arps, G. F. (1943). Correlation of Army Alpha Intelligence Test with academic grades in high schools and military academies. *Journal of Applied Psychology, 4,* 289–293.

Busato, V. V., Prins, F. J., Elshout, J. J., & Hamaker, C. (1999). The relation between learning styles, the Big Five personality traits and achievement motivation in higher education. *Personality and Individual Differences, 26,* 129–140.

Busato, V. V., Prins, F. J., Elshout, J. J., & Hamaker, C. (2000). Intellectual ability, learning style, achievement motivation and academic success of psychology students in higher education. *Personality and Individual Differences, 29,* 1057–1068.

Byravan, A., & Ramanaiah, N. V. (1995). Structure of the 16 PF fifth edition from the perspective of the five-factor model. *Psychological Reports, 76,* 555–560.

Byrd, M., & Stacey, B. (1993). Bias in IQ perception. *The Psychologist, 6,* 16.

Byrd, M., & Stacey, B. (1994). Estimation of parental IQ. *Psychological Reports, 75,* 89–90.

Callard, M. P., & Goodfellow, L. L. (1962). Three experiments using the Junior Maudsley Personality Inventory. Neuroticism and Extraversion in school boys as measured by JEPI. *British Journal of Educational Psychology, 32,* 241–251.

Campbell, J. (1990). Modelling the performance prediction problem in industrial and organizational psychology. In M. Dunette & L. Hough (Eds.), *Handbook of industrial and organizational psychology* (pp. 687–732). Palo Alto: Consulting Psychologists Press.

Carroll, H. A. (1932). A preliminary report on a study of the relationship between ability in art and certain personality traits. *School and Society, 36,* 285–288.

Carroll, H. A. (1933). What do the Meier-Seashore and McAdory Art tests measure? *Journal of Educational Research, 26,* 661–665.

Carroll, J. B. (1993). *Human cognitive abilities: A survey of factor-analytic studies.* New York: Cambridge University Press.

Caspi, A., Elder, G. H., & Bem, D. J. (1988). Moving away from the world: Life-course patterns of shy children. *Developmental Psychology, 24,* 824–831.

Cattell, J. M. (1890). Mental tests and measurements. *Mind, 15,* 373–381.

Cattell, R. B. (1946). Personality structure and measurement: I. The operational determination of trait unities. *British Journal of Psychology, 36,* 88–103.

Cattell, R. B. (1957). *Personality and motivation structure and measurement.* Oxford, England: World Book.

Cattell, R. B. (1971). *Abilities: Their structure, growth, and action.* Boston: Houghton-Mifflin.

Cattell, R. B. (1973). *Personality and mood by questionnaire.* New York: Jossey-Bass.

Cattell, R. B. (1978). Matched determiners vs. factor invariance: A reply to Korth. *Multivariate Behavioral Research, 13,* 431–448.

Cattell, R. B. (1987). *Intelligence: Its structure, growth and action.* New York: Springer.

Cattell, R. B., Eber, H. W., & Tatsuoka, N. M. (1970). *Handbook for the 16 Personality Factor Questionnaire (16PF).* Champaign, IL: Institute for Personality and Ability Testing.

Cattell, R. B., & Kline, P. (1977). *The scientific analysis of personality and motivation.* New York: Academic Press.

Chamorro-Premuzic, T., & Furnham, A. (2002). Neuroticism and "special treatment" in examinations. *Social Behaviour and Personality, 30,* 807–813.

Chamorro-Premuzic, T., & Furnham, A. (2003a). Personality predicts academic performance: Evidence from two longitudinal studies on British University students. *Journal of Research in Personality, 37,* 319–338.

Chamorro-Premuzic, T., & Furnham, A. (2003b). Personality traits and academic exam performance. *European Journal of Personality, 17,* 237–250.

Chamorro-Premuzic, T., & Furnham, A. (2004). A possible model to understand the personality-intelligence interface. *British Journal of Psychology, 95,* 145–160.

Chamorro-Premuzic, T., & Furnham, A. (in press). Art judgement: A measure of personality and intelligence? *Imagination, Cognition and Personality.*

Chamorro-Premuzic, T., Furnham, A., & Moutafi, J. (2004). The relationship between estimated and psychometric personality and intelligence scores. *Journal of Research in Personality, 38*(5), 505–513.

Chen, M., Holman, J., Francis-Jones, N., & Burmester, L. (1988). Conceptions of intelligence of primary school, high school and college student. *British Journal of Developmental Psychology, 6,* 71–82.

Cherny, S. S., & Cardon, L. R. (1994). General cognitive ability. In J. C. DeFries, R. Plomin, & D. W. Fulker (Eds.), *Nature and nurture during middle childhood* (pp. 46–56). Malden, MA: Blackwell.

Child, D. (1964). The relationships between introversion-extraversion, neuroticism and performance in school examinations. *British Journal of Educational Psychology, 34,* 187–196.

Child, I. (1965). Personality correlates of esthetic judgment in college students. *Journal of Personality, 33,* 476–511.

Christie, R. (1954). Authoritarianism re-examined. In R. Christie & M. Jahoda (Eds.), *Studies in the scope and method of "the authoritarian personality."* New York: The Free Press.

Claridge, G. (1983). Schizophrenia and lateralization of galvanic skin response. *British Journal of Psychiatry, 142,* 425–426.

Cloninger, C. R. (1987). A systematic method for clinical description and classification of personality variants: A proposal. *Archives of General Psychiatry, 44,* 573–588.

Coan, R. W. (1974). *The optimal personality.* New York: Columbia University Press.

Cohen, D., & Strayer, J. (1996). Empathy in conduct-disordered and comparison youth. *Developmental Psychology, 32,* 988–998.

Cohen, J. (1977). *Statistical power analysis for the behavioural sciences.* New York: Academic.

Cohen, J. (1988). *Statistical power analysis for the behavioural sciences* (2nd ed.). Hillsdale, NJ: Lawrence Erlbaum Associates.

Cooper, C. (1998). *Individual differences.* London: Arnold.

Cooper, R., & Payne, R. (1967). Extraversion and some aspects of work behavior. *Personnel Psychology, 20,* 45–57.

Corcoran, D. W. (1965). Personality and the inverted-U relation. *British Journal of Psychology, 56,* 267–273.

Costa, P. T., Jr. (1997, July 19–23). *The five factor model as a universal passport to understanding personality.* Presidential address at the 8th biennial meeting of the International Society for the Study of Individual Differences, Aarhus, Denmark.

Costa, P. T., Jr., & McCrae, R. R. (1976). Age differences in personality structure: A cluster analytic approach. *Journal of Gerontology, 31,* 564–570.

Costa, P. T., Jr., & McCrae, R. R. (1978). Objective personality assessment. In M. Storandt, I. C. Siegler, & M. F. Elias (Eds.), *The clinical psychology of aging* (pp. 119–143). New York: Plenum.

Costa, P. T., Jr., & McCrae, R. R. (1980). Influence of extraversion and neuroticism on subjective well-being: Happy and unhappy people. *Journal of Personality and Social Psychology, 38,* 668–678.

Costa, P. T., Jr., & McCrae, R. R. (1985). *NEO Personality Inventory Manual.* Odessa, FL: Psychological Assessment Resources.

Costa, P. T., Jr., & McCrae, R. R. (1988). Personality in adulthood: A six-year longitudinal study of self-report and spouse ratings on the NEO Personality Inventory. *Journal of Personality and Social Psychology, 54,* 853–863.

Costa, P. T., Jr., & McCrae, R. R. (1989). *NEO-PI/FFI Manual Supplement.* Odessa, FL: Psychological Assessment Resources.

Costa, P. T., Jr., & McCrae, R. R. (1991). *The NEO Five Factor Inventory: Form S.* Odessa, FL: Psychological Assessment Resources.

Costa, P. T., Jr., & McCrae, R. R. (1992). *Revised NEO Personality Inventory (NEO-PI-R) and NEO Five-factor Inventory (NEO-FFI): Professional Manual.* Odessa, FL: Psychological Assessment Resources.

Craik, K. H., Ware, A. P., Kamp, J. O., O'Reilly, C., Staw, B., & Zedeck, S. (2002). Explorations of construct validity in a combined managerial and personality assessment programme. *Journal of Occupational and Organizational Psychology, 75,* 171–193.

Crawford, J. D., & Stankov, L. (1996). Age differences in the realism of confidence judgements: A calibration study using tests of fluid and crystallized intelligence. *Learning and Individual Differences, 8,* 83–103.

Crocker, A., & Cheeseman, R. (1988). The ability of young children to rank themselves for academic ability. *Educational Studies, 14,* 105–110.

Cronbach, L. J. (1984). *Essentials of psychological testing* (4th ed.). New York: Harper & Row.

Cronbach, L. J. (1989). Construct validation after thirty years. In L. L. Robert (Ed.), *Intelligence: Measurement, theory, and public policy: Proceedings of a symposium in honor of Lloyd G. Humphreys* (pp. 147–171). Champaign, IL: University of Illinois Press.

Darke, S. (1988). Anxiety and working memory capacity. *Cognition and Emotion, 2,* 145–154.

Davidson, J. E., & Downing, C. L. (2000). Contemporary models of intelligence. In R. J. Sternberg (Ed.), *Handbook of intelligence* (pp. 34–49). New York: Cambridge University Press.

Davies, M., Stankov, L., & Roberts, R. (1998). Emotional intelligence: In search of an elusive construct. *Journal of Personality and Social Psychology, 75,* 989–1015.

Deary, I. J. (1986). Inspection time: Discovery or rediscovery? *Personality and Individual Differences, 7,* 625–631.

Deary, I. J. (1994). Intelligence and auditory discrimination: Separating processing speed and fidelity of stimulus representation. *Intelligence, 18,* 189–213.

Deary, I. J. (2001). *Intelligence: A very short introduction.* Oxford: Oxford University Press.

Deary, I. J., & Matthews, G. (1993). Personality traits are alive and well. *The Psychologist, 6,* 299–308.

De Barbenza, C. M., & Montoya, O. A. (1974). Academic achievement in relation to personality characteristics in university students. *Revista Latinoamericana de Psicologia, 6,* 331–340.

De Fruyt, F., & Mervielde, I. (1996). Personality and interests as predictors of streaming and achievement. *European Journal of Personality, 10,* 405–425.

De Nisi, A., & Shaw, J. (1977). Investigation of the uses of self-reports of ability. *Journal of Applied Psychology, 62,* 641–644.

De Raad, B. (1996). Personality traits in learning and education. *European Journal of Personality, 10,* 185–200.

De Raad, B., & Schowenburg, H. (1996). Personality in learning and education: A review. *European Journal of Personality, 10,* 303–336.

Digman, J. (1990). Personality structure: Emergence of the five-factor model. *Annual Review of Psychology, 41,* 417–440.

Digman, J. M., & Inouye, J. (1986). Further specification of the five robust factors of personality. *Journal of Personality and Social Psychology, 50,* 116–123.

Dobson, P. (2000). An investigation into the relationship between neuroticism, extraversion and cognitive test performance in selection. *International Journal of Selection and Assessment, 8,* 99–109.

Dollinger, S. J., & Clancy, S. M. (1993). Identity self, and personality: II. Glimpses through the autophotographic eye. *Journal of Personality and Social Psychology, 64,* 1064–1071.

Domino, G. (1970). Identification of potentially creative persons from the Adjective Check List. *Journal of Consulting and Clinical Psychology, 35,* 48–51.

Domino, G. (1974). Assessment of cinematographic creativity. *Journal of Personality and Social Psychology, 64,* 1064–1071.

Driskell, J. E., Hogan, J., Salas, E., & Hoskins, B. (1994). Cognitive and personality predictors of individual performance. *Military Psychology, 6,* 31–46.

Dweck, C. S. (1986). Motivational processes affecting learning. *American Psychologist, 41,* 1040–1048.

Dweck, C., & Elliot, E. (1983). Achievement motivation. In P. Mussen & E. Hetherington (Eds.), *Handbook of child psychology* (Vol. 4, pp. 643–691). New York: Wiley.

Ebbinghaus, H. (1897). Uiber eine neue Methode zur Pruifung geistiger Faehigkeiten und ihre Anwendungen bei Schulkindern [On a new method for testing mental abilities and its application to school children]. *Zeitschrift fuir angewandte Psychologie, 13,* 401–459.

Edwards, A. L. (1959). *Edwards Personal Preference Schedule (2nd ed.).* Oxford, England: Psychological Corporation.

Elshout, J., & Veenman, M. (1992). Relation between intellectual ability and working method as predictors of learning. *Journal of Educational Research, 85,* 134–143.

Entwistle, N. (1972). Personality and academic attainment. *British Journal of Educational Psychology, 42,* 137–151.

Entwistle, N., & Entwistle, D. (1970). The relationships between personality, study methods and academic performance. *British Journal of Educational Psychology, 40,* 132–143.

Eurich, A. C., & Carroll, H. A. (1931). Group differences in art judgement. *School and Society, 34,* 204–206.

Eysenck, H. J. (1947). *Dimensions of personality.* New York: Praeger.

Eysenck, H. J. (1952) *The scientific study of personality.* London: Routledge & Kegan Paul.

Eysenck, H. J. (1957). *The dynamics of anxiety and hysteria.* London: Routledge & Kegan Paul.

Eysenck, H. J. (1960). *Maudsley Personality Inventory.* London: Maudsley Hospital.

Eysenck, H. J. (1967). *The biological basis of personality.* Springfield, IL: Thomas.

Eysenck, H. J. (1967a). Factor analytic study of the Maitland Graves Design Judgement Test. *Perceptual and Motor Skills, 24,* 13–14.

Eysenck, H. J. (1967b). Personality patterns in various groups of businessmen. *Occupational Psychology, 41,* 249–250.

Eysenck, H. J. (1970). An application of the Maitland Graves Design Judgement Test to professional artists. *Perceptual and Motor Skills, 30,* 584–590.

Eysenck, H. J. (1971). Relationship between intelligence and personality. *Perceptual and Motor Skills, 32,* 637–638.

Eysenck, H. J. (1972). Preference judgements for polygons, designs, and drawings. *Perceptual and Motor Skills, 34,* 396–398.

Eysenck, H. J. (1977). Psychosis and psychoticism: A reply to Bishop. *Journal of Abnormal Psychology, 86,* 427–430.

Eysenck, H. J. (1979). *The structure and measurement of intelligence.* Berlin: Springer-Verlag.

Eysenck, H. J. (1981a). *Know your own IQ.* Harmondsworth: Penguin.

Eysenck, H. J. (1981b). Psychoticism as a dimension of personality: A reply to Kasielke. *Zeitschtrift fuir Psychologie, 189,* 381–386.

Eysenck, H. J. (1982). The biological basis of cross-cultural differences in personality: Blood group antigens. *Psychological Reports, 51,* 531–540.

Eysenck, H. J. (1986). Intelligence: The new look. *Psychologische Beitraege, 28,* 332–365.

Eysenck, H. J. (1991). Dimensions of personality: 16, 5 or 3? Criteria for a taxonomic paradigm. *Personality and Individual Differences, 12,* 773–790.

Eysenck, H. J. (1992a). A reply to Costa and McCrae: P or A and C—the role of theory. *Personality and Individual Differences, 13,* 867–868.

Eysenck, H. J. (1992b). The definition and measurement of psychoticism. *Personality and Individual Differences, 13,* 757–785.

Eysenck, H. J. (1992c). The psychology of personality and aesthetics. In S. Van Toller & G. Dodd (Eds.), *Fragrance: The psychology and biology of perfume* (pp. 7–26). New York: Ebemer.

Eysenck, H. J. (1993). Creativity and personality: A theoretical perspective. *Psychological Inquiry, 4,* 147–246.

Eysenck, H. J. (1994a). Personality and intelligence: Psychometric and experimental approaches. In R. J. Sternberg & P. Ruzgis (Eds.), *Personality and intelligence* (pp. 23–31). Cambridge: Cambridge University Press.

Eysenck, H. J. (1994b). The Big Five or giant three: Criteria for a paradigm. In C. Halverson & G. Kohnstamm (Eds.), *The developing structure of temperament and personality from infancy to adulthood* (37–51). Hillsdale, NJ: Lawrence Erlbaum Associates.

Eysenck, H. J. (1995a). Can we study intelligence using the experimental method? *Intelligence, 20,* 217–228.

Eysenck, H. J. (1995b). Creativity as a product of intelligence and personality. In D. Saklofske & M. Zeidner (Eds.), *International handbook of personality and intelligence. Perspectives on individual differences* (pp. 231–247). New York: Plenum.

Eysenck, H. J., & Cookson, D. (1969). Personality in primary school children—ability and achievement. *British Journal of Educational Psychology, 39,* 109–130.

Eysenck, H. J., & Eysenck, M. W. (1985). *Personality and individual differences: A natural science approach.* New York: Plenum.

Eysenck, H. J., & Eysenck, S. B. G. (1967). On the unitary nature of Extraversion. *Acta Psychologica, 26,* 383–390.

Eysenck, H. J., & Eysenck, S. B. G. (1975). *Manual of the Eysenck Personality Questionnaire.* London: Hodder & Stoughton.

Eysenck, H. J., & Eysenck, S. B. G. (1976). *Psychoticism as a dimension of personality.* London: Hodder & Stoughton.

Eysenck, H. J., & Eysenck, S. B. G. (1991). *Manual of the Eysenck Personality Scales (EPQ Adults).* London: Hodder & Stoughton.

Eysenck, H. J., & Furnham, A. (1993). Personality and the Barron-Welsh Art Scale. *Perceptual and Motor Skills, 76,* 837–838.

Eysenck, M. W. (1982). *Attention and arousal: Cognition and performance.* New York: Springer.

Farnsworth, P., & Misumi, I. (1931). Notes on the Meier-Seashore art judgment test. *Journal of Applied Psychology, 15,* 418–420.

Farsides, T., & Woodfield, R. (2003). Individual differences and undergraduate academic success: The role of personality, intelligence and application. *Personality and Individual Differences, 34,* 1225–1243

Feist, G. J. (1998). A meta-analysis of the impact of personality on scientific and artistic creativity. *Personality and Social Psychological Review, 2,* 290–309.

Feist, G. J. (1999). Influence of personality on artistic and scientific creativity. In R. J. Sternberg (Ed.), *Handbook of Creativity* (pp. 273–296). Cambridge, England: Cambridge University Press.

Feist, G. J., & Barron, F. X. (2003). Predicting creativity from early to late adulthood: Intellect, potential, and personality. *Journal of Research in Personality, 37,* 62–88.

Ferguson, E., & Patterson, E. (1998). The five factor model of personality: Openness a distinct but related construct. *Personality and Individual Differences, 24,* 789–796.

Fergusson, D. M., Lynskey, M. T., & Horwood, L. J. (1995). Truancy in adolescence. *New Zealand Journal of Educational Studies, 30,* 25–37.

Fletcher, C. (1991). Personality tests: The great debate. *Personnel Management, 23,* 38–42.

Flett, G. L., Hewitt, P. L., Blankstein, K. R., & Gray, L. (1998). Psychological distress and the frequency of perfectionistic thinking. *Journal of Social Psychology and Personality, 75,* 1363–1381.

Flugel, J. C. (1947). An inquiry as to popular views on intelligence and related topics. *British Journal of Educational Psychology, 17,* 140–152.

Flynn, J. R. (1987). Massive IQ gains in 14 nations: What IQ tests really measure. *Psychological Bulletin, 101,* 171–191.

Fry, P. (1984). Teachers conceptions of students intelligence and intelligent functioning. In P. Fry (Ed.), *Changing conceptions of intelligence and intellectual functioning: Current theory and research* (pp. 157–174). New York: North-Holland.

Furnham, A. (1992a). Personality and learning style: A study of three instruments. *Personality and Individual Differences, 13,* 429–438.

Furnham, A. (1992b). *Personality at work: The role of individual differences in the work place.* London: Routledge.

Furnham, A. (1994). *Personality at work.* London: Routledge.

Furnham, A. (1995). The relationship of personality and intelligence to cognitive thinking style and achievement. In D. Saklofske & M. Zeidner (Eds.), *International handbook of personality and intelligence. Perspectives on individual differences* (pp. 397–413). New York: Plenum.

Furnham, A. (1996a). The big five versus the big four: The relationship between the Myers-Briggs Type Indicator (MBTI) and NEO-PI five-factor model of personality. *Personality and Individual Differences, 21,* 303–307.

Furnham, A. (1996b). The FIRO-B, the Learning Style Questionnaire, and the five-factor model. *Journal of Social Behavior and Personality, 11,* 285–299.

Furnham, A. (1997). Knowing and faking one's five-factor personality scores. *Journal of Personality Assessment, 69,* 229–243.

Furnham, A. (1999). Personality and creativity. *Perceptual and Motor Skills, 88,* 407–408.

Furnham, A. (2000a). *Management competency frameworks.* London: CRF.

Furnham, A. (2000b). Parents' estimates of their own and their children's multiple intelligences. *British Journal of Developmental Psychology, 18,* 583–594.

Furnham, A. (2001a). Test taking style, personality traits and psychometric validity. In S. Messick & J. Collins (Eds.), *Intelligence and personality: Bridging the gap on theory and measurement* (pp. 289–304). Mahwah, NJ: Lawrence Erlbaum Associates.

Furnham, A. (2001b). Self-estimates of intelligence: Culture and gender difference in self and other estimates of both general (g) and multiple intelligences. *Personality and Individual Differences, 31,* 1381–1405.

Furnham, A., & Baguma, P. (1999). Self-estimates of intelligence: A cross-cultural study from three continents. *North American Journal of Psychology, 1,* 69–78.

Furnham, A., & Chamorro-Premuzic, T. (2004a). Estimating one's own personality and intelligence scores. *British Journal of Psychology, 95,* 145–160.

Furnham, A., & Chamorro-Premuzic, T. (2004b). Personality, psychometric intelligence, and art judgement. *Personality and Individual Differences, 36,* 705–715.

Furnham, A., & Chamorro-Premuzic, T. (2004c). Personality and intelligence as predictors of statistics examination grades. *Personality and Individual Differences, 37,* 943–955.

Furnham, A., & Chamorro-Premuzic, T. (in press). Individual differences and beliefs underlying preferences for assessment methods at university. *Journal of Social Applied Psychology.*

Furnham, A., Chamorro-Premuzic, T., & McDougall, F. (2003). Personality, cognitive ability, and beliefs about intelligence as predictors of academic performance. *Learning and Individual Differences, 14,* 47–64.

Furnham, A., Chamorro-Premuzic, T., & Moutafi, J. (in press). Personality and intelligence: Gender, the Big Five, self-estimated and psychometric intelligence. *International Journal of Selection and Assessment.*

Furnham, A., Clark, K., & Bailey, K. (1999). Sex differences in estimates of multiple intelligences. *European Journal of Personality, 13,* 247–259.

Furnham, A., Fong, G., & Martin, N. (1999). Sex and cross-cultural differences in the estimated multifaceted intelligence quotient score for self, parents and siblings. *Personality and Individual Differences, 26,* 1025–1034.

Furnham, A., Forde, L., & Cotter, T. (1998a). Personality and intelligence. *Personality and Individual Differences, 24,* 187–192.

Furnham, A., Forde, L., & Cotter, T. (1998b). Personality scores and test taking style. *Personality and Individual Differences, 24,* 19–23.

Furnham, A., & Gasson, L. (1998). Sex differences in parental estimates of their children's intelligence. *Sex Roles, 38,* 151–162.

Furnham, A., Dixon, D., Harrison, T., & O'Connor, R. C. (2000). Sex, social class, and estimated IQ. *Psychology Reports, 87,* 753–758.

Furnham, A., Hosoe, T., & Tang, T. (2002). Male hubris and female humility? A cross-cultural study of ratings of self, parental and sibling multiple intelligence in America, Britain, and Japan. *Intelligence, 30*(1), 101–115.

Furnham, A., Kidwai, A., & Thomas, C. (2001). Personality, psychometric intelligence and self-estimated intelligence. *Journal of Social Behavior and Personality, 16,* 97–114.

Furnham, A., & Medhurst, S. (1995). Personality correlates of academic seminar behavior: A study of four instruments. *Personality and Individual Differences, 19,* 197–208.

Furnham, A., & Mitchell, J. (1991). Personality, needs, social skills and academic achievement: A longitudinal study. *Personality and Individual Differences, 12,* 1067–1073.

Furnham, A., Rakow, T., & Mak, T. (2003). The determinants of parents' beliefs about intelligence of their children: A study from Hong Kong. *International Journal of Psychology, 37,* 343–352.

Furnham, A., Rakow, T., Sarmany-Schiller, I., & De Fruyt, F. (1999). European differences in self-perceived multiple intelligences. *European Psychologist, 4,* 131–138.

Furnham, A., & Rao, S. (2002). Personality and the aesthetic of composition: A study on Mondrian and Hirst. *North American Journal of Psychology, 4,* 234–242.

Furnham, A., & Rawles, R. (1995). Sex differences in the estimation of intelligence. *Journal of Social Behavior and Personality, 10,* 741–745.

Furnham, A., & Rawles, R. (1999). Correlations between self-estimated and psychometrically measured IQ. *Journal of Social Psychology, 139,* 405–410.

Furnham, A., Reeves, E., & Budhani, S. (2002, March). Parents think their sons are brighter than their daughters: Sex differences in parental self-examinations and estimations of their children's multiple intelligences. *Journal of Genetic Psychology, 163*(1), 24–50.

Furnham, A., Shahidi, S., & Baluch, B. (2003). Sex and culture differences in self-perceived and family estimated multiple intelligences: A British-Iranian comparison. *Journal of Cross-Cultural Psychology, 33,* 270–285.

Furnham, A., & Walker, J. (2001). Personality and judgement of abstract, pop art, and representational paintings. *European Journal of Personality, 15,* 57–72.

Furnham, A., & Ward, C. (2001). Sex differences, test experience and the self-estimation of multiple intelligences. *New Zealand Journal of Psychology, 30,* 52–59.

Furnham, A., & Zacherl, M. (1986). Personality and job satisfaction. *Personality and Individual Differences, 7,* 453–459.

Gabriel, M. T., Critelli, J. W., & Ee, J. S. (1994). Narcissistic illusions in self-evaluations of intelligence and attractiveness. *Journal of Personality, 62,* 143–155.

Gagne, F., & St. Pere, F. (2001). When IQ is controlled, does motivation still predict achievement? *Intelligence, 30,* 71–100.

Galton, F. (1883). *An inquiry into human ability.* London: Macmillan.

Gardner, H. (1983). *Frames of mind: The theory of multiple intelligences.* New York: Basic Books.

Gardner, H. (1993a). *Creating minds.* New York: Basic Books.

Gardner, H. (1993b). *Multiple intelligences: The theory in practice.* New York: Basic Books.

Gardner, H. (1999c). *Intelligence re-framed: Multiple intelligences for the 21st century.* New York: Basic Books.

Geen, R. G. (1985). Test anxiety and visual vigilance. *Journal of Personality and Social Psychology, 49,* 963–970.

Geisler-Brenstein, E., & Schmeck, R. (1996). The revised Inventory of Learning Processes: A multifaceted perspective on individual differences in learning. In M. Birenbaum & F. Dochy (Eds.), *Alternatives in assessment of achievements, learning processes and prior knowledge. Evaluation in education and human services* (pp. 283–317). New York: Kluwer Academic.

George, J. M., & Zhou, J. (2001). When openness to experience and conscientiousness are related to creative behavior: An interactional approach. *Journal of Applied Psychology, 86,* 513–524.

Getzels, J. W., & Jackson, P. W. (1962). *Creativity and intelligence: Explorations with gifted students.* Oxford, England: Wiley.

Gill, R., & Keats, D. (1980). Elements of intellectual competence: Judgements by Australian and Malay university students. *Journal of Cross Cultural Psychology, 11,* 233–243.

Ginton, A., Urca, G., & Lubow, R. E. (1975). The effects of preexposure to non-attended stimulus on subsequent learning: Latent inhibition in adults. *Bulletin of the Psychonomic Society, 5,* 5–8.

Goff, M., & Ackerman, P. L. (1992). Personality-intelligence relations: Assessment of typical intellectual engagement. *Journal of Educational Psychology, 84,* 537–553.

Goh, D., & Moore, C. (1987). Personality and academic achievement in three educational levels. *Psychological Report, 43,* 71–79.

Goldberg, L. R. (1982). From ace to zombie: Some explorations in the language of personality. In C. D. Spielberger & J. N. Butcher (Eds.), *Advances in personality assessment* (Vol. 1, pp. 203–234). Hillsdale, NJ: Lawrence Erlbaum Associates.

Goldberg, L. R. (1990). An alternative "description of personality": The Big-Five factor structure. *Journal of Personality and Social Psychology, 59,* 1216–1229.

Goldberg, L. R. (1994). Resolving a scientific embarrassment: A comment on the articles in this special issue. *European Journal of Personality, 8,* 351–356.

Goleman, D. (1996). *Emotional intelligence*. London: Bloomsbury.

Goodnow, J. (1980). Everyday concepts of intelligence and its development. In N. Warren (Ed.), *Studies in cross-cultural psychology* (Vol. 2, pp. 191–219). London: Academic Press.

Gottfredson, L. (1996). What do we know about intelligence? *The American Scholar, Winter*, pp. 15–30.

Gottfredson, L. S. (1997). Why g matters: The complexity of everyday life. *Intelligence, 24*, 79–132.

Gottfredson, L. S. (2000). Skills gaps, not tests, make racial proportionality impossible. *Psychology, Public Policy, and Law, 6*, 129–143.

Gottfredson, L. S. (2002). Where and why g matters: Not a mystery. *Human Performance, 15*, 25–46.

Götz, K. O., & Götz, K. (1973). Introversion-extraversion and neuroticism in gifted and ungifted art students. *Perceptual and Motor Skills, 36*, 675–678

Götz, K. O., & Götz, K. (1974). The Maitland Graves Design Judgement Test judged by 22. *Perceptual and Motor Skills, 39*, 261–262.

Götz, K. O., & Götz, K. (1979a). Personality characteristics of professional artists. *Perceptual and Motor Skills, 49*, 327–334

Götz, K. O., & Götz, K. (1979b). Personality characteristics of successful artists. *Perceptual and Motor Skills, 49*, 919–924.

Gough, H. G. (1957). *Manual for the California Psychological Inventory*. Palo Alto, CA: Consulting Psychology Press.

Gough, H. G. (1976). Studying creativity by means of association tests. *Journal of Applied Psychology, 61*, 348–353.

Gough, H. G. (1979). A creative personality scale for the Adjective Check List. *Journal of Personality and Social Psychology, 37*, 1398–1405.

Graves, M. (1948). *Design Judgement Test*. San Antonio, TX: Psychological Corporation.

Grigorenko, E. L. (2000). Heritability and intelligence. In R. J. Sternberg (Ed.), *Handbook of intelligence* (pp. 53–91). New York: Cambridge University Press.

Guilford, J. P. (1950). Creativity. *American Psychologist, 5*, 444–454.

Guilford, J. P. (1967). *The nature of human intelligence*. New York: McGraw-Hill.

Guilford, J. P. (1977). *Way beyond the IQ: Guide to improving intelligence and creativity*. New York: McGraw-Hill.

Guilford, J. P. (1981). Higher-order structure of intellect abilities. *Multivariate Behavioral Research, 16*, 411–435.

Guilford, J. P. (1985). A sixty-year perspective on psychological measurement. *Applied Psychological Measurement, 9*, 341–349.

Guion, R. M., & Gottier, R. F. (1965). Validity of personality measures in personnel selection. *Personnel Psychology, 18*, 135–164.

Hakstian, A. R., & Cattell, R. B. (1976). *Comprehensive Ability Battery*. Institute for Personality and Ability Testing, Inc.

Halamandaris, K. F., & Power, K. G. (1999). Individual differences, social support and coping with examination stress: A study of the psychosocial and academic adjustment of first year home students. *Personality and Individual Differences, 26*, 665–685.

Hamilton, V., & Freeman, P. (1971). Academic achievement and student personality characteristics: A multivariate study. *British Journal of Sociology, 22*, 31–52.

Harrell, T. W. (1969). The personality attributes of high earning MBAs in big business. *Personnel Psychology, 22,* 457–463.

Harris, D. (1940). Factors affecting college grades: A review of the literature, 1930–1937. *Psychological Bulletin, 37,* 125–166.

Hathaway, S. R., & McKinley, J. C. (1967). *Manual of the Minnesota Multiphasic Personality Inventory.* New York: The Psychological Corporation.

Haun, K. W. (1965). A note on the prediction of academic performance from personality test scores. *Psychological Reports, 16,* 294.

Heaven, P. C. (1990). Attitudinal and personality correlates of achievement motivation among high school students. *Personality and Individual Differences, 11,* 705–717.

Heaven, P. C., Mak, A., Barry, J., & Ciarrochi, J. (2002). Personality and family influences on adolescent attitudes to school and self-rated academic performance. *Personality and Individual Differences, 32,* 453–462.

Hein, J. G. (1997). International medical graduates and communication. In S. A. Husain, R. A. Munoz, & R. Balon (Eds.), *International medical graduates in psychiatry in the United States: Challenges and opportunities. Issues in psychiatry* (pp. 31–44). Washington, DC: American Psychiatric Association.

Hembree, R. (1988). Correlates, causes, effects, and treatment of test anxiety. *Review of Educational Research, 58,* 47–77.

Herrnstein, R. J., & Murray, C. (1994). *The Bell Curve: Intelligence and class structure in American life.* New York: The Free Press

Heston, L. L. (1966). Psychiatric disorders in foster home reared children of schizophrenic mothers. *British Journal of Psychiatry, 112,* 1103–1110.

Hill, K. R., & Junus, F. (1979). Individual differences in concept learning of painting style. *Perceptual and Motor Skills, 49,* 255–261.

Hirschberg, N., & Itkin, S. (1978). Graduate student success in psychology. *American Psychologist, 33,* 1083–1093.

Hofstee, W. K. (2001). Personality and Intelligence: Do they mix? In M. J. Collis & S. Messick (Eds.), *Intelligence and personality: Bridging the gap in theory and measurement* (pp. 43–60). England: Plymouth.

Hogan, R., & Hogan, J. (2002). Assessing leadership: A view from the dark sign. International Journal of Selection and Assessment, 9, 40–51.

Hogan, J., & Holland, B. (2003). Using theory to evaluate personality and job-performance relationships: A socioanalytic perspective. *Journal of Applied Psychology, 88,* 100–112.

Hogan, R., Johnson, J., & Briggs, S. (Eds.). (1997). *Handbook of personality psychology.* San Diego, CA: Academic Press.

Hogan, W. (1978). IQ self-estimates of males and females. *Journal of Social Psychology, 106,* 137–138.

Holland, D., Dollinger, S., Holland, C., & McDonald, D. (1995). The relationship between psychometric intelligence and the five-factor model of personality in a rehabilitation sample. *Journal of Clinical Psychology, 51,* 79–88.

Hough, L. M. (1992). The Big Five personality variables—construct confusion: Description versus prediction. *Human Performance, 15,* 139–155.

Hough, L. M., Eaton, N. K., Dunnette, M. D., Kamp, J. D., & McCloy, R. A. (1990). Criterion-related validities of personality constructs and the effect of the response distortion on those validities. *Journal of Applied Psychology, 75,* 581–595.

Hough, L. M., Ones, D. S., & Viswesvaran, C. (1998). *Personality correlates of managerial performance constructs.* Paper presented in R. C. Page (Chair) Personality Determinants of Managerial Potential Performance, Progression and Ascendancy. Symposium conducted at the 13th annual conference of the society for Industrial Organizational Psychology, Dallas.

Howard, A., & Bray, D. W. (1988). *Managerial lives in transition: Advancing age and changing times. Adult development and aging.* New York: Guilford.

Howe, M. (1997). *IQ in question: The truth about intelligence.* London: Sage.

Humphreys, M. S., & Revelle, W. (1984). Personality, motivation and performance: A theory of the relationship between individual differences and information processing. *Psychological Review, 91,* 153–184.

Hunter, J. E. (1986). Cognitive ability, cognitive aptitudes, job knowledge, and job performance. *Journal of Vocational Behavior, 29,* 340–362.

Hunter, J. E., & Hunter, R. F. (1984). Validity and utility of alternate predictors of job performance. *Psychological Bulletin, 96,* 72–98.

Hurtz, G. M., & Donovan, J. J. (2000). Personality and job performance: The Big Five revisited. *Journal of Applied Psychology, 85,* 869–879.

Hussain, S., & Kumari, M. (1995). Eysenck's personality dimensions in relation to ego--strength and adjustment. *Journal of Personality and Clinical Studies, 11,* 43–48.

Hyde, J. S. (1981). How large are cognitive gender differences? A meta-analysis using 2 and d'. *American Psychologist, 36,* 892–901.

Irvine, S. (1966). Towards a rationale for testing attainments and abilities in Africa. *British Journal of Educational Psychology, 36,* 24–32.

Irvine, S. (1969). The factor analysis of African abilities and attainments: Constructs across cultures. *Psychological Bulletin, 71,* 20–32.

Jackson, C. J., & Corr, P. J. (1998). Personality-performance correlations at work: Individual and aggregate levels of analyses. *Personality and Individual Differences, 24,* 815–820.

Jackson, C. J., Furnham, A., Forde, L., & Cotter, T. (2000). The dimensional structure of the Eysenck Personality profiler. *British Journal of Psychology, 91,* 223–239.

Jackson, D. N. (1984a). *Multidimensional Aptitude Battery Manual.* Port Huron, MI: Research Psychologists Press.

Jackson, D. N. (1984b). *Personality research forum manual* (3rd ed.). Port Huron, MI: Research Psychologists Press.

Jensen, A. R. (1980). Uses of sibling data in educational and psychological research. *American Educational Research Journal, 17,* 153–170.

Jensen, A. R. (1982). Level I/Level II: Factors or categories? *Journal of Educational Psychology, 74,* 868–873.

Jensen, A. R. (1987). Individual differences in the Hick paradigm. In P. A. Vernon (Ed.), *Speed of information-processing and intelligence* (pp. 101–175). Norwood: Ablex.

Jensen, A. R. (1998). *The g factor.* Westport, CT: Praeger

Jessup, G., & Jessup, H. (1971). Validity of the Eysenck Personality Inventory in pilot selection. *Occupational Psychology, 45,* 111–123.

John, O. P. (1990). The "Big Five" factor taxonomy: Dimensions of personality in the natural language and questionnaires. In L. Pervin (Ed.), *Handbook of personality theory and research* (pp. 66–100). New York: Guilford.

John, O. P., Donahue, E. M., & Kentle, R. L. (1991). *The Big-Five Inventory—Versions 4a and 54.* Berkeley, CA: University of California, Berkeley, Institute of Personality and Social Research.

Johnson, J. A. (1994). Clarification of factor five with the help of the AB5C model. *European Journal of Personality, 8,* 311–314.

Jones, R. G., & Whitemore, M. D. (1995). Evaluating developmental assessment centers as interventions. *Personnel Psychology, 48,* 377–388.

Judge, T., & Bono, T. (2000). Five factor model of personality and transformational leadership. *Journal of Applied Psychology, 85,* 751–765.

Judge, T., Bono, J., Illies, R., & Gerhordt, M. (2002). Personality and leadership: A qualitative and quantitative review. *Journal of Applied Psychology, 87,* 765–780.

Judge, T. A., Heller, D., & Mount, M. (2002). Five-factor model of personality and job satisfaction. *Journal of Applied Psychology, 87,* 530–541.

Judge, T. A., Higgins, C. A., Thoresen, C. J., & Barrick, M. R. (1999). The Big Five personality traits, general mental ability, and career success across the life span. *Personnel Psychology, 52,* 621–652.

Judge, T. A., & Ilies, R. (2002). Relationship of personality to performance motivation: A meta-analytic review. *Journal of Applied Psychology, 87,* 797–807.

Jung, C. G. (1921). The Question of the Therapeutic Value of "Abreaction." *British Journal of Psychology, 2,* 13–22.

Kalmanchey, G. M., & Kozeki, B. (1983). Relation of personality dimensions to social and intellectual factors in children. *Personality and Individual Differences, 4,* 237–243.

Kamin, L. J. (1974). *The science and politics of IQ.* London, England: Lawrence Erlbaum Associates.

Kant, I. (1796/1996). *Anthropology from a pragmatic point of view.* Carbondale, IL: Southern Illinois University Press.

Karaeng, G., & Sandstroem, C. (1959). Advaendbarheten ar esteliska bedoemrugstest. *Pedagogisk Forkning: Nordisk Tidsskiyi fur Pedagogik, 1,* 44–56.

Keats, D. (1982). Cultural bases of concepts of intelligence: A Chinese vs Australian comparison. *Proceedings: Second Asian Workshop on Child and Adolescent Development,* 67–75.

Keehn, J., & Prothero, E. (1958). The meaning of "intelligence" to Lebanese teachers. *British Journal of Educational Psychology, 58,* 339–342.

Kent, G. H., & Rosanoff, A. J. (1910). A study of association in insanity. *American Journal of Insanity, 67,* 37–96, 317–390.

Kihlstrom, J. F., & Cantor, N. (2000). Social intelligence. In R. J. Sternberg (Ed.), *Handbook of intelligence* (pp. 359–379). New York: Cambridge University Press.

King, L., Walker, L., & Broyles, S. (1996). Creativity and the five factor model. *Journal of Research in Personality, 30,* 189–203.

Kline, P., & Cooper, C. (1986). Psychoticism and creativity. *The Journal of Genetic Psychology, 147,* 183–188.

Kline, P., & Gale, A. (1971). Extraversion, Neuroticism and performance in a psychology examination. *British Journal of Educational Psychology, 41,* 90–94.

Kling, K. C. (2001, July). *The role of personality, academic ability, and gender in predicting academic achievement.* Poster presented at the 2001 meeting of the International Society for the Study of Individual Differences, Edinburgh.

Koivula, N., Hassmen, P., & Fallby, J. (2002). Self-esteem and perfectionism in elite athletes: Effects on competitive anxiety and self-conscience. *Personality and Individual Differences, 32,* 865–875.

Kuncel, N. R., Hezlett, S. A., & Ones, D. S. (2001). A comprehensive meta-analysis of the predictive validity of the graduate record examinations: Implications for graduate student selection and performance. *Psychological Bulletin, 127,* 162–181.

Kyllonen, P. (1997). Smart testing. In R. Dillon (Ed.), *Handbook on testing* (pp. 347–368). Westport, CT: Greenwood.

Lathey, J. (1991). Temperament style as a predictor of academic achievement in early adolescence. *Journal of Psychological Type, 22,* 52–58.

Lazarus, R. S., & Folkman, S. (1984). Coping and adaptation. In W. D. Gentry (Ed.), *The handbook of behavioral medicine* (pp. 282–325). New York: Guilford.

Leon, G. R., Gillum, B., Gillum, R., & Gouze, M. (1979). Personality stability and change over a 30-year period—middle age to old age. *Journal of Consulting and Clinical Psychology, 47,* 517–524.

Lippmann, W. (1992). The mental age of Americans. *New Republic, 32,* 213–215.

Locke, J. (1997). Prime movers: The traits of great business leaders. In C. Cooper & S. Jackson (Eds.), *Creating tomorrow's organization* (pp. 75–96). Chichester: Wiley.

Loehlin, J. C. (1992). *Genes and environment in personality development.* Thousand Oaks, CA: Sage.

Lubow, R. E., Ingberg-Sachs, Y., Zalstein-Orda, N., & Gerwitz, J. C. (1992). Latent inhibition in low and high "psychotic-prone" normal subjects. *Personality and Individual Differences, 15,* 563–572.

Lynn, D. B. (1959). A note on sex differences in the development of masculine and feminine identification. *Psychological Review, 66,* 126–135.

Lynn, R. (1994). Sex differences in intelligence and brain size: A paradox resolved. *Personality and Individual Differences, 17,* 257–271.

Lynn, R. (1998). Sex differences in intelligence: A rejoinder to Mackintosh. *Journal of Biosocial Science, 30,* 529–572.

Lynn, R. (1999). Sex differences in intelligence and brain size: A developmental theory. *Intelligence, 27,* 1–12.

Lynn, R., & Gordon, I. E. (1961). The relation of neuroticism and extraversion to intelligence and educational attainment. *British Journal of Educational Psychology, 31,* 194–203.

Lynn, R., & Pagliari, C. (1994). The intelligence of American children is still rising. *Journal of Biosocial Science, 26,* 65–67.

Maccoby, E. E., & Jacklin, C. N. (1974). *The psychology of sex differences.* Stanford, CA: Stanford University Press.

Maccoby, E., & Jacklin, C. (1980). Sex differences in aggression: A rejoinder and reprise. *Child Development, 51,* 964–980.

MacKinnon, D. W. (1965). Personality and the realization of creative potential. *American Psychologist, 20,* 273–281.

Mackintosh, N. J. (1998). *IQ and human intelligence.* Oxford: Oxford University Press.

Maqsud, M. (1993). Relationships of some personality variables to academic attainment of secondary school. *Educational Psychology, 13,* 11–18.

Markham, R., & Darke, S. (1991). The effects of anxiety on verbal and spatial task performance. *Australian Journal of Psychology, 43,* 107–111.

Martindale, C., & Dailey, A. (1996). Creativity. Primary process cognition and personality. *Personality and Individual Differences, 20,* 409–414.

Matarazzo, J. D. (1972). *Wechsler's measurement and appraisal of adult intelligence* (5th ed.). Baltimore: Williams & Wilkins.

Matthews, G. (1986). The effects of anxiety on intellectual performance: When and why are they found? *Journal of Research in Personality, 20,* 385–401.

Matthews, G. (1989). The factor structure of the 16PF: Twelve primary and three secondary factors. *Personality and Individual Differences, 10,* 931–940.

Matthews, G. (1992). Extraversion. In A. P. Smith & D. M. Jones (Eds.), *Handbook of human performance: Vol. 3. State and trait* (pp. 95–126). London: Academic.

Matthews, G. (1997). The Big Five as a framework for personality assessment. In N. Anderson & P. Herriot (Eds.), *International handbook of selection and appraisal* (2nd ed., pp. 175–200). London: Wiley.

Matthews, G. (1999). Personality and skill: A cognitive-adaptive framework. In P. L. Ackerman, P. C. Kyllonen, & R. D. Roberts (Eds.), *Learning and individual differences: Process, trait, and content determinants* (pp. 437–462). Atlanta: Georgia Institute of Technology.

Matthews, G., Davies, D. R., Westerman, S. J., & Stammers, R. B. (2000). *Human performance. Cognition, stress, and individual differences.* London: Psychology Press.

Matthews, G., & Deary, I. J. (1998). *Personality traits.* Cambridge: Cambridge University Press.

Matthews, G., & Gilliand, K. (1999). The personality theories of H. J. Eysenck & J. A. Gray: A comparative review. *Personality and Individual Differences, 26,* 583–626.

Mayer, A. (1955). Die gegenwaertige Problematik der Arbeits- und Betriebspsychologie [The present problematic situation of labor and industrial psychology]. *Psychologisch Rundschau, 6,* 6–18.

Mayer, J. D. (2000). Spiritual intelligence and spiritual consciousness. *International Journal for the Psychology of Religion, 10,* 47–56.

Mayer, J. D., & Salovey, P. (1997). What is emotional intelligence? In P. Salovey & D. J. Sluyter (Eds.), *Emotional development and emotional intelligence: Educational implications* (pp. 3–34). New York: Basic Books.

Mayer, J. D., Salovey, P., & Caruso, D. R. (2000). Models of emotional intelligence. In R. J. Sternberg (Ed.), *The handbook of intelligence* (pp. 396–420). New York: Cambridge University Press.

McCrae, R. R. (1987). Creativity, divergent thinking, and openness to experience. *Journal of Personality and Social Psychology, 52,* 1258–1265.

McCrae, R. R. (1993). Openness to Experience as a basic dimension of personality. *Imagination, Cognition and Personality, 13,* 39–55.

McCrae, R. R. (1994). Openness to experience: Expanding the boundaries of Factor V. *European Journal of Personality, 13,* 39–55.

McCrae, R. R., & Costa, P. T. (1982). Self-concept and the stability of personality: Cross-sectional comparisons of self-reports and ratings. *Journal of Personality and Social Psychology, 43,* 1282–1292.

McCrae, R. R., & Costa, P. T. (1985). Updating Norman's "adequacy taxonomy": Intelligence and personality dimensions in natural language and in questionnaires. *Journal of Personality and Social Psychology, 49,* 710–721.

McCrae, R. R., & Costa, P. T. (1987). Validation of the five-factor model of personality across instruments and observers. *Journal of Personality and Social Psychology, 52,* 81–90.

McCrae, R. R., & Costa, P. T. (1989). Reinterpreting the Myers-Briggs Type Indicator from the perspective of the five-factor model of personality. *Journal of Personality, 57,* 17–40.

McCrae, R. R., & Costa, P. T. (1997a). Conceptions and correlates of Openness to Experience. In R. Hogan & J. Johnson (Eds.), *Handbook of personality psychology* (pp. 825–847). Tulsa, OK: Hogan Assessment Systems.

McCrae, R. R., & Costa, P. T. (1997b). Personality trait structure as a human universal. *American Psychologist, 52,* 509–516.

McGue, M., Bouchard, T. J. J., Iacono, W. G., & Lykken, D. T. (1993). Behavioral genetics of cognitive ability: A life-span perspective. In R. Plomin & G. E. McClearn (Eds.), *Nature, nurture & psychology* (pp. 59–76). Washington, DC: American Psychological Association.

McHenry, J., Hough, L., Toquam, J., Hanson, M., & Ashworth, S. (1990). Project A validity results: The relationship between predictor and criterion domains. *Personnel Psychology, 43,* 335–354.

McNemar, Q. (1942). *The revision of the Stanford–Binet scale.* Oxford, England: Houghton Mifflin.

Mednick, S. A., & Mednick, M. T. (1967). *Examiner's manual: Remote Associates Test.* Boston: Houghton-Mifflin.

Meier, N. C. (1940). *The Meier art tests: I. Art judgment.* Oxford, England: Bureau of Educational Research.

Meier, N. C., & Seashore, C. E. (1929). *The Meier-Seashore Art judgement test.* Iowa City: University of Iowa, Bureau of Educational Research.

Melamed, T. (1996a). Career success: An assessment of a gender-specific model. *Journal of Occupational and Organizational Psychology, 69,* 217–242.

Melamed, T. (1996b). Validation of a stage model of career success. *Applied Psychology: An International Review, 45,* 35–65.

Merten, T. (1993). Word association responses and psychoticism. *Personality and Individual Differences, 14,* 837–839.

Merten, T. (1995). Factors influencing word-association responses: A reanalysis. *Creativity Research Journal, 8,* 249–263.

Merten, T., & Fischer, I. (1999). Creativity, personality and word association responses: Associative behaviour in forty supposedly creative persons. *Personality and Individual Differences, 27,* 933–942.

Metalsky, G., & Abramson, L. (1981). Attributional styles and life events in the classroom: Vulnerability and invulnerability to depressive mood reactions. *Journal of Personality and Social Psychology, 43,* 612–617.

Metha, P., & Kumar, D. (1985). Relationships of academic achievement with intelligence, personality, adjustment, study habits and academic motivation. *Journal of Personality and Clinical Studies, 1,* 57–68.

Montagliani, A., & Giacalone, R. A. (1998). Impression management and cross-cultural adaptation. *The Journal of Social Psychology, 138,* 598–608.

Moon, H. (2001). The two faces of conscientiousness: Duty and achievement striving in escalation of commitment dilemmas. *Journal of Applied Psychology, 86,* 533–540.

Morris, G., & Liebert, R. (1969). Effects of anxiety on timed and untimed intelligence tests: Another look. *Journal of Consulting and Clinical Psychology, 33,* 240–244.

Mount, M. K., & Barrick, M. R. (1995). The Big Five personality dimensions: Implications for research and practice in human resources management. *Research in Personnel and Human Resources Management, 13,* 153–200.

Mount, M. K., Barrick, M. R., & Strauss, J. P. (1999). The joint relationship of Conscientiousness and ability with performance: Test of the interaction hypothesis. *Journal of Management, 25,* 707–721.

Moutafi, J., Furnham, A., & Crump, J. (2003). Demographic and personality predictors of intelligence: A study using the NEO-Personality Inventory and the Myers-Briggs Type Indicator. *European Journal of Personality, 17,* 79–94.

Moutafi, J., Furnham, A., & Paltiel, L. (2005). Can demographic and personality factors predict intelligence? *Personality and Individual Differences*.

Muller, C., & Dweck, C. (1998). Praise for intelligence can undermine children's motivation and performance. *Journal of Personality and Social Psychology, 75*, 33–42.

Muller, J. H. (1992). Anxiety and performance. In A. P. Smith & D. M. Jones (Eds.), *Handbook of human performance* (3rd ed., pp. 127–160). London: Academic Press.

Mumford, M. D., & Gustafson, S. B. (1988). Creativity syndrome: Integration, application, and innovation. *Psychological Bulletin, 103*, 27–43.

Nauta, M. M., Epperson, D. L., & Wagoner, K. M. (1999). Perceived causes of success and failure: Are women's attributions related to persistence in engineering majors? *Journal of Research in Science Teaching, 36*, 663–676.

Neisser, U., Boodoo, G., Bouchard, T., Boykin, A., Brody, N., Ceci, S., Halpern, D., Loehlin, J., Perloff, R., Sternberg, R., & Urbina, S. (1996). Intelligence: Knowns and unknowns. *American Psychologist, 51*, 77–101.

Neubauer, A. C. (1997). The mental speed approach to the assessment of intelligence. In J. Kingma & W. Tomic (Eds.), *Advances in cognition and educational practice: Reflections on the concepts of intelligence* (pp. 49–174). Greenwich, CT: JAI Press.

Nevo, B., & Khader, A. (1995). Cross-cultural, gender and age differences in Singaporean mothers' conceptions of children's intelligence. *Journal of Social Psychology, 135*, 509–517.

Newman, H. H., Freeman, F. N., & Holzinger, K. J. (1937). *Twins: A study of heredity and environment*. Chicago, IL: University of Chicago Press.

Norman, W. (1967). *2800 personality trait descriptors: Normative operating characteristics for a university population*. Ann Arbor: Department of Psychological Sciences, University of Michigan.

Ones, D. S., Viswesvaran, C., & Reiss, A. D. (1996). The role of social desirability in personality testing for personal selection: The red herring. *Journal of Applied Behavior, 81*, 660–679.

Orpen, C. (1983). The development and validation of an adjective check-list measure of managerial need for achievement. *Psychology, 20*, 38–42.

Paulhus, D., Lysy, D., & Yik, M. (1998). Self-report measures of intelligence: Are they useful as proxy IQ tests? *Journal of Personality, 66*, 525–554.

Pelechano, V. (1972). Personality, motivation and academic achievement. *Revista de Psicologia General y Aplicada, 27*, 69–86.

Pervin, L., & John, O. P. (1997). *Personality: Theory and research* (7th ed.). Oxford: Wiley.

Pervin, L. A. (1996). *The science of personality*. Oxford: Wiley.

Peterson, J. B., & Carson, S. (2000). Latent inhibition and openness to experience in a high-achieving student population. *Personality and Individual Differences, 28*, 323–332.

Petrides, K. V., Chamorro-Premuzic, T., Frederickson, N., & Furnham, A. (in press). Accounting for individual differences in scholastic behavior and achievement. *British Journal of Educational Psychology*.

Petrides, K. V., & Furnham, A. (2000). On the dimensional structure of emotional intelligence. *Personality and Individual Differences, 29*, 313–320.

Petrides, K. V., & Furnham, A. (2001). Trait emotional intelligence: Psychometric investigation with reference to established trait taxonomies. *European Journal of Personality, 15*, 425–448.

Piaget, J. (1952). *The origins of intelligence in children*. Oxford, England: International Universities Press.

Piaget, J., & Inhelder, B. (1969). *The psychology of the child.* New York: Basic Books.

Pichot, P., Volmat, R., & Wiart, C. (1960). Exploration of aesthetic aptitudes in the mental patient. *Revue de Psychologie Appliquee, 10,* 165–181.

Plomin, R., & DeFries, J. C. (1979). Multivariate behavioral genetic analysis of twin data on scholastic abilities. *Behavior Genetics, 9,* 505–517.

Plomin, R., Fulker, D. W., Corley, R., & DeFries, J. C. (1997). Nature, nurture, and cognitive development from 1 to 16 years: A parent–offspring adoption study. *Psychological Science, 8,* 442–447.

Pommerantz, E., & Ruble, O. (1997). Distinguishing multiple dimensions of conceptions of ability. *Child Development, 68,* 1165–1180.

Rajaram, S., & Roediger, H. L., III. (1993). Direct comparisons of four implicit memory tests. *Journal of Experimental Psychology: Learning, Memory and Cognition, 19,* 765–775.

Raven, J. C. (1956). *Standard Progressive Matrices, sets A, B, C, D, E.* London: Lewis.

Raven, J. C. (1963). *Standard Progressive Matrices.* London: Lewis.

Rawlings, D., & Carnie, D. (1989). The interaction of EPQ Extraversion and WAIS subtest performance under timed and untimed conditions. *Personality and Individual Differences, 10,* 453–458.

Rawlings, D., & Skok, M. (1993). Extraversion, venturesomeness and intelligence in children. *Personality and Individual Differences, 15,* 389–396.

Rawls, D. J., & Rawls, J. R. (1968). Personality characteristics and personal history data of successful and less successful executives. *Psychological Reports, 23,* 1032–1034.

Reilly, J., & Mulhern, G. (1995). Gender differences in self-estimated IQ: The need for care in interpreting group data. *Personality and Individual Differences, 18,* 189–192.

Reitan, R. M. (1992). *Trail Making Test. Manual for administration and scoring.* South Tucson, AZ: Reitan Neurological Laboratory.

Revelle, W., Amara, P., & Tariff, S. (1976). Introversion/extroversion, time stress, and caffeine: Effect on verbal performance. *Science, 192,* 149–150.

Rhodewalt, F. (1990). Self-handicappers: Individual differences in the preference for anticipatory, self-protective acts. In R. L. Higgins (Ed.), *Self-handicapping: The paradox that isn't. The Plenum series in social/clinical psychology* (pp. 69–106). New York: Plenum.

Riggio, R. E., Messamer, J., & Throckmorton, B. (1991). Social and academic intelligence: Conceptually distinct but overlapping constructs. *Personality and Individual Differences, 12,* 696–702.

Rindermann, H., & Neubauer, A. (2001). The influence of personality on three aspects of cognitive performance: Processing speed, intelligence and school performance. *Personality and Individual Differences, 30,* 829–842.

Roberts, M. J. (2002). The relationship between extraversion and ability. *Personality and Individual Differences, 32,* 517–522

Roberts, W., & Strayer, J. (1996). Empathy, emotional expressiveness, and prosocial behavior. *Child Development, 67,* 449–470.

Robertson, I. T., Baron, H., Gibbons, P., MacIver, R., & Nyfield, G. (2000). *Journal of Occupational and Organizational Psychology, 73,* 171–180.

Robertson, I. T., & Kinder, A. (1993). Personality and job competencies: The criterion related validity of some personality variables. *Journal of Occupational and Organizational Psychology, 66,* 225–244.

Robinson, D. L. (1985). How personality relates to intelligence test performance: Implications for a theory of intelligence, aging research, and personality assessment. *Personality and Individual Differences, 6,* 203–216.

Robinson, D. L. (1989). The Neurophysiological Bases of High IQ. *International Journal of Neuroscience, 46,* 209–234.

Robinson, D. L. (1991). On the neurological bases of intelligence and intellectual factors. In H. A. H. Rowe (Ed.), *Intelligence: Reconceptualization and measurement.* Hillsdale, NJ: Lawrence Erlbaum Associates.

Robinson, D. L. (1993). The EEG and intelligence: An appraisal of methods and theories. *Personality and Individual Differences, 15,* 695–716.

Robinson, D. L. (1996). *Brain, mind and behavior: A new perspective on human nature.* Westport, CT: Praeger.

Robinson, D. L. (1998). Sex differences in brain activity, personality and intelligence: A test of arousability theory. *Personality and Individual Differences, 25,* 1133–1152.

Robinson, D. L. (1999). The "IQ" factor: Implications for intelligence theory and measurement. *Personality and Individual Differences, 27,* 715–735.

Robinson, D. L., Gabriel, N., & Katchan, O. (1993). Personality and second language learning. *Personality and Individual Differences, 16,* 143–157.

Rocklin, T. (1994). Relation between typical intellectual engagement and openness: Comment on Goff & Ackerman. *Journal of Educational Psychology, 86,* 145–149.

Rolfhus, E., & Ackerman, P. L. (1996). Self-report knowledge: At the crossroads of ability, interest, and personality. *Journal of Educational Psychology, 88,* 174–188.

Rolfhus, E., & Ackerman, P. L. (1999). Assessing individual differences in knowledge: Knowledge, intelligence, and related traits. *Journal of Educational Psychology, 91,* 511–526.

Roth, E. (1964). Die Geschwindigkeit der Verarbeitung von Informationen und ihr Zusammenhang mit Intelligenz [Speed of information processing and its relationship to intelligence]. *Zeitschrift fuir Experimentelle und Angewandte Psychologie, 11,* 616–622.

Rothstein, M., Paunonen, S., Rush, J., & King, G. (1994). Personality and cognitive ability predictors of performance in graduate business school. *Journal of Educational Psychology, 86,* 516–530.

Rushton, J. (1999). *Race, evolution and behaviour.* Somerset, NJ: Transaction Publishers.

Ryans, D. G. (1938). A study of the observed relationship between persistence test results, intelligence indices, and academic success. *Journal of Educational Psychology, 29,* 573–580.

Ryckman, D. B., & Peckham, P. D. (1987). Gender differences in attributions for success and failure. *Journal of Early Adolescence, 7,* 47–63.

Sackett, P. R., Gruys, M. L., & Ellingson, J. E. (1998). Ability–personality interactions when predicting job performance. *Journal of Applied Psychology, 83,* 545–556.

Salgado, J. F. (1997). The five factor model of personality and job performance in the European Community. *Journal of Applied Psychology, 82,* 30–43.

Salovey, P., & Mayer, J. D. (1990). Emotional intelligence. *Imagination, Cognition and Personality, 9,* 185–211.

Sanchez-Marin, M., Rejano-Infante, E., & Rodriguez-Troyano, Y. (2001). Personality and academic productivity in the university student. *Social Behavior and Personality, 29,* 299–305.

Sanders, W. B., Osborne, R. T., & Greene, J. E. (1955). Intelligence and academic performance of college students of urban, rural, and mixed backgrounds. *Journal of Educational Research, 49,* 185–193.

Sarason, I. G. (1975). Test anxiety, attention, and the general problem of anxiety. In C. D. Spielberger & I. G. Sarason (Eds.), *Stress and anxiety* (Vol. 1, pp. 165–210). New York: Hemisphere/Halstead.

Sarason, I. G. (Ed.). (1980). *Test anxiety: theory, research and applications.* Hillsdale, NJ: Lawrence Erlbaum Associates.

Sarason, I. G., Sarason, B. R., & Pierce, G. R. (1995). Cognitive interference: At the intelligence–personality crossroads. In D. H. Saklofske & M. Zeidner (Eds.), *International handbook of personality and intelligence* (pp. 91–112). New York: Plenum.

Saucier, G. (1994a). Mini-markers: A brief version of Goldberg's unipolar Big-Five markers. *Journal of Personality Assessment, 63,* 506–516.

Saucier, G. (1994b). Trapnell versus the lexical factor: More ado about nothing? *European Journal of Personality, 8,* 291–298.

Savage, R. D. (1962). Personality factors and academic performance. *British Journal of Educational Psychology, 32,* 251–253.

Schaie, K. W. (1996). Intellectual development in adulthood. In J. E. Birren & K. W. Schaie (Eds.), *Handbook of the psychology of aging: The handbooks of aging* (4th ed., pp. 266–286). San Diego: Academic Press.

Schmidt, F. L., & Hunter, J. E. (1998). The validity and utility of selection methods in personal psychology: Practical and theoretical implications of 85 years of research findings. *Psychological Bulletin, 124,* 262–279.

Schmitt, N., Gooding, R. Z., Noe, R. A., & Kirsch, M. (1984). Meta-analyses of validity studies published between 1964 and 1982 and the investigation of study characteristics. *Personnel Psychology, 37,* 407–422.

Schoenthaler, S. (1991). *Improve your child's I.Q. and behaviour.* London: BBC Books.

Schoppe, K.-J. (1975). *Verbaler Kreativitäts-Test (V-K-T). Ein Verfahren zur Erfassung verbal produktiver Kreativitätsmerkmale [Verbal creativity test (V-K-T). A method for conceiving productive creative invention].* Handandweisung [Manual]. Göttingen: Hogrefe.

Seashore, C. E. (1929). Meier-Seashore art judgement test. *Science, 69,* 380.

Sen, A. K., & Hagtvet, K. A. (1993). Correlations among creativity, intelligence, personality, and academic achievement. *Perceptual and Motor Skills, 77,* 497–498.

Serpell, R. (1976). *Cultures influence on behaviour.* London: Methuen.

Seth, N. K., & Pratap, S. (1971). A study of the academic performance, intelligence and aptitude of engineering students. *Education and Psychology Review, 11,* 3–10.

Seyle, H. (1976). *The stress of life.* New York: McGraw-Hill.

Shafer, A. (1999). Relation of the Big Five and Factor V subcomponents to social intelligence. *European Journal of Personality, 13,* 225–240.

Sharma, S., & Rao, U. (1983). The effects of self-esteem, test anxiety and intelligence on academic achievement of high school girls. *Personality Study and Group Behavior, 3,* 48–55.

Shipstone, K., & Burt, S. (1973). Twenty-five years on: A replication of Flugel's (1947) work on lay popular vies of intelligence and related topics. *British Journal of Educational Psychology, 56,* 183–187.

Siegler, R., & Richards, D. (1982). The development of intelligence. In R. Sternberg (Ed.), *Handbook of human intelligence* (pp. 897–971). Cambridge: Cambridge University Press.

Siepp, B. (1991). Anxiety and academic performance: A meta-analysis of findings. *Anxiety Research, 4,* 27–41.

Singh, R., & Varma, S. K. (1995). The effect of academic aspiration and intelligence on scholastic success of XI graders. *Indian Journal of Psychometry and Education, 26,* 43–48.

Smith, C. A., Organ, D. W., & Near, J. P. (1983). Organizational citizenship behavior: Its nature and antecedents. *Journal of Applied Psychology, 68,* 658–663.

Smith, G. (1969). Personality correlates of academic performance in three dissimilar populations. *Proceedings of the Annual Convention of the American Psychological Association, 4,* 303–304.

Sneed, T., Carlson, J., & Little, T. (1994). The relationship of teacher and parent ratings of academically related personality traits to academic performance in elementary age students. *Learning and Individual Differences, 6,* 37–64.

Snow, R. (1992). Aptitude theory: Yesterday, today, and tomorrow. *Educational Psychologist, 27,* 5–32.

Snow, R. (1995). Foreword. In D. H. Saklofske & M. Zeidner (Eds.), *International handbook of personality and intelligence* (pp. 11–15). New York: Plenum.

Snow, W. G., & Weinstock, J. (1990). Sex differences among non-brain-damaged adults on the Wechsler Adult Intelligence Scales: A review of the literature. *Journal of Clinical and Experimental Neuropsychology, 12,* 873–886.

Soldz, S., & Vaillant, G. E. (1999). The big five personality traits and the life course: A 45 year longitudinal study. *Journal of Research in Personality, 33,* 208–232.

Spangler, W., House, R., & Palrecha, R. (2004). Personality and leadership. In B. Schneider & D. Smith (Eds.), *Personality and organization* (pp. 251–290). New York: Maliwah.

Spearman, C. (1904). "General intelligence," objectively determined and measured. *American Journal of Psychology, 15,* 201–293.

Spearman, C. (1927). *The abilities of man.* New York: Macmillan.

Spielberger, C. D. (1962). The effects of manifest anxiety on the academic achievement of college students. *Mental Hygiene New York, 46,* 420–426.

Spielberger, C. D. (1972). Anxiety as an emotional state. In C. D. Spielberger (Ed.), *Anxiety: Current trends in theory and research* (Vol. 1, pp. 23–49). London: Academic Press.

Springsteen, T. (1940). A Wyoming State Training School survey on emotional stability, intelligence, and academic achievement. *Journal of Exceptional Children, 7,* 54–64.

Stanger, F. (1933). The relation of mental deficiency to crime. *Training School Bulletin, 30,* 22–27.

Stankov, L. (1999). Mining on the "no man's land" between intelligence and personality. In P. L. Ackerman, P. C. Kyllonen, & R. D. Roberts (Eds.), *Learning and individual differences: Process, trait, and content determinants* (pp. 315–337). Atlanta: Georgia Institute of Technology.

Stankov, L. (2000). Complexity, metacognition, and fluid intelligence. *Intelligence, 28,* 121–143.

Stankov, L., Boyle, G. J., & Cattell, R. B. (1995). Models and paradigms in personality and intelligence research. In D. Saklofske & M. Zeidner (Eds.), *International handbook of personality and intelligence. Perspectives on individual differences* (pp. 15–43). New York: Plenum.

Steiner, H. (1997). *Treating preschool children.* San Francisco, CA: Jossey-Bass/ Pfeiffer.

Stelmack, R. M. (1981). The psychophysiology of extraversion and neuroticism. In H. J. Eysenck (Ed.), *A model for personality* (pp. 38–64). Berlin: Springer.

Stern, W. (1912). *Die Psychologische Methoden der Intelligenzpruifung [The psychological methods of intelligence testing].* Barth: Leipzig.

Sternberg, R. J. (1982). Who's intelligent. *Psychology Today,* pp. 30–39.

Sternberg, R. J. (1985). *Beyond IQ: A triarchic theory of human intelligence.* Cambridge: Cambridge University Press.

Sternberg, R. J. (1988). A triarchic view of intelligence in cross-cultural perspective. In S. H. Irvine & J. W. Berry (Eds.), *Human abilities in cultural context* (pp. 60–85). New York: Cambridge University Press.

Sternberg, R. J. (1990). *Metaphors of mind: Conceptions of the nature of intelligence.* Cambridge: Cambridge University Press.

Sternberg, R. J. (1997). *Successful intelligence.* New York: Plume.

Sternberg, R. J., Conway, B. E., Ketron, J. L., & Bernstein, M. (1981). People's conceptions of intelligence. *Journal of Personality and Social Psychology, 41,* 37–55.

Sternberg, R. J., & Kaufman, J. (1998). Human abilities. *Annual Review of Psychology, 49,* 479–502.

Sternberg, R. J., & O'Hara, L. A. (2000). Intelligence and creativity. In R. J. Sternberg (Ed.), *Handbook of intelligence* (pp. 611–630). New York: Cambridge University Press.

Sternberg, R. J., & Wagner, R. K. (1993). The *g*-ocentric view of intelligence and job performance is wrong. *Current Directions in Psychological Science* pp. 2–4.

Stewart, G. L., & Carson, K. P. (1995). Personality dimensions and domains of service performance: A field investigation. *Journal of Business and Psychology, 9,* 365–378.

Stipek, D., & Gralinski, J. (1996). Children's beliefs about intelligence and school performance. *Journal of Educational Psychology, 88,* 397–407.

Stolz, A., & Manuel, H. T. (1931). The art ability of Mexican children. *School and Society, 34,* 379–380.

Stough, C., Brebner, J., Nettelbeck, T., Cooper, C. J., Bates, T., & Mangan, G. L. (1996). The relationship between intelligence, personality and inspection time. *British Journal of Psychology, 81,* 255–268.

Strelau, J., Zawadzki, B., & Piotrowske, A. (2001). Temperament and intelligence: A psychometric approach to the links between both phenomena. In J. M. Collins & S. Messick (Eds.), *Intelligence and personality: Bridging the gap in theory and measurement* (pp. 25–42). London: Lawrence Erlbaum Associates.

Szymura, B., & Wodnjecka, Z. (2003). What really bothers neurotics? In search for factors impairing attentional performance. *Personality and Individual Differences, 34,* 109–126.

Tenopyr, M. L. (1967). Social intelligence and academic success. *Educational and Psychological Measurement, 27,* 961–965.

Terman, L. M. (1916). *The measurement of intelligence (An explanation of and a complete guide for the use of the Stanford revision and extension of the Binet-Simon intelligence scale).* Oxford: Houghton.

Terman, L. M. (1925). *Genetic Studies of Genius: Vol 1. Mental and physical traits of a thousand gifted children.* Palo Alto, CA: Stanford University Press.

Terman, L. M., & Merrill, M. A. (1937). *Measuring intelligence.* London: Harrap.

Tett, R., Jackson, D., & Rothstein, M. (1991). Personality measures as predictors of job performance: A meta-analytic review. *Personnel Psychology, 44,* 703–734.

Thompson, D. M. (1934). On the detection of emphasis in spoken sentences by means of visual, tactual, and visual-tactual cues. *Journal of General Psychology, 11,* 160–172.

Thompson, L. A., Detterman, D. K., & Plomin, R. A. (1991). Associations between cognitive abilities and scholastic achievement: Genetic overlap but environmental differences. *Psychological Science, 2,* 158–165.

Thorndike, E. L. (1920). Intelligence examinations for college entrance. *Journal of Educational Research, 1,* 329–337.

Thorndike, R. L. (1940). "Constancy" of the IQ. *Psychological Bulletin, 37,* 167–186.

Thurstone, L. L. (1919). *Intelligence tests for college students.* Pittsburgh: Carnegie Institute of Technology.

Thurstone, L. L. (1938). *Primary mental abilities.* Chicago: University of Chicago Press.

Tobias, J. J. (1977). Suburban school vandalism: A growing concern. *Journal of Police Science and Administration, 5,* 112–114.

Tokar, D. M., & Subich, L. M. (1997). Relative contributions of congruence and personality dimensions to job satisfaction. *Journal of Vocational Behavior, 50,* 482–491.

Torrance, E. P. (1966). *Torrance tests of creative thinking: Directions manual and scoring guide.* Prince, NJ: Personnel Press.

Torrance, E. P. (1974). *The Torrance tests of creative thinking.* Bensenville, IL: Scholastic Testing Press.

Torrance, E. P. (1979). Unique needs of the creative child and adult. In A. H. Passow (Ed.), *The gifted and talented: Their education and development. 78th NSSE Yearbook* (pp. 352–371). Chicago: National Society for the Study of Education.

Trapnell, P. D. (1994). Openness versus Intellect: A lexical left turn. *European Journal of Personality, 8,* 273–290.

Tupes, E. C., & Christal, R. E. (1961). *United States Air Force ASD Technical Report.* San Antonio: Lackland Air Force Base.

Tupes, E. C., & Christal, R. E. (1992). Recurrent personality factors based on trait ratings. *Journal of Personality, 60,* 225–251.

Uduehi, J. (1996). A cross-cultural assessment of the Maitland Graves Design Judgement Test using IS and Nigerian subjects. *Visual Arts Research, 21,* 11–18.

Upmanyu, V. V., Bhardwaj, S., & Singh, S. (1996). Word-association emotional indicators: Associations with anxiety, psychoticism, neuroticism, extraversion, and creativity. *Journal of Social Psychology, 136,* 521–529.

Vernon, P. A. (1987). Relationship between speed-of-processing, personality, and intelligence. *Educational Psychology, 25,* 293–304.

Walberg, H. J., Strykowski, B. F., Rovai, E., & Hung, S. S. (1984). Exceptional performance. *Review of Educational Research, 54,* 87–112.

Wallach, M. A., & Kogan, N. (1965). *Modes of thinking in young children.* New York: Holt, Rinehart & Winston.

Watson, D., & Slack, A. K. (1993). General factors of affective temperament and their relation to job satisfaction over time. *Organizational Behavior and Human Decision Process, 54,* 181–202.

Webb, E. (1915). *Character and Intelligence: An attempt at an exact study of character.* Cambridge: Cambridge University Press.

Wechsler, D. (1944). *The measurement of adult intelligence.* Baltimore: Williams & Wilkins.

Wechsler, D. (1950). Cognitive, conative, and non-intellective intelligence. *American Psychologist, 5,* 78–83.

Wechsler, D. (1997). *Weschsler Adult Intelligence Scale–III.* San Antonio, TX: The Psychological Corporation.

Weiss, L. (1998). The relationship between personality variables and the completion of a doctoral dissertation. *Dissertation Abstracts International, 48,* 2814–2815.

Wells, A., & Matthews, G. (1994). *Attention and emotion: A clinical perspective.* Hove: Lawrence Erlbaum Associates.

Welsh, G. (1959). *Preliminary manual for the Welsh figural preference test.* Palo Alto, CA: Consulting Psychologists Press.

Welsh, G. (1975). *Creativity and intelligence: A personality approach.* Chapel Hill, NC: Institute for Research in Social Science.

Whipple, G. M. (1922). *The national intelligence tests.* New York: The Public School Company.

Wieczerkowski, W., Nickel, H., Janowski, A., Fittkau, B., & Rauer, W. (1986). *AFS Angstfragebogen fur Schuller.* Westermann, Braunschweig.

Wiggins, N., Blackburn, M., & Hackman, R. (1969). Prediction of first-year graduate success in psychology: Peer ratings. *Journal of Educational Research, 63,* 81–85.

Williamson, I., & Cullingford, C. (1998). Adolescent alienation: Its correlates and consequences. *Educational Studies, 24,* 333–343.

Willingham, W. W. (1974). Predicting success in graduate education. *Science, 183,* 273–278.

Wilson, G. D., & Patterson, J. R. (1968). A new measure of conservatism. *British Journal of Social and Clinical Psychology, 7,* 264–269.

Wine, J. D. (1982). Evaluation anxiety: A cognitive-attentional construct. In H. W. Krohne & L. Laux (Eds.), *Achievement, stress and anxiety* (pp. 207–219). Washington, DC: Hemisphere.

Wober, M. (1972). Distinguishing centri-cultural from cross-cultural tests and research. *Perceptual and Motor Skills, 28,* 488.

Wober, M. (1973). East African undergraduates' attitudes concerning the concepts of intelligence. *British Journal of Social and Clinical Psychology, 12,* 431–432.

Wolfe, R., & Johnson, S. (1995). Personality as a predictor of college performance. *Educational and Psychological Measurement, 55,* 77–185.

Wolfradt, U., & Pretz, J. (2001). Individual differences in creativity: Personality, story writing, and hobbies. *European Journal of Personality, 15,* 297–310.

Wonderlic, E. (1992). *Wonderlic Personnel Test.* Libertyville, IL: Wonderlic & Associates, Inc.

Woody, E., & Claridge, G. (1977). Psychoticism and thinking. *British Journal of Social and Clinical Psychology, 16,* 241–248.

Wuthrich, V., & Bates, T. C. (2001). Schizotypy and latent inhibition: Non-linear linkage between psychometric and cognitive markers. *Personality and Individual Differences, 30,* 783–798.

Yussen, S., & Kane, P. (1985). Children's concept of intelligence. In S. Yussen (Ed.), *The growth of reflection in children* (pp. 207–241). New York: Academic Press.

Zeidner, M. (1995). Personality trait correlates of intelligence. In D. Saklofske & M. Zeidner (Eds.), *International handbook of personality and intelligence. Perspectives on individual differences* (pp. 299–319). New York: Plenum.

Zeidner, M. (1998). *Test anxiety: The state of the art.* New York: Plenum.

Zeidner, M., & Matthews, G. (2000). Intelligence and personality. In R. Sternberg (Ed.), *Handbook of intelligence* (pp. 581–610). New York: Cambridge University Press.

Ziller, R. C. (1990). *Photographing the self: Observing self, social environmental orientations.* San Francisco, CA: Sage.

Zuckerman, G. A. (1991). Invariants of cognitive development and educational patterns. *Gestalt Theory, 13,* 86–97.

# Author Index

# Subject Index